Architecture and the Modern Hospital

More than any other building type in the twentieth century, the hospital was connected to transformations in the health of populations and expectations of lifespan. From the scale of public health to the level of the individual, the architecture of the modern hospital has reshaped knowledge about health and disease and perceptions of bodily integrity and security. However, the rich and genuinely global architectural history of these hospitals is poorly understood and largely forgotten.

This book explores the rapid evolution of hospital design in the twentieth century, analysing the ways in which architects and other specialists reimagined the modern hospital. It examines how the vast expansion of medical institutions over the course of the century was enabled by new approaches to architectural design and it highlights the emerging political conviction that physical health would become the cornerstone of human welfare.

Julie Willis is Professor of Architecture and Dean of the Faculty of Architecture, Building and Planning at the University of Melbourne, Australia. She is a distinguished architectural scholar, with expertise in Australian architectural history of the late nineteenth and twentieth centuries. Her current research examines the transmission and translation of architectural knowledge through professional networks in architecture. Major works include the *Encyclopedia of Australian Architecture* (2012, with Philip Goad) and, with Kate Darian-Smith, the recently published edited collection *Designing Schools: Space, Place and Pedagogy* (Routledge, 2017).

Philip Goad is Redmond Barry Distinguished Professor and Chair of Architecture at the Faculty of Architecture, Building and Planning at the University of Melbourne, Australia. He is an architect and architectural historian, and is renowned for his extensive scholarship on modern Australian architecture. His current research examines the role and influence of the Bauhaus on Australian architecture. His most recent book, with Geoffrey London and Conrad Hamann, is *An Unfinished Experiment in Living: Australian Houses 1950–65* (2017).

Cameron Logan is Senior Lecturer and Director of Heritage Conservation at the Sydney School of Architecture, Design and Planning at the University of Sydney, Australia. His work is concerned with civic culture, public architecture and the political, architectural and urban implications of heritage conservation practice. He is the author of *Historic Capital: Preservation, Race and Real Estate in Washington, DC* (2017).

Routledge Research in Architecture

The *Routledge Research in Architecture* series provides the reader with the latest scholarship in the field of architecture. The series publishes research from across the globe and covers areas as diverse as architectural history and theory, technology, digital architecture, structures, materials, details, design, monographs of architects, interior design and much more. By making these studies available to the worldwide academic community, the series aims to promote quality architectural research.

Architecture and the Modern Hospital
Nosokomeion and *Hygeia*
Julie Willis, Philip Goad and Cameron Logan

Housing, Architecture and the Edge Condition
Dublin is building, 1935–1975
Ellen Rowley

Unorthodox Ways to Think the City
Representations, Constructions, Dynamics
Teresa Stoppani

Flexibility and Design
Learning from the School Construction Systems Development (SCSD) Project
Joshua D. Lee

Visual Spatial Enquiry
Diagrams and Metaphors for Architects and Spatial Thinkers
Edited by Robyn Creagh and Sarah McGann

For a full list of titles, please visit: https://www.routledge.com/Routledge-Research-in-Architecture/book-series/RRARCH

Architecture and the Modern Hospital
Nosokomeion to *Hygeia*

Julie Willis, Philip Goad and Cameron Logan

LONDON AND NEW YORK

First published 2019
by Routledge
2 Park Square, Milton Park, Abingdon, Oxon OX14 4RN

and by Routledge
52 Vanderbilt Avenue, New York, NY 10017

First issued in paperback 2020

Routledge is an imprint of the Taylor & Francis Group, an informa business

© 2019 Julie Willis, Philip Goad and Cameron Logan

The right of Julie Willis, Philip Goad and Cameron Logan to be identified as authors of this work has been asserted by them in accordance with sections 77 and 78 of the Copyright, Designs and Patents Act 1988.

All rights reserved. No part of this book may be reprinted or reproduced or utilised in any form or by any electronic, mechanical, or other means, now known or hereafter invented, including photocopying and recording, or in any information storage or retrieval system, without permission in writing from the publishers.

Trademark notice: Product or corporate names may be trademarks or registered trademarks, and are used only for identification and explanation without intent to infringe.

British Library Cataloguing-in-Publication Data
A catalogue record for this book is available from the British Library

Library of Congress Cataloging-in-Publication Data
Names: Willis, Julie, Ph. D., author. | Goad, Philip, author. | Logan, Cameron, 1974- author.
Title: Architecture and the modern hospital : Nosokomeion to Hygeia / Julie Willis, Philip Goad, and Cameron Logan.
Description: Abingdon, Oxon ; New York, NY : Routledge, 2019. | Series: Routledge research in architecture | Includes bibliographical references and index.
Identifiers: LCCN 2018027233 | ISBN 9780415815338 (hardback) | ISBN 9780429434495 (ebook)
Subjects: LCSH: Hospital architecture—History—20th century. | Hospital buildings—Design and construction.
Classification: LCC RA967 .W55 2019 | DDC 725/.51—dc23
LC record available at https://lccn.loc.gov/2018027233

ISBN 13: 978-0-367-66510-4 (pbk)
ISBN 13: 978-0-415-81533-8 (hbk)

Typeset in Sabon
by Apex CoVantage, LLC

Contents

List of figures vi
Preface xiv
Acknowledgements xvi

1 From *Nosokomeion* to *Hygeia*: foundations of an architecture for health 1

2 Everyone's own "healing machine": the hospital bed 24

3 Knowledge, care and control: nurses' stations and nurses' homes 56

4 Incision and anaesthesia: the operating theatre 78

5 Treating outside, looking inside: diagnosis and therapy 101

6 Full steam ahead! Servicing the modern hospital 129

7 Health, hygiene and progress: designing the hospital of tomorrow 152

8 Health city, healing landscapes and the hospital campus 188

9 The modern hospital: the rise, fall and rise again of architecture 214

Index 235

Figures

1.1 "Dawn – and the night nurses relieved from duty conjure up visions of another dawning. From the mists of hope long deferred will soon rise their 'sunshine' hospital". 2
1.2 Paimio is an iconic health building of the twentieth century, but not as important for the international hospital movement. Building A from the south. Patients' room and the sun terraces. Paimio Tuberculosis Sanatorium, Paimio, Finland. Architect: Alvar Aalto, 1928–1932. Photograph: Gustaf Welin, 1933. 8
1.3 The Chicago-based journal *Modern Hospital* was published monthly between 1913 and 1974. 10
1.4 Irwin conceived his hospital as "a mighty part of a militant machine whose function is to safeguard mankind against forces inimical to life" (Leighton Irwin & Co 1935). Prince Henry's Hospital, Melbourne, Victoria, Australia. Architect: Leighton Irwin & Company, 1936–1940. Photograph: unknown, c. 1946. 12
1.5 St Thomas' Hospital, London, England: an example of the 1960s modern block hospital. Architects: Yorke, Rosenberg & Mardall, 1966–1975. Photograph: Chris Pettit, 2017. 15
2.1 Nightingale ward in the Royal Herbert Hospital, Woolwich, England. Architect: Douglas Galton, 1859–1864. Photograph: Qualis Photography Co., 1920. 26
2.2 An adjustable hospital bed placed beside floor to ceiling windows in the Zürcher Höhenklinik (Zurich Heights Clinic), Clavadel, Switzerland. Architect: Rudolf Gaberel, 1930–1933. Photograph: Albert Steiner, c. 1935. 28
2.3 Advertisement for Bassick Hospital Castors. 30
2.4 Advertisement by Will Ross & Co. for the Dr Urie "Patient Comfort" spring bed. 32
2.5 Dr. John F. Alksne of the Medical College of Virginia demonstrated a Circ-O'lectric Bed to the hospital that would be used for neurosurgical and neurological patients. The

Figures vii

	Circ-O'lectric Bed was developed by Dr Homer Hartman Stryker, 1958. Photograph: unknown, c. 1970.	34
2.6	Patient bedroom and terrace, Krankenhaus Waiblingen (Waiblingen Hospital), Stuttgart, Germany. Architect: Richard Döcker, 1926–1928. Photograph: unknown.	36
2.7	Advertisement for "Vita" glass produced by Pilkington Brothers Limited.	38
2.8	Advertisement for the "Teleoptic" System produced by the Teleoptic Corporation.	42
2.9	Aural service at the bedside. Photograph: unknown, c. 1937.	43
2.10	Comparative drawing of Nightingale (1915) and Rigs (1938) wards. Delineator: unknown.	46
2.11	Patients' room. Paimio Tuberculosis Sanatorium, Paimio, Finland. Architect: Alvar Aalto, 1928–1932. Photograph: Gustaf Welin, 1933.	49
2.12	Sketch showing the "horizontal man" occupying a patient room at Paimio Sanatorium. Delineator: unknown.	50
2.13	Plan of single, two- and four-bed rooms arranged in a Rigs ward format in a typical thirty-two-bed wing, Södersjukhuset (Southern Hospital), Stockholm, Sweden. Architects: Hjalmar Cederström and Hermann Imhäuser, 1937–1944. Delineator: unknown.	51
2.14	Nurse bottle-feeding a baby in a humidicrib. Echuca Base Hospital, Echuca, Victoria, Australia. Photograph: Wolfgang Sievers, 1966.	53
3.1	A student nurse enjoys an afternoon of recreation on the tennis courts provided for the employees and staff doctors of the New York Hospital–Cornell Medical Center, Manhattan, New York, USA. Architects: Coolidge, Shepley, Bulfinch & Abbott, 1932. Photograph: Paul Parker, 1943.	58
3.2	Graduate student nurses relax in the living room of a nurses' home. Photograph: Fritz Henle, 1942.	59
3.3	Aided by binoculars, student nurses watch an operation through the glazed ceiling of an operating theatre. Photograph: Fritz Henle, 1942.	60
3.4	Nurses in the landscaped grounds of the Rudolf Virchow Krankenhaus (Rudolf Virchow Hospital), Berlin, Germany. Architect: Ludwig Hoffmann, 1898–1906. Photograph: Ernst von Brauchitsch.	62
3.5	Maternity ward in the Los Angeles County General Hospital, Los Angeles, California, USA, a characteristic tall block hospital of the 1930s. The centrally located nurses' station was situated just 15 steps from the furthest bed. Architects: Allied Architects' Association, 1932. Delineator: unknown.	64

viii   *Figures*

3.6   Plan of first floor, Sandringham and District Hospital, Sandringham, Victoria, Australia. Architects: J.H. Esmond Dorney and G. M. Hirsch, 1957–1964. Delineator: unknown.   65
3.7   A nurse presents the image of administrative efficiency at her station. Glass partitions allowed nurses to both see and be seen. St George's Hospital, Kew, Victoria, Australia. Architects: Leighton Irwin and Louis R. Williams, architects in association, 1937. Photograph: Commercial Photographic Co., c. 1940.   67
3.8   Pneumatic tube system for transporting medical records in use at the University of Chicago Clinics and Lying-In Hospital, Chicago, Illinois, USA. Photograph: unknown.   69
3.9   Nurses' home, Mount Sinai Hospital, 5th Avenue, Manhattan, New York, USA. Photograph: Wurts Bros., 1931.   74
4.1   Trainees watch Stanley Boyd about to perform surgery in the old operating theatre, Charing Cross Hospital, London, England. Photograph: unknown, 1900.   79
4.2   Surgical amphitheatre at the Lying-In Hospital, Manhattan, New York, USA. Architect: Robert H. Robertson, 1902.   80
4.3   This operating room includes green tiles, grey walls and a star-shaped light pendant for optimum surgical lighting conditions.   82
4.4   Carl Erikson proposed an elliptical paraboloid as the ideal shape for an operating room, with focused lighting, television and the separation of patient and audience. Plan and sectional drawings of Carl Erikson's "Ideal Operating Room" exhibited at the "Century of Progress" exhibition. Delineator: unknown.   84
4.5   Jean Walter's domed operating theatre saw the patient transferred to a gondola and passed through a preparation area and anaesthesis prior to entering the operating room. The operating suite carefully separated the movements of patient, medical staff, equipment and attendants to maintain as sterile a space as possible. Plan and section of the new Cité Hospitalière de Lille (Lille Hospital Complex), Lille, France. Architects: Walter, Cassan & Madeline, 1934–1958. Delineator: unknown.   86
4.6   Australian architects were inspired by Walter's domed operating theatre, and created versions of their own. Operating theatre at King George V Hospital for Mothers and Babies, Camperdown, New South Wales, Australia. Architects: Stephenson & Turner, 1939–1941. Photograph: unknown, c. 1941.   87

Figures   ix

4.7 To create the perfect shadowless environment, every
     individual light in the Saint-Lô operating theatre could be
     individually controlled. Operating theatre at Centre
     Hospitalier Mémorial France États-Unis (France United States
     Memorial Hospital), Saint-Lô, France. Architect: Paul Nelson,
     1946–1956. Photograph: studio Henri Baranger, 1959.   88
4.8 Drawing of Chirurgische Universitätsklinik (University
     Surgical Clinic) in Tübingen, Germany, showing top lighting
     and air handling. Architect: Hans Daiber, 1936. Delineator:
     unknown.   90
4.9 The complexity of traffic in operating rooms is clearly
     demonstrated by this kinetic diagram. Delineator: unknown.   93
4.10 It was important to ensure that movement of key actors in
     operating suites was carefully considered to allow for
     optimum efficiency and surgical outcomes. Delineator:
     unknown.   95
4.11 A televised surgical session in progress at St Luke's Hospital,
     Chicago, Illinois, USA. Photograph: unknown, 1949.   97
5.1 Postcard depicting the Gläserner Mensch (Transparent
     Man). Photograph: unknown, 1930.   102
5.2 Gymnastics and physiotherapy, Kantonsspital (Cantonal
     Hospital) (now Universitätsspital Basel [Basel University
     Hospital]), Switzerland. Architects: H. Baur, E. & P. Vischer
     and Bräuning Leu Dürig, 1939–1945. Photograph:
     unknown, c. 1945.   105
5.3 Zander Machines for abdominal massage or chest movement
     were often used in early twentieth century hospitals.
     Photograph: unknown.   106
5.4 Burns room, Cincinnati General Hospital, Cincinnati, Ohio,
     USA, planned, designed and constructed by dermatologist
     Dr H. Jerry Lavender, 1937. Photograph: unknown.   107
5.5 An oxygen tent in use, Beth Israel Hospital, Manhattan, New
     York, USA. Photograph: Samuel H. Gottscho, 1935.   110
5.6 School lessons on the sundeck, Frankston Children's Hospital,
     Frankston, Victoria, Australia. Architects: Stephenson &
     Meldrum, 1928. Photograph: Lyle Fowler, 1936.   112
5.7 The Finsen Lamp, devised for the treating of lupus using
     ultraviolet rays, presented by Princess Alexandria to the
     London Hospital, London, England, 1900. Photograph:
     unknown.   114
5.8 Advertisement for Carbon Arc Solarium Units produced by
     the Eveready National Carbon Company Inc.   115
5.9 A child having an X-ray at the Universitäts-Kinderklinik
     (University Children's Hospital), Vienna, Austria.
     Photograph: unknown, 1921.   116

x *Figures*

5.10   Comparison of old and new X-ray department plans, Alfred Hospital, Prahran, Victoria, Australia. Architects: A. & K. Henderson, 1940. Delineator: unknown. 118
5.11   X-ray filing system, Columbia-Presbyterian Medical Center, Manhattan, New York, USA. Architect: James Gamble Rogers, 1928. Photograph: Wurts Bros., 1936. 119
5.12   CT brain scanner of 1970–1971 in use at Atkinson Morley Hospital, Wimbledon, England. Photograph: unknown, 1980. 124
6.1   "Arteries, veins and nerves", opening photograph to the article, "Hospital Heating Systems" by Alfred Kellogg, in *Architectural Forum*. Photograph: Woodhead, c. 1932. 130
6.2   Plan of 15th floor, Bellevue Hospital, Manhattan, New York, USA. Architects: Katz, Waisman, Blumenkranz, Stein & Weber with Pomerance & Breines, 1960–1974. Delineator: unknown. 135
6.3   Rendering for the power plant for the New York Hospital–Cornell Medical Center, Manhattan, New York, USA. Architects: Coolidge, Shepley, Bulfinch & Abbott, 1932. Rendering: Dadmun Company, c. 1932. 138
6.4   The interior of the power plant, New York Hospital–Cornell Medical Center, Manhattan, New York, USA. Architects: Coolidge, Shepley, Bulfinch & Abbott, 1932. Photograph: Edward Beckwith, c. 1930s. 139
6.5   Creating order from chaos: workers hand-sort large volumes of linen in the busy in-house laundry and linen department, New York Hospital–Cornell Medical Center, Manhattan, New York, USA. Architects: Coolidge, Shepley, Bulfinch & Abbott, 1932. Photograph: Ewing Galloway, c. 1940s. 141
6.6   Cover image, "The Story of a Sheet". Artist: unknown. 142
6.7   Central kitchen, Hôpital Beaujon (Beaujon Hospital), Clichy, Paris, France. Architects: Walter, Plousey & Cassan, 1932–1935. Photograph: unknown, c. 1938. 145
6.8   Morgue caravan and gurney, Hôpital Beaujon (Beaujon Hospital), Clichy, Paris, France. Architects: Walter, Plousey & Cassan, 1932–1935. Photograph: unknown, c. 1938. 147
6.9   Morgue caravan being towed through the hospital grounds, Hôpital Beaujon (Beaujon Hospital), Clichy, Paris, France. Architects: Walter, Plousey & Cassan, 1932–1935. Photograph: unknown, c. 1938. 148
6.10   Sectional drawing, McMaster University Health Sciences Centre, Hamilton, Ontario, Canada. Architects: Craig, Zeidler & Strong, 1967–1972. Delineator: unknown. 149
7.1   Fifth Avenue Hospital, Manhattan, New York, USA, was one of the many structures visited by Australian architect

	Arthur Stephenson in 1926. Architects: York & Sawyer, 1921. Photograph: Irving Underhill, 1922.	155
7.2	New York Hospital–Cornell Medical Center, Manhattan, New York, USA. Architects: Coolidge, Shepley, Bulfinch & Abbott, 1932. Photograph: William Frange, c. 1930s.	158
7.3	Columbia-Presbyterian Medical Center, Manhattan, New York, USA, one of the earliest multistoreyed block hospitals, captured the imagination as a "colossus" and a "Fortress of Health". Architect: James Gamble Rogers, 1928. Photograph: Wurts Bros., 1937.	159
7.4	Krankenhaus Waiblingen (Waiblingen Hospital), Stuttgart, Germany. Architect: Richard Döcker, 1926–1928. Photograph: Fotographisches Atelier Ullstein, 1929.	163
7.5	Stephenson admired the "extreme originality of thought" evident in the design of Zonnestraal Sanatorium (Sunburst Sanatorium), Hilversum, Netherlands (Stephenson c. 1933: 6). Architects: Jan Duiker & Bernard Bijvoet, 1925–1931. Photograph: unknown, c. 1930s.	165
7.6	For Stephenson, Stadt Krankenhaus (State Hospital), Vienna, Austria, exemplified "a lesson in beauty and form of colour" (Stephenson n.d.: 179). Architects: Fritz Judtmann & Egon Riss, 1929–1931. Photograph: Österreichische Lichtbildstelle, c. 1930.	166
7.7	Mercy Hospital, East Melbourne, Victoria, Australia. Architects: Stephenson & Meldrum, 1933–1935. Delineator: unknown, c. 1934.	167
7.8	Kantonsspital (Cantonal Hospital), Basel, Switzerland. Architects: H. Baur, E. & P. Vischer and Bräuning Leu Dürig, 1939–1945. Photograph: Werner Freidli, 1945.	169
7.9	Angles of sunlight and progressive design governed the form of the Hospital for Chronic Diseases, Welfare Island (now Roosevelt Island), New York, USA. Architects: Rosenfield, Butler & Kohn, with York & Sawyer, c. 1938. Photograph: unknown, 1938.	171
7.10	Design by Richard Neutra for a five-hundred-bed hospital in an unnamed city in California, USA. Delineator: Richard Neutra.	172
7.11	Södersjukhuset (Southern Hospital), Stockholm, Sweden. Architects: Hjalmar Cederström and Hermann Imhäuser, 1937–1944. Photograph: unknown, c. 1950s.	174
7.12	Charité Berlin-Campus Klinikum Benjamin Franklin (Benjamin Franklin Campus Clinic), Steglitz, Berlin, Germany. Architects: Arthur Q. Davis, Curtis & Davis, 1955–1958, 1959–1968. Photograph: Schöning, 2012.	179

xii *Figures*

7.13 McMaster University Health Sciences Centre, Hamilton, Ontario, Canada. Architects: Craig, Zeidler & Strong, 1967–1972. Photograph: Historic Hamilton, 2010. 183
8.1 General plan for the Cité Hospitalière de Lille (Lille Hospital Complex), Lille, France. Architect: Paul Nelson, 1932–1933. Photograph: Man Ray, 1932. 189
8.2 The collegiate Gothic form of the Chicago Lying-In Hospital, Chicago, Illinois, USA, complemented its university surroundings. Architects: Schmidt, Garden & Erikson, 1931. Photograph: Capes Photo, c. 1931. 192
8.3 Nuovo Ospedale Maggiore di Brescia (New Major Hospital), Brescia, Italy. Architect: Angelo Bordoni, 1930–1953. Delineator: unknown. 194
8.4 Hôpital Louis Pasteur (Louis Pasteur Hospital), Colmar, France. Architect: William (Willy) Vetter, 1935–1937. Photograph: unknown. 195
8.5 Vehicular arrival at the Fort Hamilton Veterans' Administration Hospital, Brooklyn, New York, USA. Architects: Skidmore Owings & Merrill, 1947–1952. Photograph: unknown, c. 1950s. 200
8.6 Postcard depicting the Los Angeles County General Hospital, Los Angeles, California, USA. Architects: Allied Architects' Association, 1932. Artist: unknown. 202
8.7 Site plan of Södersjukhuset (Southern Hospital), Stockholm, Sweden. Architects: Hjalmar Cederström and Hermann Imhäuser, 1937–1944. Delineator: unknown. 204
8.8 Stephenson & Turner publicly proposed plans to create a large hospital precinct, consisting of multiple specialist hospitals and the existing Royal Melbourne Hospital. Melbourne Medical Centre, proposal. Architects: Stephenson & Turner, c. 1944. Delineator: unknown, 1944. 206
9.1 Rear view, Hôpital Beaujon (Beaujon Hospital), Clichy, France. Architects: Walter, Plousey & Cassan, 1932–1935. Photograph: Henri Manuel, c. 1935. 216
9.2 A speculative design for an underwater hospital. Architects: E. Todd Wheeler/Perkins & Will, 1971. Delineator: E. Todd Wheeler, 1971. 219
9.3 Aerial view, Universitätsklinikum (University Hospital), Aachen, Germany. Architects: Weber & Brand, 1972–1982. Photograph: Hans Blossey, 2015. 220
9.4 The elevated main hospital "street", Northwick Park Hospital, Harrow, England. Architects: Llewelyn-Davies & Weeks, 1962, 1966–1970. Photograph: Henk Snoek, 1973. 223

9.5	Exterior, Nuffield Transplantation Surgery Unit, Western General Hospital, Edinburgh, Scotland. Architect: Peter Womersley, 1963–1968. Photograph: Sam Lambert, 1968.	224
9.6	The hospital in the twenty-first century: the atrium of the Royal Children's Hospital, Melbourne, Victoria, Australia. Architects: Bates Smart and Billard Leece Partnership, 2006–2011. Photograph: Shannon McGrath, 2012.	228
9.7	Interior, Universitätsspital Basel (formerly Kantonsspital [Cantonal Hospital]), Basel, Switzerland. Architects: H. Baur, E. & P. Vischer and Bräuning Leu Dürig, 1939–1945. Photograph: Cameron Logan, 2010.	232
9.8	Centre Hospitalier Mémorial France États-Unis (France United States Memorial Hospital), Saint-Lô, France. Architect: Paul Nelson, 1946–1956. Photograph: studio Henri Baranger, 1959.	233

Preface

The impetus for this book comes from our long-standing interest in the design of hospitals as a vehicle for architectural innovation. In Australia, the arrival of international modernism was heralded by a series of key hospitals built in the mid-1930s: these were arguably the first prominent buildings that embraced a functional aesthetic, tying the latest in medical care to a progressive architectural idiom in the eyes of the public, at a time when hospitals were emerging as foundational in the community's expectations around a functioning welfare state. And these buildings had an impressive pedigree, born of a seminal worldwide tour that Melbourne architect Arthur Stephenson, dominant partner in the architecture firm that designed them, undertook in the early 1930s; a trip that led him to witness the latest in hospital and housing design and to meet the leading lights of hospital architecture. His admiration for works like the Weissenhof Siedlung in Stuttgart and the Zonnestraal Sanatorium in Hilversum, as well as scores of other buildings, were writ large in the designs for hospitals his firm produced on his return to Australia. Stephenson's position of distance from the two key loci of architectural development of hospitals, North America (Canada and the United States) and Europe, particularly Germany and Scandinavia, meant that he was a prolific correspondent with and consumer of information from both networks, without belonging to either camp. His documentation of this tour, published in the *Modern Hospital* journal in a series of articles over several years, gave a prominence to European ideas in the American context in a way not seen before.

Our research commenced with a project, funded by an Australian Research Council Discovery Grant (DP0771644), to examine the development of the modern hospital in Australia, to understand the international influence on, but also the international significance of, these hospitals. However, it soon became clear that the buildings that had influenced Stephenson, and many other architects, had received limited attention. Some of the key sources were published only in Italian, German or French; and other publications had focused – understandably – on particular geographical locations. Hospitals, as they developed particularly in the twentieth century, are large and complex sites; their scale is overwhelming. Many scholars have concentrated on aspects of these conditions, examining hospitals from the perspective of their planning and functional arrangements. We have taken a different position, instead building up our examination of the twentieth-century hospital through a number of different lenses, or sites, which have been pivotal in the design of the modern hospital. These sites show the hospital at different scales – we start with the bed and end at the campus – but also from different perspectives such as the position of the nurse in the hospital. We do not comprehensively review every aspect of the design of hospitals, but instead seek to reveal how medical needs in providing therapy and care to patients have been deeply affected by, and have had deep effect on, architecture and design. Many of these design lessons remain relevant today. We found it a fascinating research journey and marvelled at the inventiveness designers and medical professionals demonstrated in their search for solutions to effectively treat and investigate the human body through the mode of the twentieth century hospital.

Julie Willis, Philip Goad and Cameron Logan

Acknowledgements

Research for this book was partially funded by the Australian Government through the Australian Research Council (DP0771644).

We thank all the hospitals that allowed us to visit and access their archival collections, as well as the collecting institutions and individuals who allowed us to include the illustrated material in this book. All reasonable efforts were made to contact the copyright holders for permission to reproduce the works illustrated.

The authors would like to thank Katti Williams and Ann Standish for their exemplary assistance in the production of this manuscript. Giorgio Marfella, Simon Elchlepp and Xavier Cadorel provided helpful translation advice to the project, for which we are most grateful. We would also like to thank Annmarie Adams for her long-standing advice and encouragement of this project.

1 From *Nosokomeion* to *Hygeia*
Foundations of an architecture for health

Hospitals of the recent past can be miserable places. And when they are not miserable, they can often be dreary looking and stale smelling. So it will no doubt strike some readers as counter-intuitive that this book is based around the contention that the modern hospital was a beacon of hope. The modern hospital, defined here as the distinctive product of international hospital discourse between 1918 and 1960, emerged as a bulwark against the hopelessness of disease and persistent ill-health that, in spite of the great advances in medical science, beset industrialised countries through the first half of the twentieth century. One Australian hospital's annual report in the late 1930s linked new hospitals with hope in an illustration captioned "The Vision Splendid" (Figure 1.1). Nurses standing on the balcony of an old hospital, with its traditional stylistic trappings, point towards a new hospital building, an unadorned modern edifice that emerges clear and bright from the storm clouds. The caption for the image begins, "Dawn – and the night nurses relieved from duty conjure up visions of another dawning. From the mists of hope long deferred will soon rise their 'sunshine' hospital" (Royal Melbourne Hospital 1939: 36). The image conjured the hope that hospital staff – proxies for the wider community – had invested in the idea of the modern hospital. The change was depicted in very clear terms: as one from darkness to light and from tradition to modernity.

The "Vision Splendid" image framed a transition in institutional identity, a move from charitable care to rationally organised health and welfare. This idea resonated with hospital experts in the period. As Yale Professor of Public Health Charles-Edward Winslow noted in 1932, the hospital of the past "was in its essence a work of mercy, an expression of pity rather than organized knowledge" (Winslow 1932: 222). Winslow's career, like that of other hospital experts of the time, was dedicated to furthering the process by which hospitals became institutions of knowledge where research, treatment and education would all be conducted on a single campus.

The hope invested in the modern hospital rested, therefore, on more than just architectural expression and dreamlike images of the new. The great height and expressive modernism of new hospital buildings were also powerful markers of a whole apparatus of healthcare and medical knowledge that

2 *From* Nosokomeion *to* Hygeia

Figure 1.1 "Dawn – and the night nurses relieved from duty conjure up visions of another dawning. From the mists of hope long deferred will soon rise their 'sunshine' hospital".
Source: Royal Melbourne Hospital. "Annual Report, 1938–1939". Melbourne: The Royal Melbourne Hospital, 1939: rear cover.
Courtesy: The Royal Melbourne Hospital Archives.

would enable major transformations in the health of populations and increased expectations of lifespan in the period. The international network of hospital experts that coalesced in the 1920s and 1930s – a group that included architects, doctors and economists, as well as management and organisational specialists – shared a belief that the properly planned modern hospital could treat the individual with unprecedented scientific rigour. As medical specialist and historian Joel D. Howell has argued:

> By around 1925 the people who ran and financially supported the general hospital in the United States, as well as those who delivered health care within it, had come to see science as the essential tool for making the institution a central part of twentieth century medicine.
> (Howell 1995: 4–5)

This was a wide view of science that incorporated everything from Taylorist organisational principles to advanced uses of pathology laboratories in everyday diagnosis. The collective implication of this wide embrace of science, experts believed, would be the improved health and wellbeing of whole societies. Though in reality, of course, different populations within each society experienced that promise differently and access to the benefits of new hospitals was uneven.

The conscious project to modernise the hospital through a rationalisation of its architectural plan and its procedures was in part a response to the depredations of World War I. Medical and political leaders in Europe, in particular, in the 1920s and 1930s believed that future economic expansion and military strength demanded fitter, healthier populations. The modern hospital was a key piece of infrastructure that would help realise that ambition. Consequently, the hospital, more than any other building type, was integral to the biopolitical social policy of the interwar decades.

The economic and political upheavals of the interwar period ensured that social policy was far from consistent. Yet there was an increasingly explicit ambition across Europe, North America and in other industrialised societies to govern using techniques that took the body and the health of populations as their explicit object. The hospital was a key instrument in this process. Writing in the Stuttgart-based quarterly hospital review *Nosokomeion* in 1936, the American economist and healthcare specialist C. Rufus Rorem argued that the hospital "is not merely a hotel, nor is it merely a place from which to dispense medical care at a reasonable price. It is a focal point for the concentration and dissemination of knowledge concerning life itself" (Rorem 1936: 245).

Medical historians have acknowledged that in this period, hospitals became vital educational institutions, forging themselves decisively as the profession's training ground. But for Rorem and other hospital specialists, the implications of the modern hospital were more far reaching. Dr Wilhelm C.F. Alter (1875–1943), editor of *Nosokomeion*, the official journal of the International Hospital Association, from its founding in 1929 for almost a decade, highlighted the great scope and ambition of hospitals. In his editorials and at conferences throughout the 1930s, Alter asserted that hospitals must be redesigned and rebuilt to reflect the era of health. A doctor, administrator and researcher into hospital practices and nursing, Alter regularly articulated his view that the hospital must no longer be a home of illness, but must become a "Maison de Sainte", a centre of the activities of health. In a 1933 editorial he wrote:

> health training of the people is the fundamental task of a hospital ... Materially, [the hospital] must be the efficient central institution for the organization of all preventative and curative work of the district. Spiritually it must be the centre from which new ideas emanate, and which provides the fertile soil of their growth.
>
> (Alter 1933: 2)

Writing in the same venue in 1937, architect Vladimir Uklein (1898–1986) underlined Alter's great theme, arguing that hospitals must be developed according to the principle of health (*Hygeia*[1]) and that this should replace the older idea of the hospital as a place to care for the sick (*Nosokomeion*[2]) (Uklein 1937). The idea and ambition of the modern hospital, therefore, was not simply to assist the professionalisation process for nursing and for medicine generally, though hospitals in the first half of the twentieth century unquestionably did this. They were also centrally implicated in what political theorists, following Michel Foucault, have described as "the modern conception of power as a way to enhance, render productive, compose, maximise, and administer life" (Wallenstein 2008: 9).

As has been widely noted, this account of power is productive rather than repressive and depends upon the consent of political subjects rather than a coercive state. Individuals under such a regime accept responsibility for their own biological enhancement and productive powers, and are provided with incentives and infrastructure to do so. The normalisation of hospital birthing across this period is an excellent case in point. As hospital administrator and leader of the American Hospital Association, Malcolm T. MacEachern (1881–1956), noted in 1935, "the hospital is quickly becoming the birthplace of mankind" (MacEachern 1935: 97). This happened not because women were coerced into attending hospital to give birth. Rather doctors and hospital managers, people such as MacEachern, with the strong support of governments in almost all industrialised societies, persuaded their citizens that the birthing process would be administered more safely, efficiently and, at least from a certain viewpoint, more humanely in hospitals than was typical in the home.

The various national hospital networks and associations and the International Hospital Association (IHA), formed in 1929, were almost unanimous in this period in their support for a liberal model of health promotion and service delivery, even though governments, both regional and national, supported very different economic models for funding the provision of healthcare. Indeed, the IHA was explicitly liberal and internationalist, despite maturing as an organisation just as aggressive nationalisms and totalitarianism were on the rise in the 1930s. Sigismund Schultz Goldwater (1873–1942), a leading figure in the field of public health in New York and an expert on hospital planning and administration, articulated the internationalist aspirations of the hospital movement in a 1929 article for the American journal *Modern Hospital*. He noted: "In a humanitarian field as important and significant as that of hospitals, geographical barriers and linguistic obstacles must be swept away and the totality of human experience made universally available" (Goldwater 1929: 50).

After a string of successful international biannual conferences held in Atlantic City, New Jersey, USA (1929); Vienna, Austria (1931); the coastal town of Knokke in Flanders (1933); Rome, Italy (1935) and Paris, France (1937), the IHA was split by war and by the hardening eugenic outlook of German public health under Nazism in the late 1930s. In 1935, Swiss-born German psychiatrist and geneticist, Professor Ernst Rüdin (1874–1952), a key proponent of racially based eugenic theories in Germany, gave a paper to the IHA's World Congress in Rome, discussing the uses of sterilisation. The condemnation of Rüdin's views was swift and clear. The Dutch delegation protested that his paper propagandised for the "active application of eugenic methods in hospitals" without regard for the ethical and religious convictions of delegates ("Declaration" 1935: 314). Pope Pius XI addressed the conference and underlined the Catholic Church's opposition to eugenic methods, arguing that hospital specialists and others in the health field should protest their application. The French delegation, who had agreed to host the next conference in Paris, made it clear that they would not allow the discussion of eugenics or sterilisation to be part of their official programme in 1937 (Leon 2013).

The presence of Rüdin and his advocacy of ethically unsound and morally repugnant eugenic practices did not destroy the spirit of international cooperation in the hospital movement at that time, nor disrupt its liberal foundations. But it did point to a fault line within the hospital movement and international public health in the period. Eugenics was an unstable discourse embraced to some degree by public health advocates across the political spectrum as histories of eugenics have shown (Nye 1993; Turda 2010). Eugenic policies were a logical extension of the conviction that the individual political subject and populations as a whole should be governed at the level of biological life and physical health. Nevertheless, the sovereign, state-centred biopolitics of Nazi eugenics served to highlight the limits and character of the liberal international ideals of the hospital movement. Once the enhancement of life was no longer based around the active consent and participation of citizens and patients, then the very effective operations of liberal governmentality were clearly undone.

The eugenics controversy in 1935 highlighted an important shared assumption for the hospital movement. But the line between the broad social consent of patients and the morally charged mission of health promotion was difficult to discern. Wilhelm Alter, for example, adopted a bellicose tone in some of his editorialising for *Nosokomeion*. In a 1933 editorial he wrote:

> Civilised humanity demands a science of health. The immense intensification of our social, political, and economic life forces the individual and society as a whole to become disciples of the creed of health, and to support a movement for the combating of disease through prevention. This journal has from its very beginning called attention to the fact that the hospital occupies the deciding strategic position in this movement. The hospital is holding this key position not only in the defensive war against disease, but also in the great offensive war of our time, in the war for health. No other institution or organisation is better adapted

and has a more legitimate calling to be the pioneer in safeguarding human life for health.

(Alter 1933: 2)

While most active participants in the hospital movement shared Alter's zeal for their work, they framed their mission in more moderate terms, more as a form of progressive humanity and care than a war for health. Nevertheless, evocations of fortification and war were common in the discussion of hospitals. New York's Columbia-Presbyterian Medical Center, New York, USA (Architect: James Gamble Rogers, 1928), for example, was repeatedly described as a great fortress raised against disease (Betsky 1994). But the question of how the architect should treat the problem of the hospital was not circumscribed by martial images and ideas. It was in fact a surprisingly complex arena for thinking through and expressing modern aspirations for health and architecture.

Architecture as medical equipment

Referring to architectural discourse during the 1920s and early 1930s, architectural historian Beatriz Colomina has remarked that modern architecture was "understood as a kind of medical equipment, a mechanism for protecting and enhancing the body" (Colomina 1997: 61). Margaret Campbell has highlighted the centrality of the tuberculosis sanatorium to this discourse, but importantly, she qualifies its earnest enthusiasm where, "[s]uperstition, myth and subjectivity partnered modernist functional lifestyles that emphasized purity, hygiene, fresh air and sunlight" (Campbell 2005). One might assume then that the hospital would be at the centre of the modernist architectural project. Wallenstein has suggested, moreover, that architectural modernity is "intertwined with the ordering and administering of life" and that within this regime the hospital becomes "a kind of laboratory for the testing of new ideas, which are then extended to the whole of urban space" (Wallenstein 2008: 31).

Despite the obvious overlapping concerns and the explicit modernism of the architectural avant-garde and the modern hospital movement, the relationship between hospitals and modern architecture is quite complicated, even ambivalent. For the most part, the hospital was not a signal building type for promoting the claims and ideas of the modern movement. Just one year before the establishment of the IHA in 1929, a celebrated and influential group of modernist architects and urban planners formed the *Congrès Internationaux d'Architecture Moderne* (International Congresses of Modern Architecture) (CIAM) at a meeting in Château de la Sarraz in Switzerland. Organised by Swiss-French architect Le Corbusier, Hélène de Mandrot (owner of the château) and Swiss art historian Sigfried Giedion, the group was initially comprised of twenty-eight European architects. It rapidly expanded its membership internationally, meeting at eleven congresses before it was disbanded in 1959. While CIAM's overarching goal was the modernist recasting of urbanism and housing, the number of its members involved in the design of hospitals was modest. At various times, noted hospital and sanatorium designers like Swiss architects Rudolf Steiger, Werner M. Moser and Max Ernst Haefeli, French-American architect Paul Nelson, German Richard Döcker, Dutchman Jan Duiker, Finnish architect Alvar Aalto and Belgian Gaston Brunfaut all had associations with CIAM but, while active to varying degrees, they were never its key leaders nor did the modern hospital ever feature as a key plank in CIAM's urban discourse (Mumford 2000).

Histories of modernism in architecture written before 1960 barely mentioned modernism's connections with health and hygiene; they feature the occasional tuberculosis sanatorium but never the comprehensive modern hospital. Nikolaus Pevsner's *Pioneers of Modern Design* (1936) illustrated Josef Hoffman's Sanatorium Purkersdorf in Austria (1904–1905) and J.M. Richards's *An Introduction to Modern Architecture* (1940) included Aalto's Paimio Tuberculosis Sanatorium, Paimio, Finland (1928–1932) and Tecton's Finsbury Borough Health Centre, London, England (1938), but the commentary in each of those texts focused on formal composition and little else. Sigfried Giedion's *Space, Time and Architecture* (1941) stated: "As far as we can see, there are three institutional buildings inseparably linked to the rise of contemporary architecture", of which Aalto's Paimio Sanatorium was one (Giedion 1941: 463).[3] But his book mentioned no other twentieth-century hospital. Perhaps the most balanced account in historical terms was American architectural historian Talbot Hamlin's edited four-volume set, *Forms and Functions of Twentieth Century Architecture* (1952). In a section titled "Buildings for Public Health", Hamlin wrote a brief introduction before dividing it into three sections: "Hospitals", "Dispensaries and Health Centers" and "Sanatoriums and Asylums", each authored by an American specialist hospital architect, respectively Charles Butler, Isadore Rosenfield and William L. Pereira. Hamlin's book did three things that other histories of twentieth-century architecture in that period did not. It acknowledged the significance of the modern hospital for twentieth-century architecture more generally, it clearly recognised the complexity of its subject and it placed Aalto's sanatorium in a category that better defined its important but lesser place in the overall picture of the development of healthcare buildings in the first half of the twentieth century (Hamlin 1952).

By 1960, of the most famous names of twentieth-century modern architecture, arguably only Erich Mendelsohn and Gordon Bunshaft of Skidmore Owings & Merrill had produced a significant body of hospital work. Le Corbusier's widely discussed Venice hospital proposal (1963–1965) remained unbuilt, while Walter Gropius provided advice as a consultant for extensions to the Michael Reese Hospital (1946–1953), a middle-sized postwar hospital in Chicago, Illinois, USA – a building that has rarely been discussed in either

8 *From* Nosokomeion *to* Hygeia

the specialist hospital literature or the architecture press, only really garnering any architectural attention when it was slated for demolition in 2009. Alvar Aalto's Paimio Sanatorium was perhaps the most iconic health building of the twentieth century (Figure 1.2). But, as already discussed, it was highly significant for modern architecture, but not as important for the international hospital movement. It was not, after all, a major general hospital and so, for all its aesthetic refinement, it lacked the scientific rigour and organisational complexity demanded by the leading medical institutions.

In many respects, the discourse that arose around the modern hospital in the 1920s and 1930s grew from the establishment of the IHA in 1929, and continued after the organisation reformed and was renamed the International Hospital Federation (IHF) in 1947 following a hiatus during World War II. Unlike CIAM, which disbanded after eleven congresses, the IHF's biannual congresses, now numbering more than forty, continue to this day. The IHA brought together medical practitioners and specialists, hospital directors and administrators, and architects and planners from across the globe. A strong interdisciplinary network, the IHA published

Figure 1.2 Paimio is an iconic health building of the twentieth century, but not as important for the international hospital movement. Building A from the south. Patients' room and the sun terraces. Paimio Tuberculosis Sanatorium, Paimio, Finland. Architect: Alvar Aalto, 1928–1932. Photograph: Gustaf Welin, 1933.

© Alvar Aalto Museum, used with permission.

its congress proceedings as well as the quarterly journal, *Nosokomeion* (1930–1939), published originally from Stuttgart, with articles in German, French, English, Italian and Spanish.[4] The journal's pages attracted all the leading experts in the field and its breadth and authority was widely recognised. A review in March 1932 by the *Canadian Medical Association Journal* of the latest issue underlined *Nosokomeion*'s global reach:

> The twenty contributed articles give an excellent panorama of the latest ideas in hospital construction throughout the world, and include contributions by authorities well known in this country. Prof. B.P. Watson writes from the viewpoint of the obstetrician; the well known architect E.F. Stevens reviews hospital construction in the United States; Mr. C.E. Elcock contributes the British viewpoint; Doctor Rollier has written well on the sun treatment of tuberculosis in the Alps; Dr. G.B. Roatta reviews progress in Italy. The roentgenological department is considered by Grossman, of Berlin, Holfelder, of Frankfurt – A.M., and Seth Hirsch, of New York. Professor Holfelder warns against injudicious purchases of radium because of the uncertain future demarcation between the fields of roentgen and curie-therapeutics.
>
> ("Review: Nosokomeion" 1932: 392)

The official discourse was supplemented by other journals, most notably the monthly English-language *Modern Hospital* (1913–1974), published out of Chicago (Figure 1.3), and a daunting range of large, comprehensively detailed books, written not just by medical specialists but also by hospital architects from Europe, United Kingdom and the United States, that indicate the scale and importance of these buildings to twentieth-century social, architectural and urban development. The key texts among them, written by leading medical practitioners and architects and consistently cited across the period, include Edward F. Stevens' *The American Hospital of the Twentieth Century* (1918, updated 1928), J.E. Stone's *Hospital Organization and Management* (1927), Wilhelm Alter's *Das Deutsche Krankenhaus 1925* (1927) and *Das Krankenhaus* (1936), Jean Walter's *Renaissance de l'architecture médicale* (1945), Charles Butler and Addison Erdman's *Hospital Planning* (1946) and Isadore Rosenfield's *Hospitals: Integrated Design* (1947). B. Franco Moretti, administrative director of Clinical Training Institutes in Milan, compiled the most comprehensive review of contemporary hospitals across the world, the magisterial *Ospedali*, published first in 1935 with a second edition in 1940 and a third in 1951. Copiously illustrated and with over five hundred pages, it documented hospitals in Europe, the United States, South America and Australia, and remains one of the most thoroughgoing studies of any building type of the twentieth century. Other key sources were the numerous manual-like publications on hospitals produced by the US Public Health Service (USPHS). As a means of coming to grips with the technical and spatial complexity of the modern hospital,

Figure 1.3 The Chicago-based journal *Modern Hospital* was published monthly between 1913 and 1974.

Source: *Modern Hospital* 31, no. 4 (October 1928): front cover.

these publications gave excellent and easily digestible expert advice. All these books were remarkable for their authors' willingness to share and compare practices and expertise across continents. If there was ever an open international dialogue about the future of a modern building type, this was it (Stone 1944).

For most of the period, the field of hospital architecture was dominated by specialists rather than by the prevailing figures in modern architecture internationally. Edward F. Stevens (1860–1946, North America), Hermann Distel (1875–1945, Germany), Jean Walter (1883–1957, France), Hjalmar Cederström (1880–1953, Sweden) and Arthur Stephenson (1890–1967, Australia) were among the most prolific hospital designers from the 1920s to the 1950s, and each was closely connected with the modern hospital movement as an expert and interlocutor. None were major figures in the international discourse on modernism in architecture. But the modernism of the hospital movement and modern movement in architecture influenced their work in important, though quite different, ways.

Some hospital specialists proclaimed a modernism that echoed Wilhelm Alter's epochal rhetoric about health and the hospital. For example, Leighton Irwin (1892–1962), an Australian hospital architect and *Nosokomeion* editorial board member, wrote of his Prince Henry's Hospital project in Melbourne, Victoria, Australia in 1935 (Figure 1.4):

> The hospital is an essential factor in modern living, for two equally important reasons. It is a mighty part of a militant machine whose function is to safeguard mankind against forces inimical to life ... [And as] part of the educational structure of modern civilization it teaches its patients how to live.
>
> (Leighton Irwin & Co 1935)

The influential Swedish hospital architect and expert Hjalmar Cederström shared some of Irwin's convictions about the fight against disease. But his articles and pamphlets highlighted that social planning and the wider problem of the healthy urban organism were as vital to the process of planning and building a hospital as purely architectural considerations. Indeed, for Cederström, the architectural considerations could only proceed on the basis of thorough social and technical investigations of the problem. He argued, for example, that the techniques of regional planning be applied to the hospital problem, and that hospital planning should be based on a clear understanding of the demographic characteristics of the city and its districts. Architecture was to be integrated into social science and the health and wellbeing of populations in Cederström's vision. In North America, this expanded field of action for architecture became a keynote of modern architecture during and immediately after World War II. But the planning for Cederström and Imhäuser's Södersjukhuset (Southern

Figure 1.4 Irwin conceived his hospital as "a mighty part of a militant machine whose function is to safeguard mankind against forces inimical to life" (Leighton Irwin & Co 1935). Prince Henry's Hospital, Melbourne, Victoria, Australia. Architect: Leighton Irwin & Company, 1936–1940. Photograph: unknown, c. 1946.

Courtesy: Pictures Collection, State Library of Victoria, H2014.1020/16.

Hospital) (1937–1944) in Stockholm, Sweden, highlighted that it was already prominent in the 1930s (Cederström 1932, c. 1946; Shanken 2009).

Edward F. Stevens was the leading hospital architect in North America from the 1900s until World War II. Prolific as both a designer and an expert commentator, he produced reams of published material, including a major manual on hospital design. In contrast to Irwin and Cederström, who created buildings with striking modern elevations, Stevens' modernism was almost entirely focused on "the making of the plan" (Adams 2008: 90). He drew upon analogies with the factory and other business enterprises to describe the objectives of hospital design. In his 1918 book, he wrote:

> Hospital planning demands the same careful thought that is the foundation of any modern successful business enterprise. It is essential in the shoe factory, the paper mill, or the business establishment to so plan that the raw materials may be assembled and the finished product delivered with fewest possible intervening motions. In the hospital the patient, the food and the treatment may be termed raw material.... In the factory the saving of time in any of the processes adds to the annual product, and in the hospital, likewise ... everything that can help early convalescence, add to the efficiency of the institution.
>
> (Stevens 1918: 2)

The analogy with the factory became something of a commonplace for promoting the productiveness of the modern hospital during the 1930s. However, unlike the architectural avant-garde of the interwar decades, Stevens did not draw upon a factory aesthetic for his hospital projects. Instead, he treated the problem of hospital expression just as other conventional architects of the period might have designed a municipal office building or perhaps a large hotel. As architectural historian Annmarie Adams has argued, the work of Stevens' firm was as advanced, or more so, technically and in terms of spatial organisation as any other in the period. He was a genuine functionalist, but he did not adopt advanced architectural expression. Instead, he favoured what he described as "comforting associations" for the patient, relying on traditional stylistic trappings, sturdy looking masonry construction and carefully designed timber furnishings that militated against an industrial feel (Adams 2008: 109–21).

This complex articulation of "the modern" in hospital design, especially before World War II, enriches received understandings of the scope of modern architecture as defined by its historiography. But this is not simply because of relentless commitment to the functional efficiency of the plan. The modernism of the hospital was the plan, as Stevens insisted, with all its implications for capacity and "throughput". But the modernism of the hospital was also embodied in the technical servicing and operation of the building and its site. It was evident in the commitment to research and the integration of the hospital into the urban tissue and its social situation, as Cederström and others insisted. And, in the end, it was also intrinsic to the commitment to articulate the functional and technical rationales for the hospital as a formally modern entity, whether in diagram form or as a fully detailed building.

All the most ambitious projects of architectural modernism forged bonds between ideals of technical innovation, spatial rationality and social salvation. In the period between 1918 and 1960, the hospital movement was committed to fostering those ideals and fundamentally improving life. But as with the other prominent social projects of modernism, especially housing, the 1960s presented a fundamental challenge – even crisis – for the modern hospital movement. Some practitioners in the field in the early 1960s, such as the North American firms of Perkins & Will and Craig, Zeidler & Strong, pursued more and more sophisticated means for tempering and servicing the hospital environment, continuing a long-standing project with a distinguished set of precedents beginning in the nineteenth century as architectural historian Robert Bruegmann has shown (Bruegmann 1978). Others, such as William Tatton-Brown (1910–1997), working for the United Kingdom's Ministry of Health, continued to explore new planning models that would further rationalise patterns of movement (Hughes 1997).

These ongoing efforts to improve the capacity and comfort of hospitals in the late 1950s did not prove to be as convincing a source of optimism as earlier modern hospitals had been. As optimism about the efficacy of hospital care waned and as facilities that had been new in the 1920s and 1930s aged and lost their expressive and functional clarity, architects looked to new models and new sources of inspiration. Where the factory and skyscraper had both been important sources or reconsidering the problem of the hospital in the 1920s, by the late 1960s newly emergent urban spatial forms such as the shopping centre and airport became more relevant. Moreover, the isolated and institutionally distinct campus model gave way to ideas of urban integration and in more recent decades a more thoroughgoing concern with landscape perception, sustainability and a heightened need to address ever more conscientiously a patient-centred experience (Verderber 2010).

Those trends signalled the end of the modern hospital. As architectural historian and theorist Cor Wagenaar has noted, in the 1960s activists, designers and decision-makers all questioned the salutary qualities of the hospital and whether the monolithic, modern block hospital was in fact good for patients (Figure 1.5). Many observers believed the institutionality of hospitals – their separateness from the norms of city and town, especially from commercial activity and social interaction – as well as their diminished connections to landscape, had stripped hospitals of humanity (Wagenaar 2006). Yet the evolution of hospital design during the twentieth century represented a powerful shift in thinking about health and the body. From

Figure 1.5 St Thomas' Hospital, London, England: an example of the 1960s modern block hospital. Architects: Yorke, Rosenberg & Mardall, 1966–1975. Photograph: Chris Pettit, 2017.
Courtesy: www.flickr.com/photos/watfordquaker/32953233772 (CC BY-ND 2.0), used with permission.

a model of salubriousness which framed the body as a whole, provided healthy spaces of recuperation, fresh air, abundant light and clean-looking surfaces to a powerful arrangement of technical services and diagnostic machinery arranged to apprehend the body in its multiplicity and attack the specific causes of disease, the hospital underwent a fundamental transformation. Architects grappled with this change, often struggling to find compelling images to draw together the functions of the modern hospital in the postwar decades.

The history of the modern hospital

The historically focused literature on the modern hospital is sparse, especially compared with that focused on industrial architecture, tall commercial buildings or twentieth-century housing. But it has grown steadily in recent years and the newest book, Jeanne Kisacky's *Rise of the Modern Hospital* (2017), is the most thoroughly researched and most detailed in tracking the complex relationship between major medical developments and the form of hospital buildings. It also contains a comprehensive review of extant literature on the history of hospitals. Kisacky's book builds on work that goes back to the 1970s, beginning with John D. Thompson and Grace Goldin's *The Hospital: A Social and Architectural History* (1975), which focused on changes to ward planning across two centuries. Stephen Verderber and David J. Fine's *Healthcare Architecture in an Age of Radical Transformation* (2000) also tracked the plan as the fundamental generator of hospital design – a conviction that goes back to Edward F. Stevens in the early twentieth century – but the authors do this in relation to shifts in social and economic models of healthcare provision taking place at the time they were writing. Their interest was in understanding "present" conditions as they pertained at the end of the twentieth century, and so their book does not focus on the modernisation process and its connection with modern architecture in the wider sense, but rather on the innovations of the last third of the twentieth century. Each of these books focuses on the United States, though Verderber and Fine and Thompson and Goldin draw extensively from British and European examples. Canadian architectural historian Annmarie Adams is the other key historian of twentieth-century hospitals. Adams (2008) uses a close-up reading of one city (Montreal, Canada), one architectural firm (Boston-based Stevens & Lee) and, for the most part, one hospital (Royal Victoria, Montreal) to track major technical, social and architectural changes in hospital architecture. Each of these studies is strongly contextualised within a national framework and as such they are not finely attuned to the internationalism of the hospital movement and the flows of information that resulted from its flourishing in the interwar decades in particular.

Two further books, both of which have a more universal ambition, warrant recognition here. Cor Wagenaar's edited collection *The Architecture of Hospitals* (2006) attempts to synthesise the most important architectural developments affecting hospitals in the nineteenth and twentieth centuries, and provide a framework of historical development. The hospital has also been the focus of a recent effort to theorise the emergence of modern architecture alongside modern modes of governmentality. Sven-Olov Wallenstein's *Biopolitics and the Emergence of Modern Architecture* (2008) is a concise contribution to the study of hospitals and conveys a fundamental insight about the way in which the modern hospital is at once a mode of individuation and a mechanism by which political subjects are transformed into populations. But both this and Wagenaar's book are really only essay-length studies and do not amount to historical accounts of the modern hospital.

Diagnosing the modern hospital: seven sites of design

What this book does, which is different, is underline the development of the modern hospital as a global phenomenon, the result of a persistent and geographically interwoven network of discourse, protagonists and sites. It charts that development from around 1918 to the early 1960s. The international breadth, scale and complexity of innovations in the design of the modern hospital make it a demanding phenomenon to comprehend. For this reason, the book analyses historical developments by focusing on seven key sites of design that range from the scale of the body to the scale of the city, a structuring device that also distinguishes this book from others. These sites enable a magnified view of key areas of architectural innovation situated within a wider framework of historical development. Each of these detailed analyses outlines evolving concerns with hygienic rigour and patient wellbeing, as well as the powerful ideal of organisational efficiency that motivated architects' efforts to redesign the modern hospital.

The seven sites speak directly to the most important hospital-based developments of the period covered by the book, 1918 to the early 1960s. During more than fifty years of development, hospitals saw the consolidation of a series of innovations that had been discernible but patchy before World War I: the widening use of pathology laboratories, the redesign of operating theatres, the centralisation of kitchen and laundry services, the reconfiguration of the basic hospital ward, the development of the multilevel block hospital and the reconfiguration of the hospital campus, the almost universal expectation of hospital birthing and the vast expansion of patient record keeping. Many of these social, technical and professional changes were brought together for the first time by the hospital architecture of the interwar decades and the institutional arrangements it fostered. The second half of the twentieth century saw those developments recast both formally and technically, in some cases several times, but the underlying process of hospital modernisation – with its focus on intensive treatment of the causes of disease rather than on housing the patient – continued to be the central driver of change. The sequence of seven chapters that follow therefore examines in detail the various scales of analysis observable in the hospital, from the body-centred scale of the bed to the urban scale of the hospital campus.

Chapter 2, "Everyone's own 'healing machine': the hospital bed", examines the development of the hospital bed as a self-contained site for healing, medical servicing and enhanced patient control. By the early twentieth century, the hospital bed was well established both as the privileged site of clinical investigation and observation and as the unit by which hospitals defined their capacity. The bed now became a mobile place of patient treatment capable of movement to different parts of the hospital, carrying patients to specialised places of treatment, such as solaria or balconies for heliotherapy, or "deep therapy" in radiation departments. In the interwar decades, the bed became a command post as well as the focus of patient amusement, recreation and repose. Electronic call systems were introduced for ready communication with nursing staff and a variety of medical and non-medical technologies, from reticulated oxygen to radio, were brought to the bedside. The placement of the bed in the design and planning of wards and the shift to smaller wards thus required both efficiency and amenity, and patient comfort was carefully managed through acoustic treatment, appropriate furnishings and restful prospects.

Chapter 3, "Knowledge, care and control: nurses' stations and nurses' homes", examines the shifting position of the nurse in hospitals both organisationally and in terms of physical positioning and activity. Nurses' stations and nurses' homes were key sites of design that evolved rapidly in the era of the modern hospital. The development of the modern hospital corresponded with a period during which the role of nurses within the hospital was dramatically reconfigured. Far from simply observing and ministering to the sick, nurses became active professionals who played key roles in managing work processes, undertaking medical observations and keeping standardised records. While the need to directly observe patients remained, the physical configurations of nursing and positions of observation underwent significant change. Increasingly, their station was a mobilisation point for medical documentation and communication, encouraged by new technologies that promoted efficient and standardised methods of observation. The prominence of nurses as vital professionals and auxiliary medical staff within hospitals was also powerfully expressed via the development of large residential wings – nurses' homes – that became increasingly prominent buildings on the evolving hospital campus during the first half of the twentieth century. The designs of these buildings, which in many cases were among the largest residential buildings in their urban areas at the time, encouraged wholesome living within a carefully controlled environment. But as social expectations changed and nurses ceased living on hospital grounds, many of the great dormitory buildings were abandoned. Some have been reconfigured for other uses, some demolished, while some remain, ambivalent monuments to an earlier era of institutional development.

Chapter 4, "Incision and anaesthesia: the operating theatre", examines the operating theatre, the domain of the surgeon and their skilled team, as a space of primary importance in the modern hospital and as the ultimate challenge for architects seeking to create a "well-tempered" hospital environment (Banham 1969). Once a great auditorium where the surgeon performed daring feats for the edification of students, the operating theatre in the modern hospital became something of a closed set. Students now observed surgery through small portholes or glazed ceilings, and eventually via closed circuit television. Often high in the main hospital block, the surgical theatre was positioned within a suite of specialist spaces that serviced it, including sterilising rooms for equipment and scrub-up rooms for medical staff. Hospital architects had long understood the need for adequate light for surgery and thus favoured large windows that admitted indirect natural light, but the reliability of artificial light soon gained favour. Maintaining aseptic standards was vital in the surgical areas, and they were thus often increasingly fitted with systems of mechanical ventilation and "air purification" that made the operating suite a completely self-contained system within the hospital.

Chapter 5, "Treating outside, looking inside: diagnosis and therapy", examines the potent idea of investigating and treating the exterior and interior of the body using the techniques of diagnosis and therapy. The modern hospital was developed in parallel with the rise of hospital-based therapies and diagnostic tools. Increasing use of machinery that enabled subcutaneous investigation without surgery, such as X-ray, coupled with pathology laboratories, led to more reliable diagnosis and built a regime of testing that was separate from the physical examination of the patient. The ensuing treatments involved, first, a proliferation of equipment that relied on the mechanical or physical manipulation of the whole body, such as hydro- and heliotherapies, physiotherapy or artificial light treatments. A shift to drug and radiation therapies saw older ideas of environmental salubriousness and regimes of patient management diminish in importance.

Architectural expression echoed this inward-looking focus, with a gradual move away from the use of sun-filled balconies as an expressive device to a closed, fully controlled environmental system. The chapter documents the array of specialised spaces of treatment that appeared at various points in the twentieth century and analyses the challenges involved in designing for highly specialised functions while continually adapting to medical and technical innovation.

Chapter 6, "Full steam ahead! Servicing the modern hospital", examines the spatial implications of the ever-increasing technological and mechanical servicing of the modern hospital. As hospitals grew in size and complexity, considerable emphasis was placed on the efficient use of resources. Taylorist ideas of production encouraged centralising services to a single point of operation, resulting in huge central kitchens and laundries. Other services were also provided from a single point of origin: one boiler house, instead of one per building, to provide steam for the entire hospital site; and reticulated gases, such as oxygen, piped to the operating theatre and patient bedside from a remote location rather than provided by bottles transported to the place of need. The modern mechanical plant that served the hospital was displayed proudly behind glass walls with the towering chimneys of the incinerator rising above; towers of reticulated services and mechanical ventilation became part of the architectural expression of the modern hospital. The path of a bed sheet or the provision of an appropriate diet to a patient became exercises in scientific management with their own pathways and presence in the hospital. Architects were deeply involved in the design of each of these systems, and spent considerable energy in researching and refining their functionality. This chapter examines the evolution of the hospital as a system and explores the different ways hospital experts and designers responded to the challenges of designing systems that could be both fully integrated and flexible.

Chapter 7, "Health, hygiene and progress: designing the hospital of tomorrow", outlines the search for a modern idiom for the modern hospital, one that might clearly signal health, hygiene and progress. The impetus for the modern hospital was through its plan, with traditional pavilion planning superseded by the amalgamated block during the interwar decades. At the same time, European hospital designers embraced the new modernist idiom from the 1920s, with its pared-down aesthetics, clean lines and emphasis on healthy living; the combination of modern planning and modernist idiom was fostered by French, Australian and Swedish architects in the 1930s and 1940s before gaining wide acceptance as the standard vocabulary after World War II. Progressive medical treatment thus became bound to architectural expression during the era, emblematic of a forward-looking society. Such symbolism of health, care and progress was evident not only in exterior treatment of buildings, but in the entrance sequences with their ubiquitous sculptures dedicated to time-honoured images of vocational healing, as well as in the interior treatment of reception and waiting areas. This chapter examines the changing strategies employed by hospital architects across the twentieth century to highlight ideas of scientific progress and technical rigour, medical efficiency and patient wellbeing.

Chapter 8, "Health city, healing landscapes and the hospital campus", follows the path from garden to campus, aspect and efficiency in the site planning and the landscape of the modern hospital. The hospital as a grand edifice in a garden setting was gradually replaced by an efficient campus arrangement; the rise of the automobile meant the imposing portico was replaced by the *porte-cochère*, ambulances arrived at specially designed entrances and internal roads and tunnels became important veins by which essential services were delivered. Ideas of amenity were changing: landscape's curative associations as pleasant spaces in which to perambulate diminished, as the terrace and balcony became the formal and structured places in which patients were exposed to fresh air and sunlight. The new vision of the hospital was as an efficient system – a highly networked diagram – with the whole site considered as a healing machine.

Chapter 9, "The modern hospital: the rise, fall and rise again of architecture", concludes the book, with the admission that the design of the modern hospital had reached a point of aesthetic stasis by the mid-1960s. Yet even before that, during the 1950s, the seeds for rethinking the modern hospital had been planted, with the emergence, especially in the United Kingdom, of evidence-based research that critically reflected upon and scientifically evaluated hospital spaces, the working practices of nurses and doctors, and patient experience. There was a newly recharged emphasis on patient-centred design and an acknowledgement that specifically architectural solutions to providing flexibility in hospital planning might aid the constant need for growth and change. While some architects reverted to almost fantastic schemes, there was a general recognition that a return to first principles was required and that the heroic period of the modern hospital had passed.

More than any other building type in the twentieth century, the hospital was connected to transformations in the health of populations and expectations of lifespan. From the scale of public health to the level of the individual, the architecture of the modern hospital has reshaped knowledge about health and disease and perceptions of bodily integrity and security. However, the rich and genuinely global architectural history of these hospitals is poorly understood and largely forgotten. This book explores the rapid evolution of hospital design in the twentieth century, moving as it did from a place to care for the sick (*Nosokomeion*) to one founded on the principle of health (*Hygeia*), analysing the ways architects and other specialists reimagined the modern hospital. It examines how the vast expansion of medical institutions over the course of the century was enabled by new approaches to architectural design, and it highlights the emerging political conviction that physical health would become the cornerstone of human welfare.

Notes

1 *Hygeia*, a Latin form of the earlier Greek *Hygieia*, was the goddess of good health.
2 *Nosokomeion*, from late Greek, means a place in which to care for the sick.
3 The three buildings Giedion singled out were the Bauhaus buildings at Dessau, Germany (Architect: Walter Gropius, 1925–1926), the competition entry for the League of Nations, Geneva, Switzerland (Architect: Le Corbusier, 1927) and the Paimio tuberculosis sanatorium in Finland (Architect: Alvar Aalto, 1928–1932).
4 *Nosokomeion* was later continued as *World Hospitals* (1964–1993), then *World Hospitals and Health Services* (1993–present).

References

Adams, Annmarie. *Medicine by Design: The Architect and the Modern Hospital, 1893–1943*. Minneapolis, MN: University of Minnesota Press, 2008.
Alter, Wilhelm. *Das Deutsche Krankenhaus 1925*. Berlin: Julius Springer, 1927.
Alter, Wilhelm. "Editorial." *Nosokomeion* 4, no. 1 (January 1933): 2.
Alter, Wilhelm. *Das Krankenhaus*. Berlin: W. Kohlhammer, 1936.
Banham, Reyner. *The Architecture of the Well-Tempered Environment*. London: Architectural Press, 1969.
Betsky, Aaron. *James Gamble Rogers and the Architecture of Pragmatism*. Cambridge, MA: MIT Press, 1994.
Bruegmann, Robert. "Central Heating and Forced Ventilation: Origins and Effects on Architectural Design." *Journal of the Society of Architectural Historians* 37, no. 3 (October 1978): 143–60.
Butler, Charles and Addison Erdman. *Hospital Planning*. New York: F.W. Dodge Corporation, 1946.
Campbell, Margaret. "What Tuberculosis Did for Modernism: The Influence of a Curative Environment on Modernist Design and Architecture." *Medical History* 49, no. 4 (October 2005): 463–88.
Cederström, Hjalmar. "A Report on the Municipal Hospital Conditions of Stockholm with a Proposal for a New General Hospital Accommodating 1,500 Patients." *Nosokomeion* 3, no. 3 (1932): 320–6.

Cederström, Hjalmar. *Söderjukhuset*. Stockholm: Rydahls Boktryckeri A-B, c. 1946.
Colomina, Beatriz. "The Medical Body in Modern Architecture." *Daidalos* 64 (June 1997): 60–71.
"Declaration." *Nosokomeion* 6, no. 3–4 (1935): 314.
Giedion, Sigfried. *Space, Time and Architecture*. Cambridge, MA: Harvard University Press, 1941.
Goldwater, S.S. "An International View of Hospital Problems." *Modern Hospital* 23, no. 5 (May 1929): 50.
Hamlin, Talbot. *Forms and Functions of Twentieth Century Architecture*. New York: Harvard University Press, 1952.
Howell, Joel D. *Technology in the Hospital: Transforming Patient Care in the Early Twentieth Century*. Baltimore: Johns Hopkins University Press, 1995.
Hughes, Jonathan. "Hospital-City." *Architectural History* 40 (1997): 266–88.
Kisacky, Jeanne. *Rise of the Modern Hospital: An Architectural of Health and Healing, 1870–1940*. Pittsburgh: University of Pittsburgh Press, 2017.
Leighton Irwin & Co. (B.M. Johnston). "The Public Doesn't Know." Materials connected with Prince Henry's Hospital Project, Scrapbook, No. 1, Irwin Alsop Archive, held Group GSA, Melbourne, Australia, 1935.
Leon, Sharon M. *An Image of God: The Catholic Struggle with Eugenics*. Chicago, IL: University of Chicago Press, 2013.
MacEachern, Malcolm T. "What Every Obstetrical Supervisor Should Know." *American Journal of Nursing* 35, no. 2 (February 1935): 97.
Moretti, B. Franco. *Ospedali*. Milan: Editore Ulrico Hoepli, 1951.
Mumford, Eric. *The CIAM Discourse on Urbanism, 1928–1960*. Cambridge, MA: MIT Press, 2000.
Nye, Robert A. "The Rise and Fall of the Eugenics Empire: Recent Perspectives on the Impact of Biomedical Thought in Modern Society." *Historical Journal* 36, no. 3 (1993): 687–700.
Pevsner, Nikolaus. *Pioneers of Modern Design: From William Morris to Walter Gropius*. London: Faber & Faber, 1936.
"Review: Nosokomeion." *The Canadian Medical Association Journal* 26, no. 3 (March 1932): 392.
Richards, J.M. *An Introduction to Modern Architecture*. Harmondsworth and New York: Penguin Books, 1940.
Rorem, C. Rufus. "Hospitals as Social Capital." *Nosokomeion* 7, no. 3 (1936): 245.
Rosenfield, Isadore. *Hospitals: Integrated Design*. New York: Reinhold Publishing Corporation, 1947.
Royal Melbourne Hospital. *Annual Report, 1938–38*. Melbourne: The Royal Melbourne Hospital, 1939.
Shanken, Andrew. *194X: Architecture, Planning and Consumer Culture on the American Home Front*. Minneapolis, MN: University of Minnesota Press, 2009.
Stevens, Edward F. *The American Hospital of the Twentieth Century*. New York: Architectural Record Publishing Company, 1918.
Stone, Joseph Edmund. *Hospital Organization and Management (Including Planning and Construction)*. London: Faber & Gwyer, 1927.
Stone, Joseph Edmund. *Hospital Organization and Management*. London: Faber & Faber, 1944.
Thompson, John D. and Grace Goldin. *The Hospital: A Social and Architectural History*. New Haven, CT: Yale University Press, 1975.

Turda, Marius. *Modernism and Eugenics*. New York: Palgrave Macmillan, 2010.
Uklein, Vlad. "The Architect and Technical Economy in Hospitals." *Nosokomeion* 8, no. 2 (1937): 116–20.
Verderber, Stephen. *Innovations in Hospital Architecture*. New York: Routledge, 2010.
Verderber, Stephen and David J. Fine. *Healthcare Architecture in an Age of Radical Transformation*. New Haven, CT: Yale University Press, 2000.
Wagenaar, Cor (ed.). *The Architecture of Hospitals*. Rotterdam: NAi Publishers, 2006.
Wagenaar, Cor. "Five Revolutions: A Short History of Hospital Architecture." In *The Architecture of Hospitals*, edited by Cor Wagenaar, 26–41. Rotterdam: NAi Publishers, 2006.
Wallenstein, Sven-Olov. *Bio-Politics and the Emergence of Modern Architecture*. New York: Princeton Architectural Press, 2008.
Walter, Jean. *Renaissance de l'architecture médicale*. Paris: Impressions E. Desfossés, 1945.
Winslow, C.E.A. "The Hospital as a Preventive Institution." *Nosokomeion* 3, no. 3 (1932): 222.

2 Everyone's own "healing machine"
The hospital bed

In the nineteenth century, pavilion-plan hospitals often took on the spreading scale of a vast country estate or an institutional campus set within extensive gardens and landscaped grounds. In contrast, during the twentieth century, hospitals became very large, complex organisms that sometimes filled entire city blocks or more and took on the appearance of office skyscrapers or high-rise hotels. However, beyond the availability of land and capital funds, the determining heart of the size, layout and day-to-day organisation of all of these hospitals was one of its smallest elements – the hospital bed.

The patient in a bed – a bed that is not their own – has been the focus of the spatial understanding of a hospital ever since its inception as a building type. For a sick body to be tended to under shelter meant the bed had to function as more than just a comfortable platform on which the patient could sleep. The bed became the spatial locus and focus of medical attention, care and recuperation. The doctor, the nurse and the family could tend to the patient around the bed, meaning that immediate space became a zone of service, supervision and salvation. It served multiple functions. For the patient, the hospital bed became the place from which their body was offered up to the medical profession, a place from which they knew a return to health was possible, a place from which they might know they were being observed (for their own good) and a place from which they might observe others and the world outside, with a view to recuperation from injury or illness. The hospital bed, therefore, has multiple inward and outward forces of need: spatial, medical, psychological and – significantly, in terms of the construction of an architecture that houses more than one patient – economic.

The level and type of care, technology and amenity associated with each hospital bed generates the plan of a hospital. The number of beds becomes the key determinant of the whole functional brief for the modern hospital. It determines the scale of the hospital and the types of spaces in which the bed sits: public ward, semi-private ward or private room. The bed becomes the metric of design. Almost every manual of hospital design and construction uses bed numbers in the first line of its case studies. For instance, in

B. Franco Moretti's *Ospedali*, each example in the vast international compendium of hospitals is introduced by quoting the number of beds it contains before considering any other detail (Moretti 1951).

In the second half of the nineteenth century, the dominant spatial understanding of hospital-based medical care, the Nightingale ward plan, was linked to the bed and its envelope of space. Both military and civilian hospitals adopted this plan, which was usually characterised by a large linear open space with windows on either side and usually contained between twenty-four and thirty beds with two rows of beds, facing each other, set perpendicular to and against the perimeter walls. There would be a nurses' station and public access at one end and a bath and toilet block at the other. In her influential and popular book, *Notes on Hospitals* (1859), the English nurse and social reformer Florence Nightingale outlined the key determining factors behind this model, which strove to minimise rates of cross-infection by maximising light, air, ventilation and supervision. The Nightingale ward also offered a degree of flexibility in the configuration of hospital site plans. The wards were frequently arranged as single-storey units spread over large sites. But where space was not as easily obtainable, the wards were stacked vertically, with three- or four-storey ward pavilions common by the end of the nineteenth century. This arrangement encouraged the planning of buildings in single ward wings, and hence pavilion layouts abounded. The Royal Herbert Hospital, Woolwich, England (Architect: Douglas Galton, 1859–1864), the first hospital to be constructed entirely under Nightingale's supervision, exemplifies this arrangement best (Thompson and Goldin 1975) (Figure 2.1). But, in the first half of the twentieth century, the dominance of the Nightingale ward came to be challenged. Ideas were shifting and becoming more complex in relation to the idea of the bed, its provision, its supervision and its spatial, functional and experiential roles. During the nineteenth century, cultural and technological differences had emerged between North America, Europe and Australia, each of which was now defining different spatial practices for the modern hospital.

The idea of the hospital bed

Between 1890 and 1960, a series of factors affected the relationship of the bed to its immediate surroundings and, by extension, the subsequent design of the general hospital. Not all are related in terms of time or location, and there is no easy causal link to identify influences between them, but each contributed to the architectural evolution of the modern hospital.

The first factor was, in many respects, a desire to make the hospital bed and its immediate surroundings feel like home, or at the very least impart a sense of homeliness to the hospital experience. The second factor was related to the broad acceptance of germ theory and what was perceived as its best form of defence: hygiene. As both a practical and an intellectual concept, hygiene with all its implications of germ-free cleanliness that could

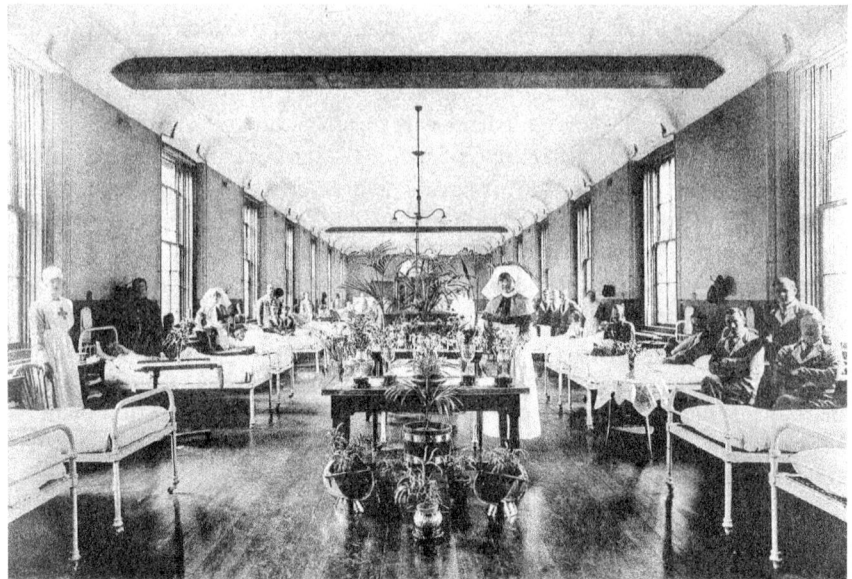

Figure 2.1 Nightingale ward in the Royal Herbert Hospital, Woolwich, England. Architect: Douglas Galton, 1859–1864. Photograph: Qualis Photography Co., 1920.

Courtesy: Trustees of the Museum of Military Medicine/Wellcome Collection (CC BY-NC 4.0), used with permission.

be easily maintained had clear material and aesthetic implications. These applied to the bed and the spaces immediately around it, not just the operating theatre and the morgue. The third factor was the presence and scourge of tuberculosis in the late nineteenth and early twentieth century, which gave rise and prominence, especially in Europe and United Kingdom, to a particular building type: the sanatorium. Much feted in the literary and architectural press in the 1920s and early 1930s as icons of modernism, sanatoria bequeathed to the general hospital many of its key architectural elements. The role of the bed in the sanatorium, and in particular its reconfiguration as a mobile site of treatment for patients, effected important changes in the design of the hospital. As such, modernism provided a distinct architectural rhetoric of hygiene that went well beyond the hygienic techniques of nineteenth-century hospitals. The bed in the modern hospital was thus not just the essential unit of planning, it became the *de facto* site of the patient, and its placement, movement, role in infection control and presentation all reflected the way patients were controlled and cared for in the hospital environment.

The ideals of homeliness and hygiene (or at least the appearance of hygiene) as expressed through the hospital bed were both intended to have a placebo effect in inducing confidence in the medical service being provided. But the rationale for each was different. Hygiene was a measure of cleanliness, a "safeguard" against infection and, by extension, a measure of the hospital's discipline and efficiency in protecting patients from falling ill via others. Homeliness was a measure of psychological comfort, intended to reassure the patient that they had not been institutionalised but rather were receiving the same care and attention they would if they were being treated at home. The design of the bed and the atmosphere of the room or ward around it vacillated in focus between hygiene and homeliness, which was reflected in different approaches to hospital design in North America compared to Europe, United Kingdom and Australia as late as the 1940s. As Annmarie Adams and Thompson and Goldin have emphasised, the North American habit was, largely, to favour homeliness and emulate the quality of a hotel, and this was encouraged by the North American preference for the private room and what was described in Canada as the "pay hospital". By contrast, in Europe, United Kingdom and Australia, the idea of the public hospital, "where an attempt is made to provide on a limited budget a decent standard of hospitalization for all citizens" (Thompson and Goldin 1975: 231), the emphasis was on hygiene and an architectural palette that expressed this. Privacy could be achieved in different "hygienic" ways.

In the 1930s, a fourth factor emerged to accompany the double placebo of hygiene and homeliness: technological services to the bedside. By 1950, technology had superseded the ideals of homeliness and hygiene. The irresistible rise of mechanical and electrical services available to the patient bedroom and the bed increased exponentially in scale as the decades of the twentieth century progressed. This technology of, for and from the bed radically liberated the patient from helplessness and complete reliance on doctors and nurses. The bed became the site of patient empowerment, enabling the patient to seek help, communicate, even self-entertain, and control – as much as possible and within reason – their surroundings.

Three themes can be used to summarise these factors at the level of the bed: mobility; technology and flexibility; and space and privacy. In 1951, in the republished preface to the second edition of Moretti's *Ospedali*, the opening photograph by Albert Steiner shows an adjustable hospital bed placed beside floor-to-ceiling windows in the Zürcher Höhenklinik (Zurich Heights Clinic) in Clavadel, Switzerland (Architect: Rudolf Gaberel, 1930–1933) with a spectacular view to an alpine landscape outside (Moretti 1951) (Figure 2.2). The bed has clearly been moved here from somewhere else. As an object, it can be adjusted to assume a desirable position for the body, and as the bed is pictured alone, it seems an idealised moment of solitude for the prospective patient who can also view an uplifting "healing" panorama. In many respects, this image highlights the challenge of the bed in the modern hospital. It is both a machine or a tool through which the patient is cared for, and the essential unit of care – a place or position

28 Everyone's own "healing machine"

Figure 2.2 An adjustable hospital bed placed beside floor to ceiling windows in the Zürcher Höhenklinik (Zurich Heights Clinic), Clavadel, Switzerland. Architect: Rudolf Gaberel, 1930–1933. Photograph: Albert Steiner, c. 1935.

© Bruno Bischofberger, Meilen-Zürich, used with permission.

from which the patient experiences the hospital environment. By 1960, the bed had become the complete machine but had not lost its significance as the determining factor for any new hospital design. What had changed dramatically was what was around the bed and what lay outside the private room and the ward.

Mobility and amenity

A bed with wheels was not a new idea in the twentieth century. In the nineteenth century, child patients at St Thomas' Hospital, London, were wheeled outside to enjoy the benefits of sunlight and the hospital's garden. The mobility afforded by the bed at that time had no direct effect on the external walls and space of the ward or the hospital per se, but the bed could perform the function of a mobile stretcher. Thus, a bed on wheels began to prescribe the width of hospital corridors and the scale of elevator openings.

A key development in the increased mobility of the hospital bed was the invention of swivel castors in 1920 by American Seibert Chesnutt. Previously castors had only permitted beds to travel in a straight line, making turning and manoeuvring difficult. The swivel castor enabled the bed to be a more completely mobile device, and bed-bound patients could be easily relocated from treatment space to ward. Increasingly, the mobile bed as a unit of size not only dictated corridor widths, but also room sizes, window widths and balcony depths. Further sophistication came with rubber-tyred castors, which brought acoustic benefit. Not only could the bed now move, it could do so without disturbing others. Reducing noise in the hospital environment was an important issue. In 1928, *Modern Hospital* featured a bed that could be "made both rigid and noiseless by the use of machined steel double locks" ("A New Type of Bed" 1928: 160). Advertisements for castors featured prominently in the 1930s in journals like *Modern Hospital* and *Hospital Magazine* (Australia). In 1933, the Bassick Company of Bridgeport, Connecticut, USA, the oldest and largest manufacturer of castors in the world, advertised an entirely new line that offered "improved appearance, efficient operation, improved construction, greater economy" with the new Bassick "Spring-Iron" Ball Bearing Castor Socket with Baco Protective Tread Wheel Castor (Bassick Hospital Castors 1933: 117) (Figure 2.3). In 1937, given a history of defective wheels, castors were considered a significant enough issue to require national quality control by the Standards Association of Australia ("A Standard Bed Castor" 1937; "Castors for Hospital Furniture: Draft Specification" 1937).

In the early decades of the century, each component of the hospital bed as a machine for healing was refined, even the mattress and the sheets. In 1928, Jacob Goodfriend, assistant general superintendent of the Montefiore Hospital for Infectious Diseases in New York, wrote a detailed account on the handling, filling, construction and care (including frequent turning) of mattresses, arguing:

> Our aim in selecting the type of bedding most suitable for hospital use is not to reduce food consumption, but we are vitally interested in giving our patients the greatest amount of bed comfort and incidentally decreasing the amount of work to be done by the nurse.
> (Goodfriend 1928: 148)

In February 1935, Assistant Superintendent G.W. Olson and Technical Assistant Carl A. Friedmann of the recently completed Los Angeles County General Hospital defended their use of specially designed mattresses:

> The decision to use an inner spring mattress was based on several reasons. It was felt that 1) this type of mattress represented the latest trend in mattress design; 2) it provided greater comfort for the

Figure 2.3 Advertisement for Bassick Hospital Castors.
Source: Modern Hospital 41, no. 3 (September 1933): 117.

patient; 3) it would contribute to a more rapid recovery of the patient, thus reducing his stay in hospital.

(Olsen and Friedmann 1935: 90)

Thus, the bed itself had the potential to assist healing and consequently reduce the length of hospital stays. Research on patient comfort and mobility also focused on enabling a patient to remain in bed. It was desirable that the bed become more adjustable, an object that could, without moving from the ward or private room, increase patient comfort and at the same time facilitate medical attention directly at the bedside.

Research was also directed towards the patient not being overly inconvenienced with normal bodily functions, even to enabling a patient to use a bedpan without leaving their bed, as defecation lying down is difficult for most patients. For example, from 1935 considerable effort was expended by researchers at the University of California Medical School on refining the design of bedpans, which, when used in conjunction with an adjustable bed, could increase patient comfort. The research was instigated at the behest of US Senator James D. Phelan, who had experienced the miseries of "that barbaric relic the bedpan" and left a sum of money for "medical research to improve the comfort of bedridden patients" (Saunders and Morgan 1939). Another American Ohio surgeon, F.L. Shively, spent six years designing and engineering a bedpan with a backrest, which was ready for sale in 1939 (Shively 1939).

Elevating the feet or the head separately from moving the rest of the body had long been a requirement for bed-based treatment of patients. Between 1815 and 1825 in England, adjustable hospital beds were developed with side rails that could be raised or lowered with a mechanical crank. But it wasn't until 1909 that Dr Willis Dew Gatch (1878–1954), chair of the Department of Surgery at the Indiana University School of Medicine, invented a hospital bed that could be manually adjusted for both head and legs, with three mechanically operated sections enabling independent elevations. It was specifically developed to aid recovery from surgery (Gatch [1909] 2009: 2). The so-called "Gatch bed" meant treatment, recuperation and servicing of the body could increasingly take place in or within the immediate environs of the bed itself. Generously, Gatch didn't patent his invention and others like Foster Beds (Foster Hospital Beds 1931) in upstate New York developed his concept over the ensuing decades. But the concept, and the term "Gatch bed", continues to be used. In July 1940, *Modern Hospital* advertised the "Dr Urie 'Patient Comfort' spring bed", a development of the Gatch bed with an inbuilt bedpan, an innovation which did not last (Will Ross & Co 1940) (Figure 2.4).

In 1945, the Gatch bed was further enhanced by the arrival of the "push button" bed, by which patient, doctor and nurse could electronically adjust the bed to the desired position ("Push-Button Bed Provides Self-Nursing Service for Hospital Patients" 1946). On 12 November 1945, *Life Magazine*

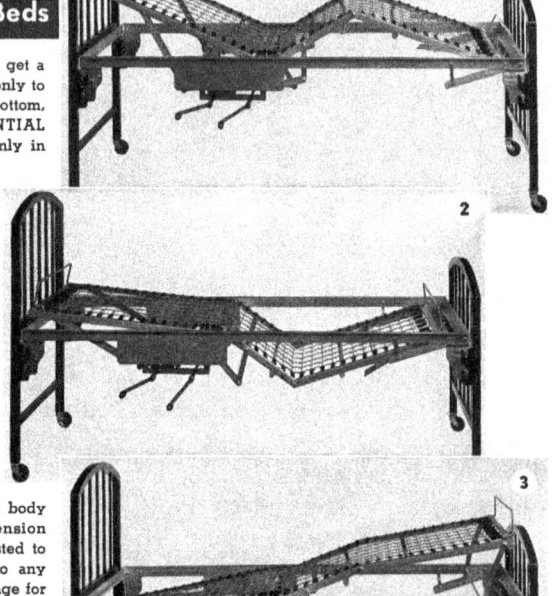

Figure 2.4 Advertisement by Will Ross & Co. for the Dr Urie "Patient Comfort" spring bed.
Source: *Modern Hospital* 55, no. 1 (July 1940): 111.

ran an article titled "Push-Button Hospital Bed", which featured Los Angeles-based Dr Marvel Darlington Beem's invention of an electrically powered bed with a full-size built-in toilet, and a control board at the foot of the bed that could be operated by the nurse. Patient freedom and nurse efficiency were touted as key benefits:

> Dr Beem's bed also includes other features which almost make it possible for patients to take care of themselves without any help at all. Piloting the bed like an airplane from a panel of switches, a patient may raise his head and feet, swing in front of him a washbasin with hot and cold running water, open and shut windows, draw blinds, heat the bed, turn on lights anywhere in the room, or call a nurse. Also built into the bed are a collapsible table, an ultraviolet lamp and an overhead trapeze bar for the patient to move himself around [...]
> By eliminating bathrooms, the beds can save 20% in space. The bed's general convenience may release 25% of the nurses in hospitals. Says Dr. Beem, "Nursing will become a profession and not a chore".
> ("Push-Button Hospital Bed" 1945)

Beem's bed never went into mass production, but in 1952 the Hill-Rom Company developed its first bed with an electric engine and began commercially producing its first fully electrical bed, the "Hill-Rom '55' All-Electric Bed" in 1956 (Ghersi, Marino and Miralles 2016). Another more advanced bed was the Circ-O'lectric Bed, developed by Dr Homer Hartman Stryker (1894–1980) of the Stryker Company in 1958, which allowed patient and doctor to electrically rotate the body and bed forward or backward. In 1960, Harriet R. Senf, clinical instructor in medical-surgical nursing at the Hockley Hospital School of Nursing in Muskegon, Michigan, USA, described this bed as "a startling departure in hospital bed design [which] has made it possible to incorporate – in one piece of furniture – the advantages of the turning frame, the Gatch bed, and the tiltboard" (Senf 1960). The hoop-like tubular steel frame bed could be electrically rotated to place the patient in any position from the Trendelenburg[1] to an erect stance, and there were various accessories such as traction bars, suspension and exercise apparatus, restraining straps and intravenous bottle holders (Figure 2.5). It remained in use until the 1970s.

In the 1960s in the United Kingdom, further development came with the King's Fund Bed. Based on research recorded in *Design of Hospital Bedsteads* (King Edward's Hospital Fund for London 1967), the King's Fund Charity worked with a design team led by the Royal College of Art's Bruce Archer to develop a bed that, using a series of foot pedals, could be easily moved, tilted, its backrest reclined and have its height adjusted to make the nurse's work at the bedside more comfortable and efficient. The nurse, rather than the patient, was in control.

34 *Everyone's own "healing machine"*

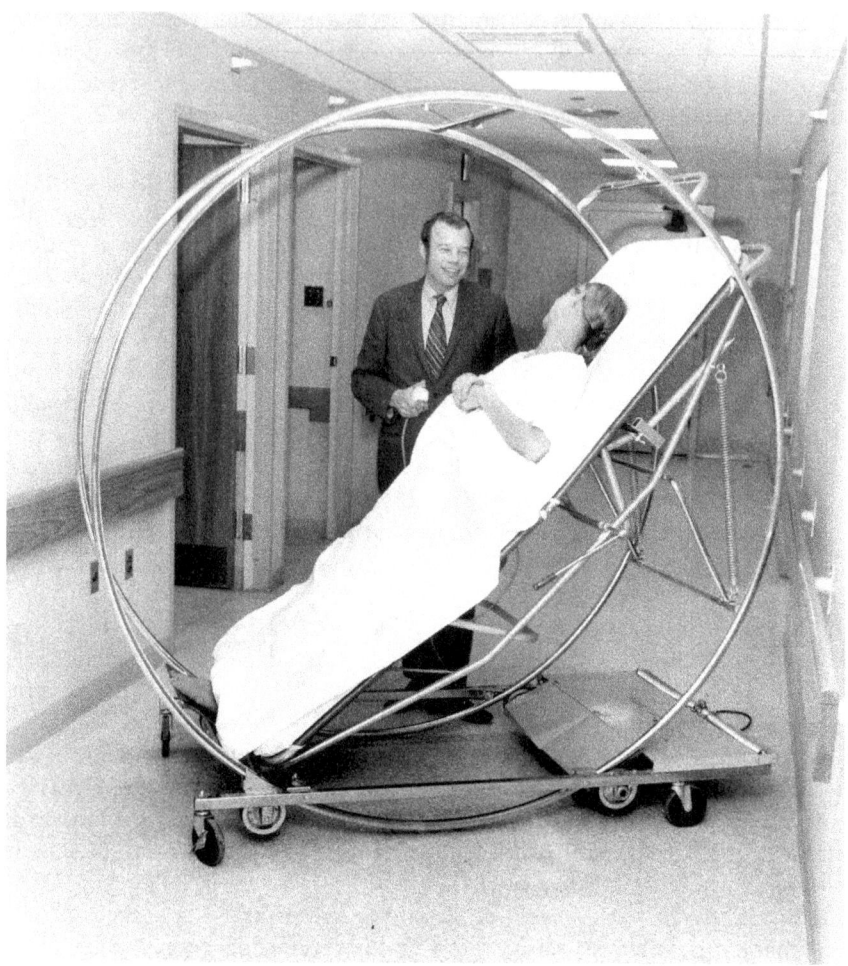

Figure 2.5 Dr. John F. Alksne of the Medical College of Virginia demonstrated a Circ-O'lectric Bed to the hospital that would be used for neurosurgical and neurological patients. The Circ-O'lectric Bed was developed by Dr Homer Hartman Stryker, 1958. Photograph: unknown, c. 1970.
Courtesy: *Richmond Times-Dispatch*.

The principle of mobility was also applied to bedside tables and particularly overbed tables on wheels, which could be used for reading or tray service. If beds and the elements around them had thus become mobile and adjustable, a corollary was that the doors and elevators of the modern hospital needed to be detailed and scaled for this mobility. By the interwar decades, beds needed to move to different treatment areas such as physiotherapy, radiation (deep therapy) and solaria. And for heliotherapy, beds needed to move outside, onto balconies, often directly from the patient bedroom or the ward. The window thus began to assume greater importance. Not all hospital architects agreed on the type and shape of window to be adopted. The ability to open all windows fully, or even a whole wall of the patient bedroom to fresh air – a proposition influenced greatly by theories related to heliotherapy and the treatment of tuberculosis patients – was followed by many European hospital designers.

Sigfried Giedion in *Befreites Wohnen: Licht, Luft, Oeffnung* (1929) extolled the virtues of light, air and openness for modern architecture. In his profile of Richard Döcker's Krankenhaus Waiblingen (Waiblingen Hospital) (1926–1928), he illustrated the relationship between the bed and window: large floor-to-ceiling sashes that slid up to allow the beds to be rolled out on the generous terrace (Figure 2.6). That relationship of the bed to the outside – both light and landscape – was considered essential, for "Der Kranke braucht Licht und psychische Erheiterung ebenso notwendig wie Antisepsis" ("The patient needs light and mental amusement as necessary as antisepsis") (Giedion 1929: 25). Giedion described the skeleton-framed construction of the hospital as dissolving the walls into glass, freeing up access to light, and no longer a "hermetisch abgeschloßner Bazillenkasten" ("hermetically sealed bacilli box") (Giedion 1929: 25).

The desire to provide fresh air to the patient in their hospital bed led to a host of new designs for operable windows. In 1935, British architect E. Stanley Hall (1881–1940) of the firm Stanley Hall, Easton & Robertson stated his preference for an ideal window that had three types of openings, such as at his firm's Maidenhead Hospital: the upper fourth was horizontally centre hung, the bottom fourth hung to open inwards and the centre half had a pair of side-hung windows that opened outwards. The ability to adjust for all manner of fresh air intake was seen as preferable to the sash window and sash boxes "where germs may breed" and which could only open to 50 per cent of their area (Hall 1935: 651). But Hall's suggestions never took hold across the hospital field.

It was not just the bedroom window which was considered in detail, but also the glass it was made from. One of the well-known products to emerge in the mid-1920s was "Vita" glass, developed in the United Kingdom with the specific objective of producing a window glass with special transparency to the sun's "vital", health-giving ultraviolet (UV) rays. Rickets, skeletal tuberculosis and imperfect bone formation caused by deficiency in Vitamin D could apparently all be alleviated with exposure to sunlight, but ordinary glass blocked the vital UV rays. Vita glass did not. At a 1929 meeting of the Royal Society of Arts in London, Francis Everard Lamplough, a former head of research for glass manufacturers Chance Bros, claimed:

> The glass has already been adopted in over 180 hospitals in this country, being used particularly for roofing open-air wards and for

Figure 2.6 Patient bedroom and terrace, Krankenhaus Waiblingen (Waiblingen Hospital), Stuttgart, Germany. Architect: Richard Döcker, 1926–1928. Photograph: unknown.

Courtesy: Akademie der Künst, Berlin, Richard-Döcker-Archiv, Nr. 280 F. 7.

sun lounges, etc. This glass is exclusively a British product, and it is interesting to note that its use is also extending rapidly in the United States.

(Lamplough 1929: 805)

Chairing the meeting was eminent physiologist Professor Leonard Hill, who had encouraged Lamplough to develop the glass. Hill stated in further support of Vita glass:

> For Vita glass to be useful far more light must be got in. We should have as big windows as we possibly could. Our buildings should be altered in order to get in more light. People did not realise how little light came into the room through an ordinary window, and a great reform had to be brought about in this respect.
>
> (Lamplough 1929: 808)

Chance teamed up with its major rival Pilkington Bros as a manufacturing partner, and, as John Sadar has observed, launched the most elaborate and expensive marketing campaign in the history of architectural glass (Sadar 2015) (Figure 2.7), but the fortunes of Vita glass dimmed swiftly and by the late 1930s it had virtually disappeared off the market. Other products such as VioRay and Lustraglass, made by the American Window Glass Co. in Pittsburgh, followed a similar trajectory, but they, like Vita glass:

> embodied a transient moment, wedged between the development of bacteriology, the medicalization of light, and the emergence of glass chemistry and technology on one hand, and the development of pharmaceutical therapies for infectious and chronic disease on the other.
>
> (Sadar 2015: 390–1)

In 1943, Chicago architect George Fred Keck (1895–1980) criticised the conventional hospital window:

> A patient, in bed, loves to look out of the window, but it is not clear – it is draped, it is screened, it is drafty, it is cold or hot with the seasons. It is altogether undesirable and old-fashioned.
>
> (Keck 1943: 59)

Keck argued that the wall of the patient bedroom might be made entirely of glass of one, two or even three layers, and there might be ventilation separate to a vision panel so patients "can be cheered and entertained by the birds, sun, moon, flowers and all nature" (Keck 1943: 60). The image he used was a bedroom in a private home with a fully glazed wall but the arrangement of the beds parallel to the window was clearly intended to simulate a possible two-bed patient room in a hospital. Keck, a long-time expert in

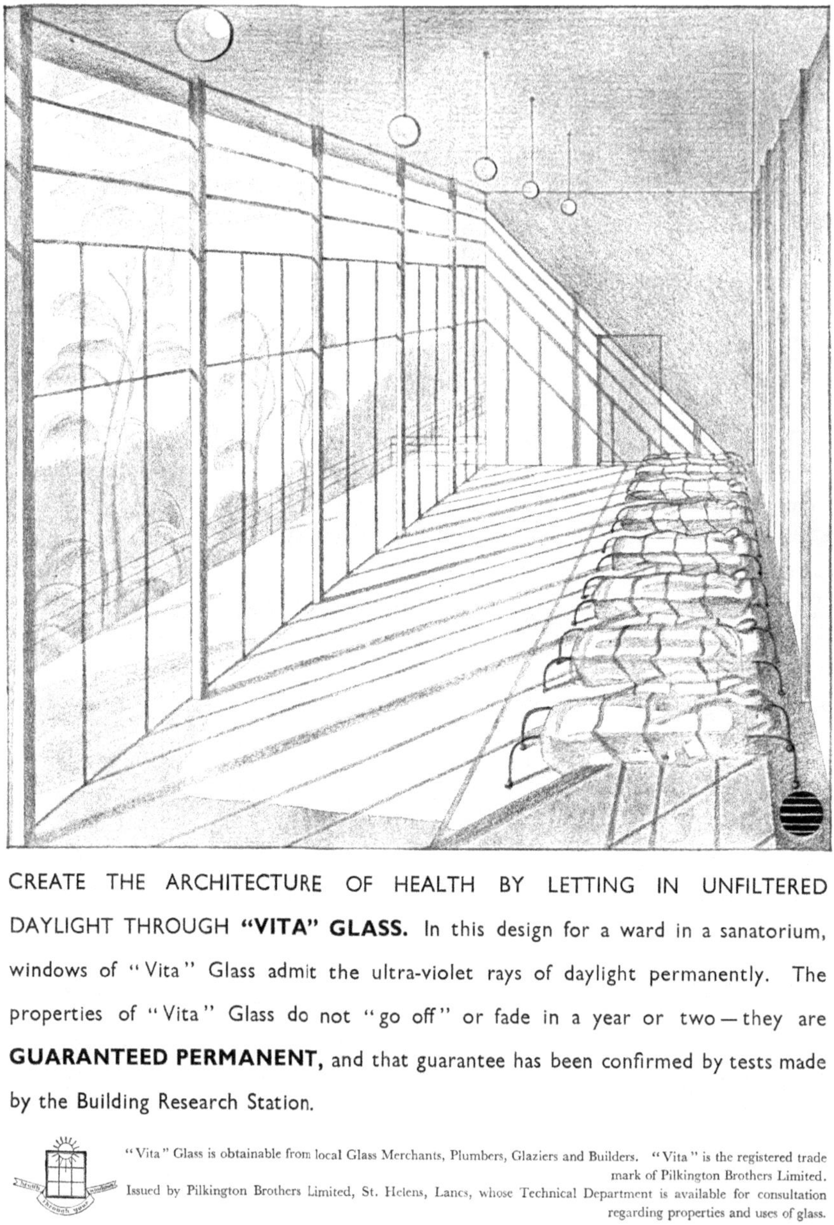

CREATE THE ARCHITECTURE OF HEALTH BY LETTING IN UNFILTERED DAYLIGHT THROUGH **"VITA" GLASS.** In this design for a ward in a sanatorium, windows of "Vita" Glass admit the ultra-violet rays of daylight permanently. The properties of "Vita" Glass do not "go off" or fade in a year or two — they are **GUARANTEED PERMANENT,** and that guarantee has been confirmed by tests made by the Building Research Station.

"Vita" Glass is obtainable from local Glass Merchants, Plumbers, Glaziers and Builders. "Vita" is the registered trade mark of Pilkington Brothers Limited. Issued by Pilkington Brothers Limited, St. Helens, Lancs, whose Technical Department is available for consultation regarding properties and uses of glass.

Figure 2.7 Advertisement for "Vita" glass produced by Pilkington Brothers Limited.
Source: *Architects' Journal*, 17 May 1933: xxiii.

passive solar design, also argued that external sun shades to a room designed to admit the low rays of winter sun and exclude the excessive radiant heat of summer sun would result in "several types of hospitals in the various parts of the United States, for we have several climatic conditions" (Keck 1943: 60). Supplementing this provision of sunlight to the bedroom, Keck also proposed radiant heating in the floor, and/or the walls and ceilings so "small children will be able to crawl over floors in comfort, and adults will never suffer the discomfort of cold feet" (Keck 1943: 61). The goal was to optimise human comfort in the patient bedroom to an extent that would, in Keck's words, "bring about a hospital of a type that will render all others obsolete" (Keck 1943: 61).

In 1947, American hospital specialist Isadore Rosenfield wrote there were three reasons why daylighting in hospitals was important: proper vision, psychological effect and protection from cross-infection. The first two reasons were clear. At the bedside, the ability to read a thermometer and to detect symptoms such as abnormalities in the patient's skin, lips or fingernails was critical. The psychological effects of daylight were also agreed on, with it acknowledged that the patient often "craves the cheerful play of daylight and a view of the sky" (Rosenfield 1947: 242). But his third reason, "the life-or-death quality of daylight", was somewhat more controversial (Rosenfield 1947: 243). In the 1890s, according to so-called "contact theory", it was believed diseases of respiratory origin could only be spread over a short distance. To prevent cross-infection, contagious disease wards were often established within hospitals with patient beds placed in partitioned cubicles. But by the late 1930s, bacteriological, epidemiological and clinical research had proven that disease could spread through the air over great distances and survive for days and weeks. Rosenfield outlined an approach that over the previous five years had comprised "interposing sanitary means (ultraviolet light, chemical sprays, floor and bedding oils) to break the chain of infection, to destroy the microorganisms in their journey from one person to another" (Rosenfield 1947: 245). But he also went further, advocating an approach not yet fully followed: "This attack involves the use of glass" (Rosenfield 1947: 245). Citing studies carried out in 1941 by Dr Leon Buchbinder at Columbia University, which showed "diffuse daylight was a patent lethal agent" (Buchbinder 1942) against streptococci and pneumococci passing through window glass and the glass covers of Petri plates, he argued it was clear that natural daylight and sunlight could reduce infection and that window areas in hospitals should be maximised (Solowey, Solotorovsky and Buchbinder 1942; Rosenfield 1947). The embrace of sunshine was, of course, not a new idea – it had long been intrinsic to tuberculosis treatment – but acceptance of this scientifically proven evidence in the early 1940s would be quickly superseded by the widespread mass production of penicillin from the mid-1940s.

The psychological impact of the window on a patient's wellbeing continued to be considered of prime importance, although not all architects followed this precept. One of the more controversial designs of the 1960s that did away with windows altogether in a single-patient bedroom (or cell) was Le Corbusier's unbuilt project for a Venice Hospital for the acutely ill (1963–1965). This design has often been celebrated for its attempt to relate to the urban fabric of Venice (Sarkis 2001; Shah 2013; Gargiani and Rosellini 2011), but criticism was levelled at Le Corbusier's ideas on the individual patient experience. Inspired by Vittore Carpaccio's painting *Funeral of Saint Ursula* (1493), Le Corbusier had the patient elevated on a high bed, rather like a bier. There was no window to the room, only a top-lit skylight that washed reflected light on the wall and ceiling overhead. Gargiani and Rosellini have argued that this was deliberate:

> In the drawings of the cells of the patients, a story is narrated of solitary bodies, stretched out to contemplate the mysterious light shaped by the surface of the ceilings, awaiting a revelation – the ultimate *maison d'homme*.... The bed is placed at such a height that the eyes of the patient are positioned at 1.4 metres from the ceiling, in the "same condition of a man standing upright" in a room with a height of 3.2 metres, to create the perceptive condition of a resurrection.
>
> (Gargiani and Rosellini 2011: 578)

Le Corbusier argued that he was designing for acute patients, and the bed might be moved occasionally so the patient could look at the sky. As recently as 2013, researchers have argued, on the basis of recently constructed ICU units in the United Kingdom, that acute patients had little need to look out the window (Shah 2013). Nevertheless, Isadore Rosenfield's criticism of the Venice project from 1969 remains robust:

> be[ing] human, he does not want the same thing all the time. He needs privacy, but when he chooses, he should be able to turn the other way and look out at the terrain and the sky ... we find the cubicles Le Corbusier proposed for Venice difficult or nearly impossible. The patient is alone in a 10 feet x 10 feet cubicle and cannot see anything outside of it, neither view nor sky nor corridor activity nor other patients.
>
> (Rosenfield 1947: 61–2)

Technology and flexibility

Empowering the patient while in they were in bed, by giving them the ability to seek help from nurses and adjust the light, air and sound around them, had already begun to assume significance by the 1920s. As New York's Edwards & Company Inc.'s advertising proclaimed in 1929, central to this was hospital signalling equipment "without which no hospital can be new and without which no hospital can ever be old" (Edwards & Company 1929: 127). One of the most sophisticated systems was the "Teleoptic" system (1930) developed in Racine, Wisconsin, USA. It connected to the broader network of nurse support and record keeping, and was silent (Figure 2.8). The patient in bed pressed a button on the side of a small hand-held box, which was connected by an electrical cord to the wall. A series of words rotated on a screen – "water", "nurse", "bedpan", and "emergency" – and on release of the button, the word chosen by the patient was recorded on a small two-way screen above the bedroom door. At the nurses' station, that request was recorded on a larger screen where a nurse could also see requests from other rooms and judge their urgency. At the same time, the signal flashed up the room number on a screen in the superintendent's office, allowing accurate checks on personnel activities and recording how long it took nurses to respond (Teleoptic Corporation 1931).

The connection between a patient's bed and the wall behind it thus began to assume greater significance. The wall became a key mechanism not just for providing the patient with greater amenity, but also for connecting the horizontal body of the patient to an entire network of assistance. In essence, medical service was brought directly to the bed. Lamps were attached to the wall behind so the patient could read in comfort, but the bed might still be easily moved, and by 1931, patients could also be equipped with headphones connected to a radio outlet. Listening to music on the radio was seen as another technique to encourage recovery. The cover of the April 1937 edition of *Hospital Magazine* (Australia), for example, showed a young boy, headphones on and smiling, the very image of a bedridden patient in happy diversion (Figure 2.9). Additional services such as a panic button and reticulated oxygen could also be made available to the bed.

In 1953, in US hospitals, bedside call systems were generally of two types: push buttons on extension cords and pull cords connected to a tumbler switch. More expensive but increasingly advocated by the Public Health Service of the US Department of Health, Education and Welfare was a microphone and loudspeaker at the bedside, which was connected to the nurses' station so a patient could signal or speak to a nurse and receive an answer (US Department of Health, Education and Welfare 1953). In the US system, it was recommended that all private and semi-private beds have telephone jacks so that a phone could be plugged in at any time with a minimum rental charge to the hospital. The Public Health Service also recommended in the early 1950s that facilities for television reception in patients' rooms be considered, given rapid advancement in that field, especially as televising surgical operations for teaching purposes had begun successfully (US Department of Health, Education and Welfare 1953).

Implicit in all these developments was the aim to increase technological service to the bed. As a result, the ability of the patient to control their surroundings and increase their personal wellbeing through personal choice

At Last!

A Hospital Signal System that Offers an Entirely New Principle—Speeds Up Service—Cuts Down Personnel—and Describes the Patient's Wish.

THE "Teleoptic" System offers a radical departure from all signaling devices heretofore available to hospitals.

In principle it has all the advantages of both the visible and the audible signal—yet it is silent, accurate, reliable, and it exactly describes the patient's wish instead of merely recording the fact that something or other is wanted.

The "Teleoptic" System in any hospital— new or old—speeds up service. The nurse, either at her station or in the corridor, knows in an instant just what the patient wants—water, bedpan, service, emergency. Time is saved, useless running back and forth is avoided, and the patient is intelligently helped.

All these merits of the "Teleoptic" System point toward savings and a new order of efficiency that will interest you.

Write for further information. "Teleoptic" Signals can be installed by your local electrician from specifications and instructions submitted by us.

The Teleoptic Corporation
9 Main St.   Racine, Wisconsin

FIRST UNIT
The patient, at her bedside, merely presses the button on the "Teleoptic" hand signal. A series of words rotate before her view. At any one—"water," "nurse," "bedpan," "emergency"—the button is released and this particular request will then be promptly and accurately fulfilled.

SECOND UNIT
The same word chosen by the patient is recorded above her door in full view of both approaches in the corridor. The nurse, if away from her station, knows in an instant what is wanted and can offer her assistance without delay and without verbal confirmation.

THIRD UNIT
The patient's wish is also recorded at the nurses' station. An extra trip to the patient is not necessary, because the request is fully understandable. If more than one signal is given, the nurse can, of her own choice, decide which request is most urgent and respond accordingly. Incidentally, special buttons showing a picture as well as the words can be substituted at any bedside for foreign-born patients.

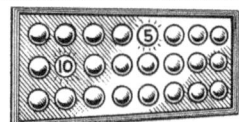

FOURTH UNIT
A signal in the superintendent's office, with room number, allows for an accurate check of personnel activities—and the time taken for the nurse to render service.

Figure 2.8 Advertisement for the "Teleoptic" System produced by the Teleoptic Corporation.
Source: *Modern Hospital* 36, no. 2 (February 1931): 125.

Everyone's own "healing machine" 43

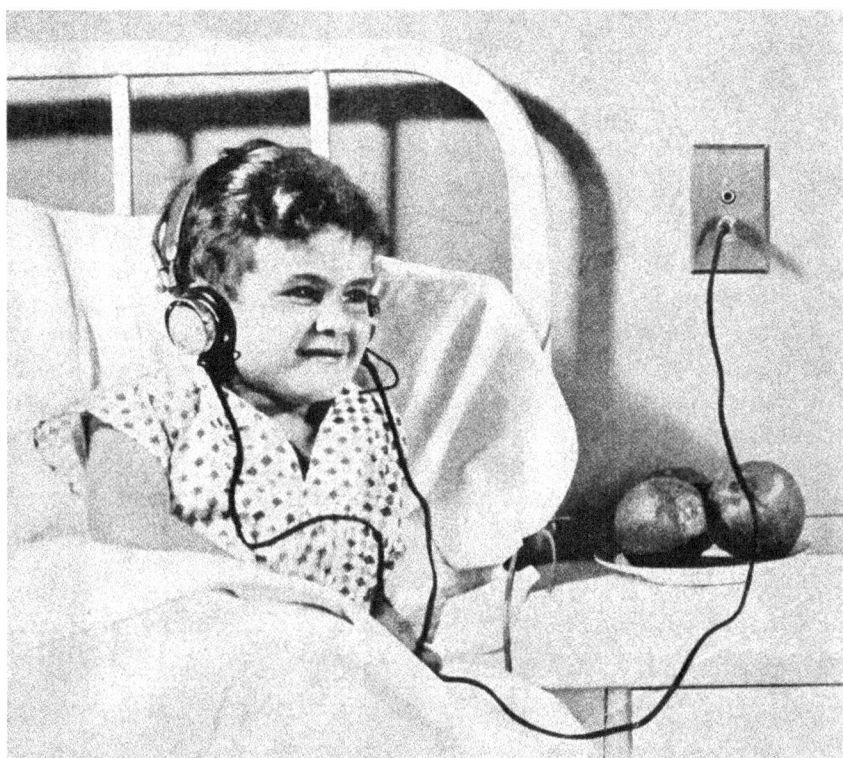

Figure 2.9 Aural service at the bedside. Photograph: unknown, c. 1937.
Source: *Hospital Magazine* (Australia) 1, no. 2 (April 1937): front cover.

was greatly enhanced, and, critically for the hospital, so too was the ability to maximise effective medical care at the bedside while minimising labour. The bed could be likened to a workbench, with the patient's body passive and positioned, through bed adjustment, in a way that was most amenable to the work of the hospital. Some of this technology was visible to the patient, but there was also a degree to which it was discreetly concealed. As well as a place where medical service could be provided as efficiently and effectively as possible, the bed was also a place for the patient to sleep and recuperate, to retreat in comfort, as much like home as possible.

The introduction of glareless lighting for wards and personal lighting at the hospital bed was another development to improve the patient experience (Ferree and Rand 1932). Eliminating glare from visible light sources was considered essential to relieve eye strain for patients and staff. The wall-mounted American "Dua-Light", positioned above the bed and fitted with upper and lower globes of different wattage, was promoted as suitable for private rooms, wards, nurses' stations and other departments, because it offered "no distress to the patient, no trying and tiring strain on optic nerves to handicap convalescence" (Curtis Lighting 1933: 113).

To satisfy the demands of medical service as well as create a sense of homeliness, a flexible approach to the furniture surrounding the bed was needed. Annmarie Adams has highlighted the bedside table advertised by Canadian department store Eaton's in *Canadian Hospital* in 1930. This looked like a typical domestic fitting, but its top could slide across and a patient bed table could be pulled up from within the unit and folded across the bed (Adams 2007). Its practical (that is, medical) function could be concealed. In 1933, Raymond P. Sloan, editor of *Modern Hospital* took readers through a complete tour of the furniture and furnishings of the recently completed New York Hospital–Cornell Medical Center, Manhattan, New York, USA, emphasising "numerous details that give a homelike touch and eliminate much of the old ward atmosphere" (Sloan 1933: 46), while at the same time admitting it was "impossible to create in a hospital room the characteristics of a home bedroom, because of the necessity of conforming to certain essential hospital requirements" (Sloan 1933: 47). Hospital beds were often higher than domestic beds, so medical staff could comfortably treat the patient at the bedside, and the need to regularly refresh the mattress and clean under the bed also meant that proportions often differed from those of a conventionally understood bedroom setting. At the same time, period style furniture supplier Stickley Bros argued that homely appearances and the modern hospital interior were not mutually exclusive:

> And now all Stickley furniture has a startlingly superior, patented finish that will save the average hospital hundreds of dollars, ordinarily spent for refinishing. It is absolutely impervious to alcohol, iodine, medicines, etc. – will not chip, check or craze. The most enduring finish known to science – guaranteed for 10 years.
>
> (Stickley Bros 1932: 151)

The concept of homeliness was not unique to North America. In 1940, architect Gio Ponti (1891–1979) designed the Columbus Clinic in Milan, Italy, after discussing patient care with one of Europe's foremost surgeons, Mario Donati (1879–1946). Ponti concluded the hospital should always look like a house rather than a clinic, so "the patient will express his gratitude to the doctors and nurses, and to the architect too, who has thought about him as a human being" (Ponti 1990: 118). Each room in the clinic was painted a different colour and had wooden – not metal – beds and armchairs. Indeed, the choice of timber for hospital furniture was an issue also championed by Alvar Aalto who, critical of the tendency to deploy the hard lines of tubular metal chairs and beds for hospitals, argued: "Tubular and chromium are good solutions technically, but psychologically these materials are not good for the human being". For him, timber was "better for the human touch" (Aalto 1998: 104).

Such thinking across hospitals, American and European, and styles, modernist and traditional, indicate simmering concerns in the interwar years over the visual state of the emerging image of the modern hospital, in almost all respects. On the one hand, the hospital – from its beds to its exterior – needed to fulfil the requirements of modern medical treatment; on the other hand, the patient – an active participant in their own recovery – needed a degree of comfort and familiarity in the hospital environment. This tension, the balance of which has swung over the course of the twentieth century, forecast how hospital designers' concerns would be redirected towards overt patient-centred design at the end of the twentieth century.

Space and privacy

The move to increase patient wellbeing and reduce the average length of patient stay in the modern hospital saw moves in the 1920s to smaller ward sizes. The number of beds in a typical Nightingale ward at the turn of the century had been 24–30, and beds were generally arranged perpendicular to the wall, forming, as Sloane and Sloane and others have described, a "perimeter" configuration (Sloane and Sloane 2003). Critics of this type of ward argued that patients in a perimeter ward risked the danger of cross-infection. Also, the patient was subject to the glare from windows opposite them and, because the beds were placed against the perimeter wall, the windows to the ward were necessarily small. The smaller the window, the darker the room. Isadore Rosenfield argued persuasively against the perimeter model:

> This is uncomfortable for the patient. The only way he can get away from the glare is to turn himself on his stomach or assume some similar difficult position which he may not be able to achieve because of his position. It also means that he has to be subjected to all the sights, noises and smells, and other unpleasantness that may be taking place in the ward. It is a rather inhuman and objectionable manner of housing patients.
>
> (Rosenfield 1947: 50)

In 1909, a Nightingale ward at the Rigshospital in Copenhagen, Denmark, was reconfigured to give patients more privacy. Instead of beds being arranged around the edge of the ward space, they were placed parallel to the windows and two beds deep with a central space acting as an open corridor. This new arrangement did not require any additional floor space. The space was further subdivided by screens held free of the floor and the ceiling to form groups of three or four beds, with one set of two beds facing another set of two. This meant that "socially, patients were now citizens of a small group rather than of the entire ward" (Thompson and Goldin 1975: 231). Another key advantage was that patients could actually look

46 *Everyone's own "healing machine"*

out the window from the bed, something the Nightingale ward did not allow, and they were no longer subject to glare. This arrangement, essentially a cubicle of four beds, was widely copied, especially in Europe and later in North America, with further refinement that saw the creation of four-bed wards divided by glass screens, and eventually the introduction of walls to define what have come to be known as Rigs wards or, in some countries, Spanish wards (Figure 2.10).

Rosenfield, in his book *Hospitals* (1947), made special mention of continental European Rigs ward planning, using the French example of a design for La Maison Medicale de Châtillon-sous-Bagneux (Medical Centre Châtillon-below-Bagneux) (Architects: Albert Thiers, J. Bardin, Marcel Favier, c. 1938) and noting that the general habit was to arrange the wards on one side of the corridor only (the south, facing the sun). This

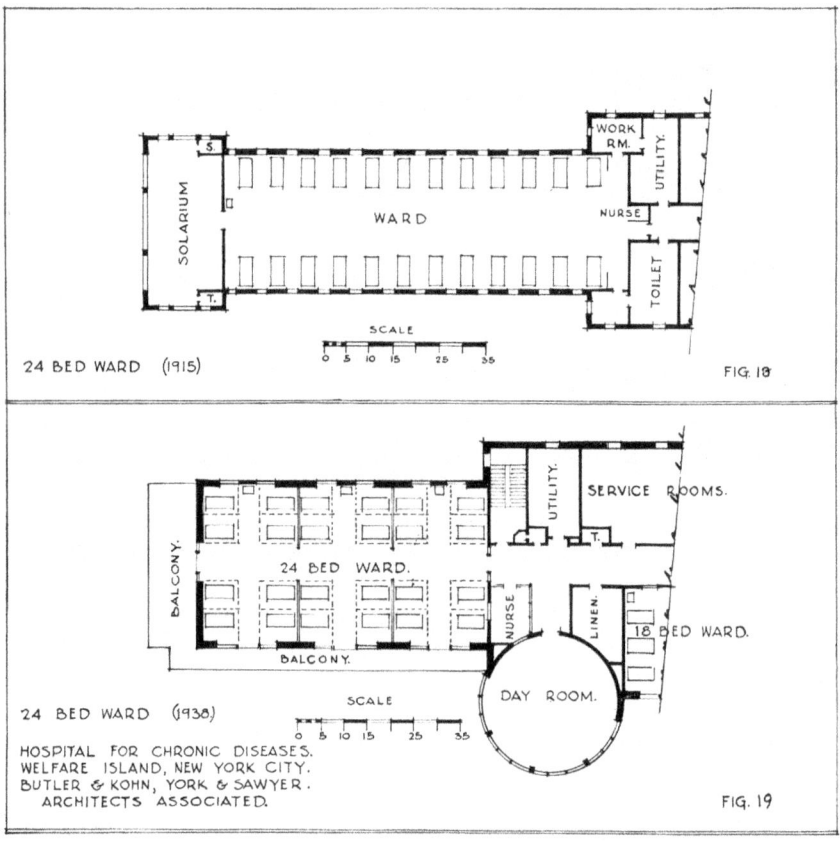

Figure 2.10 Comparative drawing of Nightingale (1915) and Rigs (1938) wards. Delineator: unknown.

Source: Butler, Charles and Addison Erdman. *Hospital Planning*. New York: F. W. Dodge Corporation, 1946: 26.

meant the hospital corridor could be naturally well lit and ventilated. Rosenfield provided two further reasons for this European arrangement, arguing Europeans had not developed or mechanised the services for the care of the patients as the Americans had and, because of this, the service spaces were small. He claimed this was because, for the most part, European labour was cheap and therefore used instead of the "mechanical aids" favoured in North America (Rosenfield 1947: 51–2).

In American hospitals, he argued, the services required so much room that they "absorb[ed] most of the space on the north side of the corridor" (Rosenfield 1947: 52). Indeed, Rosenfield's 1947 observation was prescient. After 1950, the expectation for highly equipped service spaces across the corridor from a typical single-patient bedroom, double or four-bed ward came to be the norm globally. With accompanying developments in air conditioning, many hospital plans employed Rigs wards placed on both sides of a wing with two corridors and a central double access spine of windowless service spaces. Rosenfield described this as a "double pavilion plan" and argued:

> It is an attempt at economy to meet the mounting cost of hospital construction. It places all the services in a central core available to two corridors. This arrangement has the advantage of shortening the building, relegating all patients' rooms to the perimeter where they can have light and air, but subjects the core to artificial means of illumination and ventilation.
>
> (Rosenfield 1947: 55)

The size of a hospital ward could be shrunk further through the addition of a top-hung hospital curtain that could be swiftly drawn around the patient's bed, essentially creating a single-bed enclosure within a ward. The ability to temporarily create a visually private (though not acoustically separate) space allowed immediate, sometimes delicate, investigation at bedside. Like the screens in Rigs wards, the curtains, hung on special noiseless roller curtain hooks, were held off the ceiling and above the floor, so as not to impede air flow or trap dust, and to allow for ease of cleaning the floor. These abstract space-enclosing curtains were so aesthetically effective that some modernist architects, including Ludwig Mies van der Rohe and Lilly Reich, took the hospital curtain into the everyday domestic interior in the Tugendaht House, Brno, Czechoslovakia (now Czech Republic) (1928–1930) as well as the temporary exhibition setting (Die Mode der Dame (Women's Fashion) exhibition, Berlin, Germany, 1927) (Miller 2001).

Approaches to providing space and privacy for the hospital bed included not only reducing ward size and creating a sense of an individual bedroom, but were also apparent in clever design that might promote patient recovery. Alvar Aalto, one of the most thoughtful designers of the modern medical interior, stated: "The ordinary room is a room for a vertical person: a patient's room is a room for a horizontal human being, and colours, lighting, heating and so on must be designed with that in mind" (Aalto 1998: 103). At the Paimio Sanatorium, Finland, which later became a general hospital, Aalto and his wife Aino Marsio Aalto (1894–1949) designed each of the patient bedrooms with special care, with the view of making them as comfortable and quiet as possible. The room was conceived in terms of the "patient's physical needs and the psychological effect on him of his surroundings" (Breines 1938: 7; Goldhagen 2012; Kellein 2005). Each room received full morning sunlight and housed just two patients, each with elegant tubular steel-framed beds and individual washbasins and cupboards, all designed by the Aaltos. The wall-hung basins, into which the water fell at an angle of 30 degrees, were "silent" and the faucets tilted so the noise and splash of water would not disturb the other patient. Lighting for the room was indirect, positioned behind the patient's head to minimise glare. The individual bed lamps were placed out of each patient's line of vision but close enough to provide adequate light for reading. The ceiling was painted a grey-green to avoid glare. A large part of the ceiling was a low-temperature heating panel, which in combination with draftless window ventilation ensured a constant temperature with "a minimum of dust-laden air currents" (Breines 1938: 8). Heat was directed to the foot of the beds, away from patients' faces. The wall-hung wardrobes made of light plywood were held well off the floor so that the floor beneath could be easily cleaned. The D-shaped door handles, shaped to fit the hand, swung down so clothing wouldn't catch on them. The floor immediately beneath the draft-proof window had a sloping section to stop dust buildup, which also acted as a footrest for the desk above. Acoustic privacy was enhanced by three of the room's walls being "hard" and the fourth "soft", achieved by thick slabs of insulating board covered with a jointless cellular material approximately 3 millimetres thick. This concern for the "horizontal man" was one of the earliest and most convincing examples of patient-centred design (Figures 2.11 and 2.12).

Large wards of more than twelve beds persisted even into the 1960s, but the tendency from the 1920s onwards was to seek, where possible, a realistic and economic spread of eight-, six-, four-, two- and single-patient rooms, based on the concept of the Rigs wards, with all the beds placed parallel to the window. This was the strategy pursued by Hjalmar Cederström and Hermann Imhäuser in Stockholm's Södersjukhuset (Southern Hospital), Sweden (1937–1944), where in a typical L-shaped thirty-two-bed wing, there was a spread of single, two- and four-bed rooms, with the four-bed rooms being closest to the south-facing solaria at the end of the L (Figure 2.13). By 1937, European practice had largely adopted the Rigs ward principle. Dr Hans Frey, Director of Hospitals in Bern, Switzerland, claimed, almost definitively:

> Both for building and working, the two and four [bed] ward system has, at present, proved both practical and economic, with the four

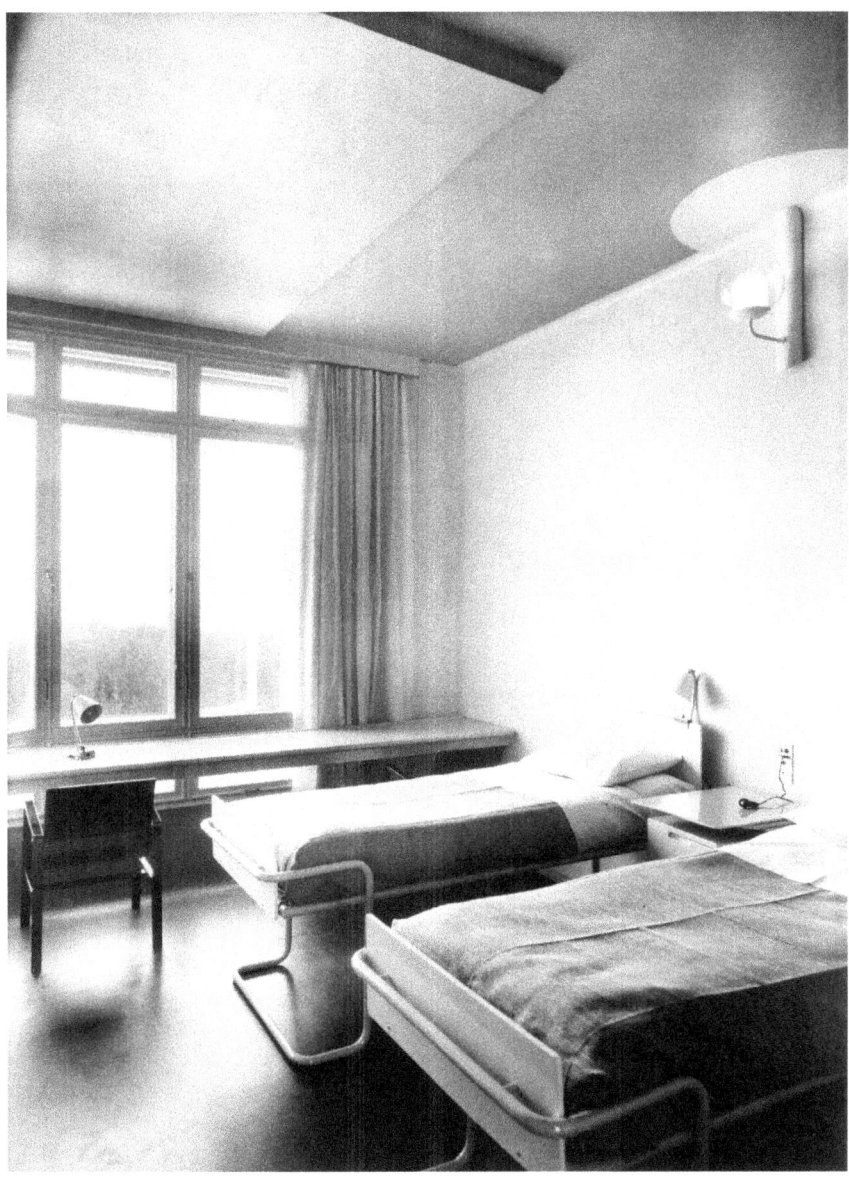

Figure 2.11 Patients' room. Paimio Tuberculosis Sanatorium, Paimio, Finland. Architect: Alvar Aalto, 1928–1932. Photograph: Gustaf Welin, 1933.
© Alvar Aalto Museum, used with permission.

50 *Everyone's own "healing machine"*

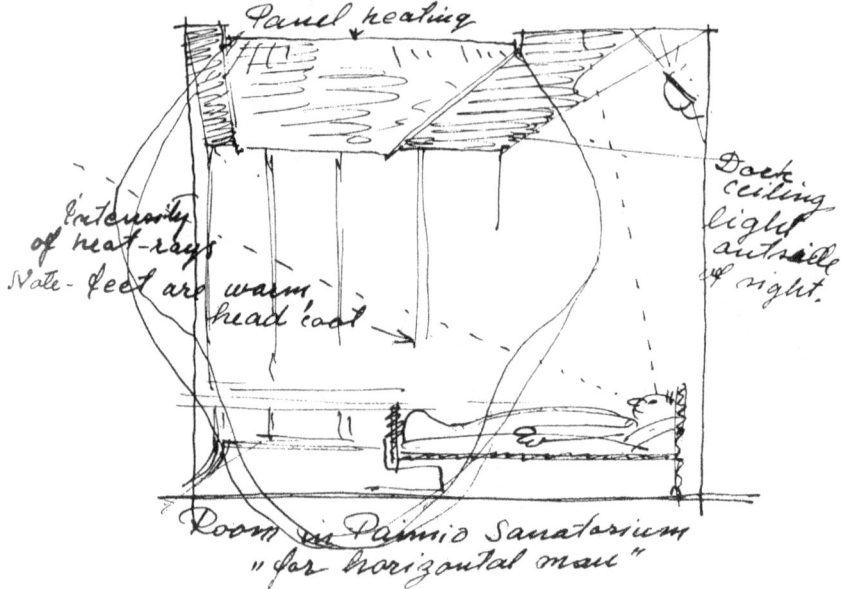

Figure 2.12 Sketch showing the "horizontal man" occupying a patient room at Paimio Sanatorium. Delineator: unknown.
Source: Aalto, Alvar. "The Humanizing of Architecture". *Technology Review* (November 1940).

> [bed] ward as the largest unit. This system is therefore most frequently adopted at present in new buildings.
>
> (Frey 1937: 131)

Privacy and community were carefully managed to maximise spatial equity and amenity. As many authors have emphasised, it was in the United States where the demand for private rooms was most evident. In the modern hospital, privacy and the single-patient bedroom were often sought but provision depended on the finances of the patient or the seriousness of their illness. The desire for the private room was most strongly expressed in the United States, where hospital directors explored ways to meet the demands of private patients, such as providing individual toilets for each room or shared between two rooms. In 1929, US hospital superintendents were frank about the demands of the paying patient:

> Sick persons are often impatient and are often justified in wondering why it takes a nurse so long to get a bedpan or an emesis basin. A patient who pays $12 or $15 a day cannot see why all his needs

Everyone's own "healing machine" 51

Figure 2.13 Plan of single, two- and four-bed rooms arranged in a Rigs ward format in a typical thirty-two-bed wing, Södersjukhuset (Southern Hospital), Stockholm, Sweden. Architects: Hjalmar Cederström and Hermann Imhäuser, 1937–1944. Delineator: unknown.

Source: Moretti, B. Franco. *Ospedali*. Milan: Editore Ulrico Hoepli, 1951: 283.

should have to be supplied from rooms half a block or even 100 feet distant.

(Munger 1929: 140)

Little wonder the demands of the private patient encouraged the pervasive idea of the "Hotel-Hospital" that dominated US hospital management thinking. But there were also medical reasons for patient isolation and privacy.

The ultimate isolated space for the hospital bed was the completely glazed cubicles for individual newborn babies, developed to eliminate any kind of contagion or cross-infection. Incubators had been used since the late nineteenth century, especially for premature babies, but in the 1930s more sophisticated equipment was developed. In 1939, the Presbyterian Hospital in Chicago, Illinois, USA, opened a new nursery for seven premature infants with each infant housed in a completely enclosed air conditioned cubicle rather like a large telephone booth, lined up as a series against a wall (Bacon 1939). The doctor and the nurse could then enter and minister to the child with all necessary equipment inside the cubicle. The next logical development was to house a premature baby in its own freestanding private cubicle, as was seen at the island-like double cubicles at Milwaukee Hospital, Wisconsin, USA, in 1939. As soon as the infants were born, they were wrapped in blankets, placed first in a basket and then in an enamelled steel cubicle with shatterproof glass on all sides. A sponge basin, weighing pan, bathing utensil and serving tray were all contained within. A counterbalanced front glass panel could be lowered for the nurse to complete her work, after which the glass was raised and complete isolation guaranteed (Fritschel 1939). Concealed fans on top blew clean air into the cubicle in a way that avoided drafts (an especially important feature because of the bradycardic reflex, whereby babies hold their breath when air is blown directly on to their face) and the baby was able to get newly cleaned air with each breath. Exhaled air was forced down by the fan and pushed out of the case at the bottom.

These artificial environments were dramatically reduced in size over the next ten years, and gained names such as "incubator" or "isolette". In Australia, the word "humidicrib" was used from 1946. The words "humidity" and "crib" were combined, indicating the advances which allowed this equipment to regulate oxygen and humidity, as well provide various monitoring and feeding options. After World War II, Tasmanian obstetrician William McIntyre and inventor Eric Waterworth invented the Waterworth Infant Respirator, which was then further developed by Adelaide inventors Edward T. Both (inventor of the "iron lung") and his younger brother Donald, which culminated in 1953 with Donald Both's refined version of what is now formally known as the humidicrib and which has since saved thousands of lives (Figure 2.14).

The development of the humidicrib and its artificial environment was in many respects symptomatic of how the patient bedroom interior would develop in the 1950s modern hospital. By the late 1950s, air conditioning was in use in most spaces of the hospital, especially in the United States, and the increased technological servicing of patient bedrooms meant the hospital room began taking on the aesthetic appearance of an efficient machine. The aura of homeliness so carefully managed in the interwar decades diminished sharply in favour of a regime of fast, efficient treatment. The idea of comfort was seen less in relation to convalescence and more as something perfectly calibrated through providing the most efficient treatment for the patient from the doctor and service from the nurse, whose tasks and professional status expanded exponentially during the 1940s and 1950s. Even Le Corbusier, reflecting on his Venice Hospital design, stated: "For the patient, a more comfortable hospitalization represents, in fact, a more effective cure which is always economical" (Le Corbusier 2001: 42). The bed had become a highly mechanised cog, which was now positioned in a much vaster machine than ever before.

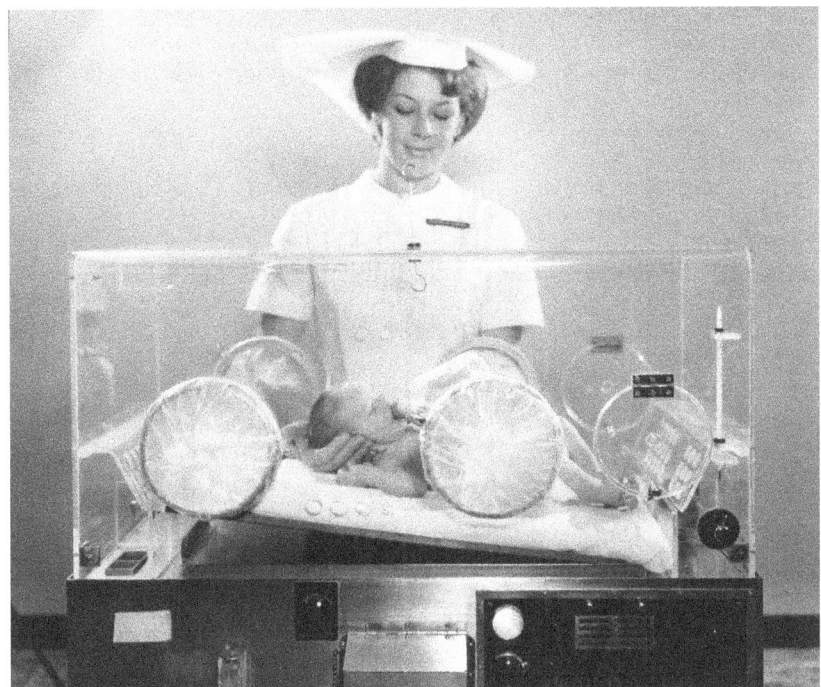

Figure 2.14 Nurse bottle-feeding a baby in a humidicrib. Echuca Base Hospital, Echuca, Victoria, Australia. Photograph: Wolfgang Sievers, 1966.
Courtesy: Pictures Collection, State Library of Victoria, H2002.99/241.

Note

1 The Trendelenburg position is defined as the body lying supine or flat on the back with the feet elevated higher than the head by 15–30 degrees. The reverse Trendelenburg position is defined as the body also lying flat but with the head raised 15–30 degrees higher than the feet.

References

Aalto, Alvar. "The Humanizing of Architecture." *Technology Review* (November 1940). In *Alvar Aalto in His Own Words*, edited by Göran Schildt. New York: Rizzoli, 1998.

Adams, Annmarie. "'That Was Then, This Is Now': Hospital Architecture in the Age(s) of Revolution, 1970–2001." In *The Impact of Hospitals, 300–2000*, edited by J. Henderson, P. Horden and A. Pastore, 227–8. Bern: Peter Lang, 2007.

Bacon, Asa S. "Designed for Premature Infants." *Modern Hospital* 52, no. 1 (January 1939): 61–2.

Bassick Hospital Castors. "Advertisement." *Modern Hospital* 43, no. 3 (September 1933): 117.

Breines, Simon. "Architecture." In *Architecture and Furniture: Aalto*, 5–12. New York: Museum of Modern Art, 1938.

Buchbinder, Leon. "The Transmission of Certain Infections of Respiratory Origin." *Journal of the American Medical Association* 118, no. 9 (28 February 1942): 718–30.

"Castors for Hospital Furniture: Draft Specification." *Hospital Magazine* (August 1937): 25.

Curtis Lighting. "Advertisement for Dua-Light." *Modern Hospital* 40, no. 3 (March 1933): 113.

Edwards & Company. "Advertisement for Edwards and Company Inc. Hospital Signaling." *Modern Hospital* 33, no. 3 (September 1929): 127.

Ferree, C.E. and G. Rand. "Glareless Lighting for Hospital Wards." *Modern Hospital* 38, no. 6 (June 1932): 128–38.

Foster Hospital Beds. "Advertisement." *Modern Hospital* 37, no. 1 (July 1931): 133.

Frey, Hans. "Das Krankenzimmer." *Nosokomeion* 8, no. 2 (1937): 131.

Fritschel, Herman L. "Isolation for Infants." *Modern Hospital* 52, no. 5 (May 1939): 62.

Gargiani, Roberto and Ana Rosellini. *Le Corbusier: Beton Brut and Ineffable Space, 1940–1965*. Abingdon, UK: EPFL Press and Routledge, 2011.

Gatch, Willis D. "The Sitting Posture; its Postoperative and Other Uses: With a Description of a Bed for Holding a Patient in this Position." *Annals of Surgery* 49, no. 3 (March 1909): 410–5. In Indiana Medical History Museum Newsletter (Fall 2009): 2.

Ghersi, I., M. Marino and M.T. Miralles. "From Modern Push-Button Hospital-Beds to 20th Century Mechatronic Beds: A Review." *Journal of Physics: Conference Series* 705 (2016): 6.

Giedion, Sigfried. *Befreites Wohnen: Licht, Luft, Oeffnung*. Zurich and Leipzig: Orell Füssli Verlag, 1929.

Goldhagen, Sarah Williams. "Aalto's Embodied Rationalism." In *Aalto and America*, edited by Stanford Anderson, Gail Fenske and David Fixler, 13–35. London: Yale University Press, 2012.

Goodfriend, Jacob. "The Handling of Mattresses." *Modern Hospital* 30, no. 2 (February 1928): 148–52.

Hall, E. Stanley. "Modern Hospital Planning." *Journal of the Royal Institute of British Architects* 42 (6 April 1935): 651–2.

Hospital Magazine (Australia) 1, no. 2 (April 1937): cover.

Keck, George Fred. "Modern Design Applied to Hospitals." *Modern Hospital* 60, no. 3 (March 1943): 59–61.

Kellein, Thomas. *Alvar & Aino Aalto: Design: Collection Bischofberger*. Ostfildern: Hatje Cantz, 2005.

King Edward's Hospital Fund for London. *Design of Hospital Bedsteads*. London: King Edward's Hospital Fund for London, 1967.

Lamplough, F.E. "The Properties and Applications of 'Vita' Glass." *Journal of the Royal Society of Arts* 77, no. 3997 (28 June 1929): 805.

Le Corbusier. "Rapport Technique." In *Le Corbusier's Venice Hospital and the Mat Building Revival*, edited by Hashim Sarkis, 19–35. Munich: Prestel Verlag, 2001.

Miller, Wallis. "Mies and Exhibitions." In *Mies in Berlin*, edited by Terence Riley and Barry Bergdoll, 340–2. New York: Museum of Modern Art, 2001.

Moretti, B. Franco. *Ospedali*. Milan: Editore Ulrico Hoepli, 1951.

Munger, C.W. "Modern Utility Units That Meet the Demands of Private Patients." *Modern Hospital* 33, no. 2 (August 1929): 140.

"A New Type of Bed with Many Advantages." *Modern Hospital* 30, no. 2 (February 1928): 160.

Nightingale, Florence. *Notes on Hospitals*. London: John W. Parker and Son, 1859.

Olson, G.W. and Carl A. Friedmann. "Two Specially Designed Pieces of Hospital Equipment." *Modern Hospital* 44, no. 2 (February 1935): 90–2.

Ponti, Lisa Licitra. *Gio Ponti: The Complete Works, 1923–1978*. London: Thames & Hudson, 1990.

"Push-Button Hospital Bed." *Life Magazine* (12 November 1945): 92.

"Push-Button Bed Provides Self-Nursing Service for Hospital Patients." *Popular Mechanics* (August 1946): 116.

Rosenfield, Isadore. *Hospitals: Integrated Design*. New York: Reinhold Publishing Corporation, 1947.

Sadar, John. "Unveiling the Ultraviolet: 'Vita' Glass, Bodies and the Marketing of Material Performance." *Architecture and Culture* 3, no. 3 (2015): 375–95.

Sarkis, Hashim (ed.). *Le Corbusier's Venice Hospital*. London: Prestel, 2001.

Saunders, James B. deC. M. and James W. Morgan. "The Bedpan Loses Its Barbarism." *Modern Hospital* 52, no. 3 (March 1939): 92.

Senf, Harriet R. "Caring for the Patient in the CircOlectric Bed." *American Journal of Nursing* 60, no. 2 (February 1960): 227.

Shah, Mahnaz. *Le Corbusier's Venice Hospital Project: An Investigation into Its Structural Formulation*. London: Taylor and Francis, 2013.

Shively, F.L. "Bedpan with Backrest." *Modern Hospital* 52, no. 3 (March 1939): 94.

Sloan, Raymond P. "The Hospital Is Known by the Furnishing It Keeps." *Modern Hospital* 39, no. 1 (July 1933): 46.

Sloane, David and Beverlie Sloane. *Medicine Moves to the Mall*. Baltimore and London: Johns Hopkins University Press, 2003.

Solowey, Mathilde, Morris Solotorovsky and Leon Buchbinder. "Studies on Microorganisms in Simulated Room Environments." *Journal of Bacteriology* (May 1942): 545–5.

"A Standard Bed Castor." *Hospital Magazine* (April 1937): 35.

Stickley Bros. "Advertisement for Stickley Bros: Furniture." *Modern Hospital* 38, no. 3 (March 1932): 151.

Teleoptic Corporation. "Advertisement." *Modern Hospital* 36, no. 2 (February 1931): 125.

Thompson, John D. and Grace Goldin. *The Hospital: A Social and Architectural History*. New Haven, CT: Yale University Press, 1975.

Will Ross & Co. "Advertisement for Dr Urie 'Patient Comfort' Spring bed." *Modern Hospital* 55, no. 1 (July 1940): 111.

US Department of Health, Education and Welfare: Public Health Service. *Design and Construction of General Hospitals*. New York: F.W. Dodge Corporation, 1953.

3 Knowledge, care and control
Nurses' stations and nurses' homes

If the bed was the technology around which the modern hospital was conceptualised, scaled and serviced, the history of hospital architecture in the nineteenth century was, to a significant degree, the history of institutionalised nursing. The desire to make nursing care more efficacious drove hospital development in the era of the pavilion-plan hospital when the duties and capacity of nurses were the central conceptual bases of ward design. The ward was, in turn, the organising unit for the plan of the hospital as a whole and consequently generated its overall form. Before World War I, nursing care meant not only observing the patients and attending to their urgent medical needs; it also involved servicing the ward. Cooking and laundry, for example, were organised at the ward level and so nurses were housekeepers and ward managers, as well as carers and guards. Practically and conceptually the nurse was at the centre of hospital activities.

This all changed in the era of the modern hospital, when centralised servicing became a driver for a radical transformation of the way resources were organised and care provided. Significantly, centralised provision of food and clean linen via industrial-scaled kitchens and laundry services freed nurses to participate in more specialised aspects of the medical process, particularly in observing and recording the patient's condition. There were changes, therefore, in the physical and conceptual relationship of nurse to bed. This in turn inspired a different approach to ward design. While nursing remained a driver of design, it was integrated into a more complex functional diagram.

In the first half of the twentieth century, the Nightingale ideal of the nurse – pious, dutiful and humble – persisted as a cultural figure, but the actual nurse, at work in the ward, was absorbed into a more functionally specialised system of care. This tension between the sentimental ideal on the one hand and her evolving practical specialisation on the other underpinned the seemingly paradoxical position of nursing within a reformulated system of hospital care. Annmarie Adams has noted that the encircling role of gender in shaping nursing meant the individual nurse of the early twentieth century (at that stage almost invariably female) was simultaneously empowered and constrained by the architecture of the modern hospital (Adams 2008).

The design of nursing stations, nurses' homes and related recreational and educational facilities in modern hospitals recognised the nurse's interests as a person, and her desire for privacy, leisure and professional respect to a much greater degree than earlier forms of hospital organisation. At the same time, hospital managers of the interwar decades prescribed a narrower, more functionally specialised domain of activity for nurses as workers. This shift in what the nurse actually did and in how she was conceived by the institution – and it was still almost always "she" – led to several notable physical changes in the modern hospital. These occurred in and around the wards, but also, importantly, in the living quarters designed for nurses and the educational and recreational spaces that were provided for nursing staff.

In the early 1940s, US government agencies such as the Office of War Information, collaborated with major US hospitals to create detailed photographic portraits of daily life in these institutions as part of the home front propaganda effort during World War II. Photographer Paul Parker created one such pictorial story focusing on nurses and nursing at the New York Hospital–Cornell Medical Center, Manhattan, New York, USA (Architect: Coolidge, Shepley, Bulfinch & Abbott, 1932) in 1943. This authorised photographic depiction of typical daily nursing activities in a large, modern hospital pointed to some of the major shifts that had occurred during the early decades of the twentieth century. In Parker's storyboard, nurses are shown attending to patients at the bedside, observing patients undergoing treatment and watching an equipment sterilisation demonstration, but also playing tennis and socialising (Figure 3.1). The clear intent was to depict nurses in three modes: working, learning and relaxing. The images and others like them, such as Fritz Henle's photographs, were highly orchestrated representations of nurses that served an ideological and promotional purpose (Figures 3.2 and 3.3). But they also provide a telling view of what institutions believed nursing was and should be in a large, metropolitan teaching hospital. As this and other depictions of nursing life in the period highlight, significant constraints on the autonomy of nurses remained firmly in place. However, earlier associations with religious sequestration in the hospital had now given way to a more collegiate life. These official transcripts of the nurse's life in the modern hospital showed nursing in a way that departed significantly from the vigilant and dutiful nurse that had been at the heart of the classic pavilion ward.

Pavilions

In Florence Nightingale's *Notes on Nursing*, first published in 1859, the godmother of British nursing pointed to the spatial, even architectural, implications of nursing practice. The idea of nursing, she argued, was not simply the administration of medicines and poultices, rather it "ought to signify the proper use of fresh air, light, warmth, cleanliness, quiet, and the proper selection and administration of diet" (Nightingale 1860: 12).

Figure 3.1 A student nurse enjoys an afternoon of recreation on the tennis courts provided for the employees and staff doctors of the New York Hospital–Cornell Medical Center, Manhattan, New York, USA. Architects: Coolidge, Shepley, Bulfinch & Abbott, 1932. Photograph: Paul Parker, 1943.

Courtesy: Medical Center Archives of New York–Presbyterian/Weill Cornell.

Figure 3.2 Graduate student nurses relax in the living room of a nurses' home. Photograph: Fritz Henle, 1942.
Courtesy: Library of Congress, Prints & Photographs Division, FSA/OWI Collection, LC-DIG-fsa-8b08221.

She defined nursing as an activity that encompassed both the nourishment of the patient and the tempering and overall management of their environment.

It was a short step from this assertion of the architectural and spatial responsibility of nursing to *Notes on Hospitals* (1859), Nightingale's treatise on hospital buildings themselves. There, Nightingale took up the problem of specifying best practices and ideal spatial conditions for a building type she regarded as a necessary evil. In her revised third edition, she suggested the very first requirement of a hospital was that "it should do the sick no harm" (Nightingale 1863: iii). It must enable efficient nursing

60 *Knowledge, care and control*

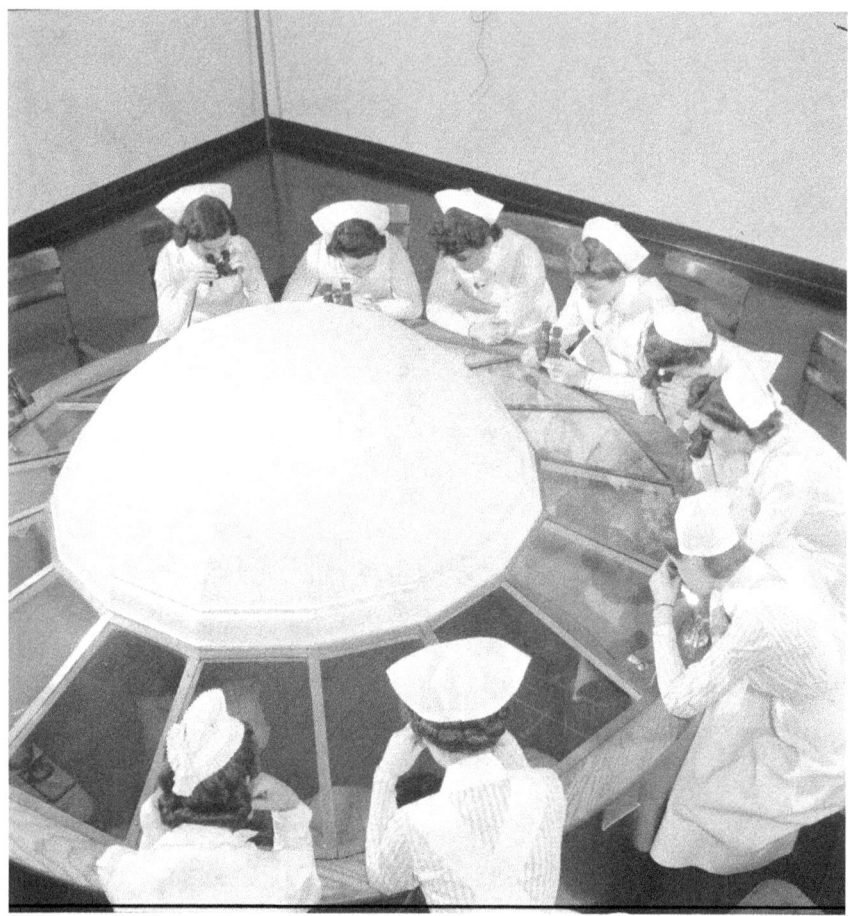

Figure 3.3 Aided by binoculars, student nurses watch an operation through the glazed ceiling of an operating theatre. Photograph: Fritz Henle, 1942.

Courtesy: Library of Congress, Prints & Photographs Division, FSA/OWI Collection, LC-DIG-fsa-8b07797.

care but not expose the patient to risk of infection from others. The challenge, therefore, was to enable the greatest number of patients to be observed while maintaining adequate distance between those patients. Hence, she supported the pavilion model of hospital planning, a formally uncomplicated and spatially separated system that she described as a "detached" model:

> The essential feature of the pavilion construction is that of breaking up hospitals of any size into a number of separate detached parts, having a

common administration, but nothing else in common. And the object sought is that the atmosphere of no one pavilion or ward should diffuse itself to any other pavilion or ward, but should escape into open air as speedily as possible, while its place is supplied by the purest obtainable air from the outside.

(Nightingale 1863: 56)

This model of detached pavilions, containing what would later be called Nightingale wards, gave hospitals their basic form and dominated hospital design thinking for the half century before World War I. Anthony King has argued that Nightingale's role in establishing the supremacy of the pavilion in British hospital planning has been overstated (King 1966). Certainly, pavilions existed well before the rise of Nightingale and her fellow sanitarians, and powerful exemplary models, such as the plans by Bernard Poyet and J.R. Tenon for the French Hospital Commission in the 1780s and new wings of St Thomas' Hospital, London, England (1840–1842), were well known and widely discussed before Nightingale became the most prominent voice in the field in England (Thompson and Goldin 1975; Pevsner 1976; Forty 1980). It is nevertheless significant that the pavilion ward model is so closely associated with Nightingale and her legacy. If it is true that, as Adrian Forty has suggested, the architectural, medical and nursing professions all "seized on and promoted the advantages of the pavilion plan" in order to advance professional claims over the form and use of hospitals, then it seems that Nightingale and nurses staked the strongest claim (Forty 1980: 79).[1]

One of the most significant examples of the pavilion-plan hospital, and certainly one of the most intact records surviving of that period of hospital development, Berlin's Rudolf Virchow Krankenhaus (Rudolf Virchow Hospital), Germany (Architect: Ludwig Hoffmann, 1898–1906), was not constructed until the turn of the twentieth century. By that time, the miasmic theory of disease to which Nightingale and many of her sanitarian colleagues subscribed in the 1850s, 1860s and 1870s had been well and truly disproven. Indeed, the pavilion hospital had prospered precisely as the work of Louis Pasteur and Joseph Lister – on disease transmission and antiseptic technique, respectively – undermined its overt theoretical justification. The microbiological research of German scientist Robert Koch, first published in the 1870s, strengthened the impetus toward laboratory medicine and away from a strictly environmental aetiology of disease. Nevertheless, the broad environmentalism that highlighted the importance of fresh air, clean sheets and wall surfaces and the absence of foul odours, as well as the salutary qualities of natural landscape settings, continued to motivate hospitals and their architects at the beginning of the twentieth century (Kisacky 2017).

The Virchow Hospital, one of the most prominent public projects in its day and one of Europe's most architecturally distinguished hospitals, was

62 *Knowledge, care and control*

constructed near the edge of Berlin just beyond the Ringbahn in the city's north. When completed in 1906 it was one of Europe's largest, containing fifty-seven separate buildings and two thousand beds served by more than one thousand employees. Its architect was Ludwig Hoffmann, Berlin's director of urban planning and construction. His rigorously controlled site planning and the immaculate landscape setting gave the hospital its character and prized environmental qualities. Edward F. Stevens, the leading North American hospital specialist in the early decades of the twentieth century, saw lessons in the Virchow model. He visited the hospital as part of his European hospital research trip in 1911 and noted approvingly in his subsequent book that patients and staff could use "the beautifully laid out grounds and parks, with their walks and drives" and that every third day they are reserved "for the sole use of the nurses" (Stevens 1918: 4) (Figure 3.4).

The example of Virchow and its ongoing currency as a model for hospital planning in the 1910s highlights the fact that, as Adrian Forty argued, there is no "clear causal relationship between scientific discovery and innovation in building form" (Forty 1980: 61). As both Forty and Adams have noted, if

Figure 3.4 Nurses in the landscaped grounds of the Rudolf Virchow Krankenhaus (Rudolf Virchow Hospital), Berlin, Germany. Architect: Ludwig Hoffmann, 1898–1906. Photograph: Ernst von Brauchitsch.

Source: *Neubauten der Stadt Berlin* 6 (1907).

Courtesy: Architekturmuseum TU Berlin, Inv. B 2376.069.

we want to understand the physical form of hospitals, it makes more sense to focus on "those who controlled hospitals" rather than on the state of scientific knowledge (Forty 1980: 61; Adams 2008). In many respects, therefore, Virchow testifies to the centrality of nurses and nursing in the organisation of hospitals in the early decades of the twentieth century. But even as Stevens wrote approvingly of Virchow's salutary environment and its benefits for staff and patients alike, new ideas and practices hinted at fundamental changes that would transform the shape of the nursing unit and make Virchow a monument to an earlier model of hospital care.

Beyond the pavilion

By the time Stevens published his hospital treatise in 1918, the rapidly professionalising field of the hospital manager had changed the ways nurses worked, the tasks they performed and, therefore, the working and living spaces they used. While Virchow and most other major hospitals that had been developed at the turn of the century reflected the environmental determinism embedded in the architecture and city planning discourses, by 1918 it was apparent that knowledge and information would be the new currency for the hospital. Information did not, of course, replace fresh air, cleanliness and the cultivation of pleasant surroundings as the only driver for hospital design. But after 1918, a demonstrable concern with how information was collected, utilised and shared suffused hospital planning and design and shaped hospital operations in important ways.

In the nineteenth century, the nurse was a physically proximate carer and guard, and the nurses' desk or station, therefore, had to be in sight and hearing of patients. This meant that in the pavilion-planned hospital, the nurses' station was always situated within the large open ward in plain view of patients. But the Rigs ward came into wide use in the 1910s and 1920s, and formerly large wards were subdivided into smaller groupings, most often of four beds, making it no longer possible for a single nurse to supervise the sixteen, twenty or twenty-four patients directly. In major new interwar hospitals such as the Los Angeles County General Hospital, California, USA, nurses took charge of the nursing unit. Such units were composed of groups of two and four beds, as well as several isolation beds and were overseen from a "nursing utility station" – in effect both a central repository for supplies and a command post for information and communications (Thompson and Goldin 1975; Stevens 1918; Goldwater 1927; Rosenfield 1947).

In a plan for the Leeds Hospital, Yorkshire, England, by Stanley Hall, Easton & Robertson, published in the British architectural press in the mid-1930s, the position of the nurses' station in a newly configured nursing unit consisting mostly of four-bed wards was a fairly simple translation of the old model. Instead of being a large open space, the nursing unit was a wing of a single floor with several four-bed wards on one side of the corridor and a variety of smaller isolation and two-bed rooms on the other. The nursing station was positioned roughly halfway along the corridor on the western side, and a separate area for "Sisters" was provided close to the entrance to the whole unit. The overall space was roughly the same as the pavilions of earlier years, with nurses' posts close to the midpoint as well as at the entrance to the area. But the rooms were divided and the corridor defined as a distinct circulation space, so the whole design created a quite different regime of observation (Hall 1935). Other hospitals from the period had deeper plans and redefined the shape of the ward more fundamentally, allowing for a different spatial relationship between nursing station and bedside. At the L.A. County General Hospital, nurses' stations and desks projected into the main circulation space and were more obviously the observational centre points of the whole unit (Hunt 1940) (Figure 3.5).

After World War II, the fundamental rethinking of the nursing unit and its planning in relation to the nurses' station was taken even further.

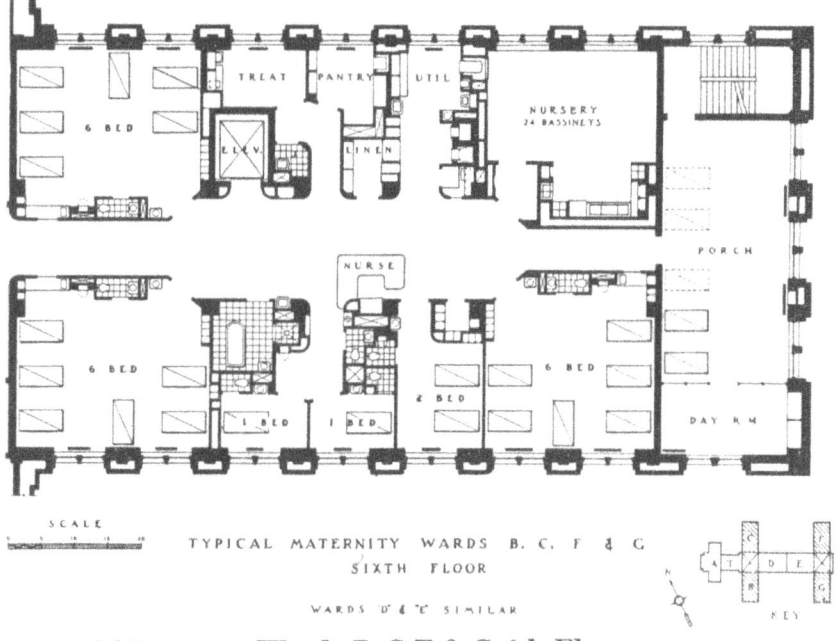

Typical Maternity Wards B C F & G 6th Floor

Figure 3.5 Maternity ward in the Los Angeles County General Hospital, Los Angeles, California, USA, a characteristic tall block hospital of the 1930s. The centrally located nurses' station was situated just 15 steps from the furthest bed. Architects: Allied Architects' Association, 1932. Delineator: unknown.

Source: *Architectural Forum* 62, no. 3 (March 1935): 224.

Architects promoted the benefits of a variety of circular and polygonal plans, harking back to some of the more radical geometric hospital plans of the late eighteenth century. In the 1950s, Australian architects J.H. Esmond Dorney and G.M. Hirsch designed the Sandringham and District Hospital (1957–1964) in suburban Melbourne, Victoria, Australia. He conceived the building as three linked polygons. The two smaller scaled polygons were ward buildings organised around central nurses' stations (Goad 2009) (Figure 3.6). Such polygonal planning with central nursing stations were also the basis of the ward planning and overall form of three US hospitals from the mid-1960s: the Lorain Community Hospital in Ohio (1964–1965); the White Memorial Hospital in Temple, Texas (1963–1965); and the Central Kansas Medical Center, Great Bend, Kansas (1963–1964) (Verderber and Fine 2000). A few years later, Chicago architect Bertrand Goldberg designed the Prentice Women's Hospital (1968–1972, demolished in 2015) for the Northwestern University hospitals, Chicago, Illinois, USA in a similar way. In this building, four interlocking cylindrical concrete ward buildings were planned with nurses' stations as the centre point of each of the ward floors. Goldberg dramatised the formal distinctiveness of the plan much more graphically than the earlier examples, with the linked cylindrical forms of the nursing units hovering above the cuboid

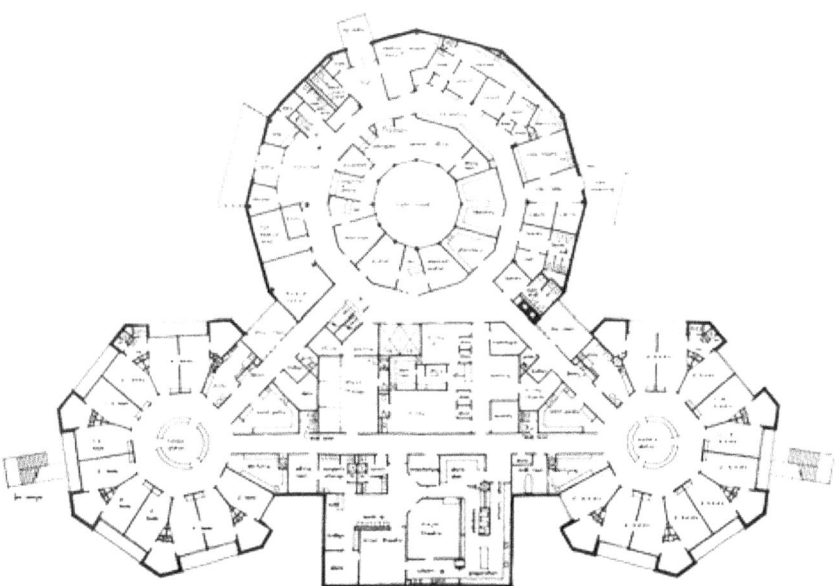

Figure 3.6 Plan of first floor, Sandringham and District Hospital, Sandringham, Victoria, Australia. Architects: J.H. Esmond Dorney and G.M. Hirsch, 1957–1964. Delineator: unknown.

Source: *Foundations* 2, no. 6 (June 1961): 43.

Courtesy: Paddy Dorney/J.H. Esmond Dorney Trust.

block below, which housed outpatient departments and reception areas (Fisher 2011).

In these postwar circular and polygonal-planned hospital buildings, the clear intent was to provide a kind of panoptic observation point for the charge nurse. In a sense, this was also the *rhetoric* of the plan, an architectural strategy that referred explicitly to the nurse-patient relationship and tried to plan for it in the most efficient way possible. In some of these examples, as well as in many more prosaic nursing unit plans, how the stations were detailed also contributed to the panoptic rhetoric. Most provided a partition, but one that was glazed to enable sight lines to corridors and, sometimes, patient rooms. In the interwar decades, some partitions were of smart curved glazing.

Information workers

Despite the development of this panoptic rhetoric in some of the later iterations of the modern hospital, direct lines of sight to all patients were relatively uncommon for most of the period in most hospitals. Without direct visual connection to all the patients in their care, nurses depended on remote communications, especially the developing nurse call button systems. The call button became an indispensable link between patient and nurse in the interwar decades, and technology companies vied to provide the most advanced systems. As noted in Chapter 2, the Teleoptic Corporation of Racine, Wisconsin, USA, claimed in 1931 to have made a "radical departure" from previous call systems. Their four-unit system not only conveyed information from bedside to nurses' station, but also relayed the information to an intervening display point above the door to the patient's room and to the superintendent's office. Moreover, the system allowed the patient to convey something of their situation or what they needed, giving them a choice between four different messages: "water", "bedpan", "nurse", "emergency" (Teleoptic Corporation 1931). But there were a host of other manufacturers, including Edwards and Company of New York, USA, which advertised a full range of call systems for hospitals in the late 1920s and 1930s (Edwards & Company 1929).

Such electronic communications between patient and nursing staff freed the hospital architect to arrange wards in new ways. Stevens noted that the changed configuration of the ward, with its flexible partitions and new divisions of space, meant there was not an obvious prime location to station the head nurse of a floor or ward. Architects differed over the degree of flexibility they felt should be possible in the arrangement of modern nursing units (Kisacky 2017). There was no unanimity of opinion among managers and hospital planners, either, and a number of contrasting positions were taken, each with its own rationale. More important than the specific location of the station, Stevens argued, was that "certain conditions and equipment should exist" (Stevens 1918: 215). In particular, he noted that

Knowledge, care and control   67

convenient office conditions should prevail at the station; it should have adequate light, a place for writing and convenient records storage. He suggested that the annunciator for the nurses' call system should also be located at the station.

By the 1930s, images of nurses at their stations on the telephone, writing or undertaking some other administrative task circulated widely in promotional material for hospitals. Such images highlighted both the modernity of the institutions and the emerging role of nurses as conduits and recorders of information (Figure 3.7). Architects put a great deal of effort into thinking through issues of information storage and even discussed in print questions such as the best type of manila folder and the best means of carrying patient case records.

As with other hospital functions, record keeping developed its own specialised spaces and staff in the interwar decades. The hospital trade publications dedicated extensive space to the question. Hospital plans likewise

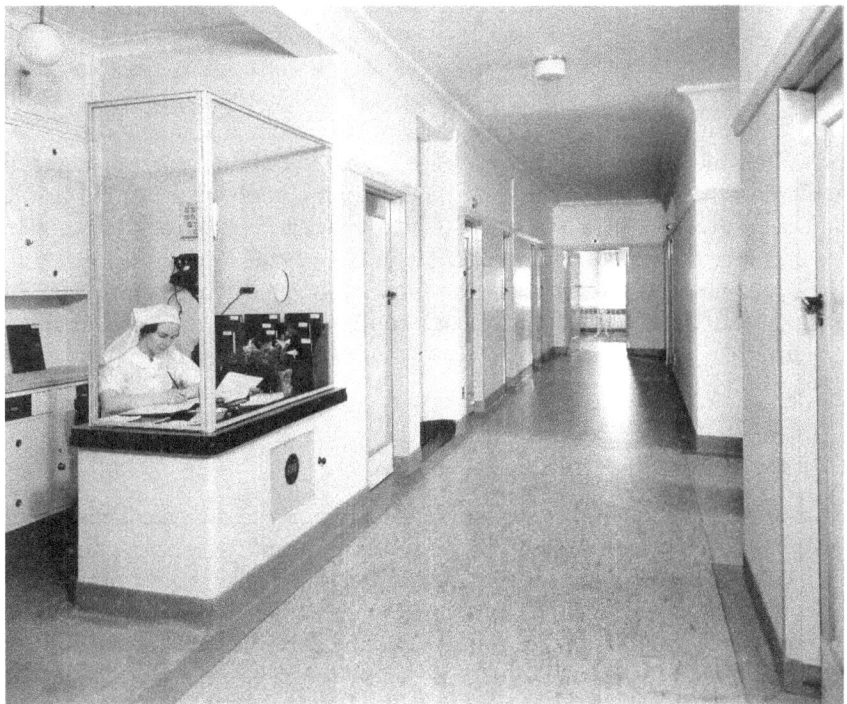

Figure 3.7 A nurse presents the image of administrative efficiency at her station. Glass partitions allowed nurses to both see and be seen. St George's Hospital, Kew, Victoria, Australia. Architects: Leighton Irwin and Louis R. Williams, architects in association, 1937. Photograph: Commercial Photographic Co., c. 1940.

Courtesy: Pictures Collection, State Library of Victoria.

reflected the growing importance of data storage to hospital operations. As hospital historian Joel D. Howell has noted, the emergence of separate departments within the hospital in the early decades of the twentieth century, such as roentgenology or radiology, threatened to fragment knowledge of the patient even as investigation of the body intensified. The institutional response to this was centralised record keeping, an attempt to reconstruct in archival form the whole patient fragmented by diverging regimes of testing and treatment (Howell 1995).

In 1928, Florence Babcock, record librarian at the University of Michigan Hospital, Ann Arbor, Michigan, USA, reported that her department employed forty-four people, including cataloguers, stenographers and Dictaphone operators. The department possessed eighteen dictation machines and a carrier system serviced the central records library, linking it to each of the outpatient clinics on the "diagnostic floor" (Babcock 1928). This sophisticated central unit method of record keeping depended on a carefully coordinated system of information technology with strong protocols for data management and retention. The idea was to move data as quickly and as safely as possible between departments and to store as much data as practicable. At the University of Chicago Clinics, Illinois, USA, this transfer of data was achieved using pneumatic tubes (Hayden 1940: 92) (Figure 3.8). The implications of these new regimes of data storage and use, of course, went beyond nursing. But they were highly significant for nursing and underline the extent to which hospitals became knowledge-centred in the interwar decades. In a system in which charity and the comfort of the patent were the primary objectives, the nurse was the heart of the hospital. This was no longer the case in the modern hospital where knowledge of disease and of the individual patient's condition became the focus of activity. The role of the nurse inevitably changed with that overarching mission (Hayden 1940).

Nurses as human resource

Historians of nursing have argued that doctors asserted medical control of hospitals in an unprecedented way in the early twentieth century, diminishing the authority of nurses and, therefore, of women in the institution (Group and Roberts 2001). The architectural sources and records of hospital planning tell a slightly different story, but one that likewise sees the authority and agency of nurses reduced in this period. The emergence of a new class of managers in hospitals eroded the position and moral authority of nurses by narrowing and specialising their role. In 1913, Johns Hopkins Hospital physician and leader W. Gilman Thompson attached pedometers to nurses to measure how far they were walking. The intent of this data gathering was very clear. He wanted to learn how much energy – or at least how much time – was expended by nurses in carrying out routine activity in the hospital so as to find ways to rationalise nursing resources. This

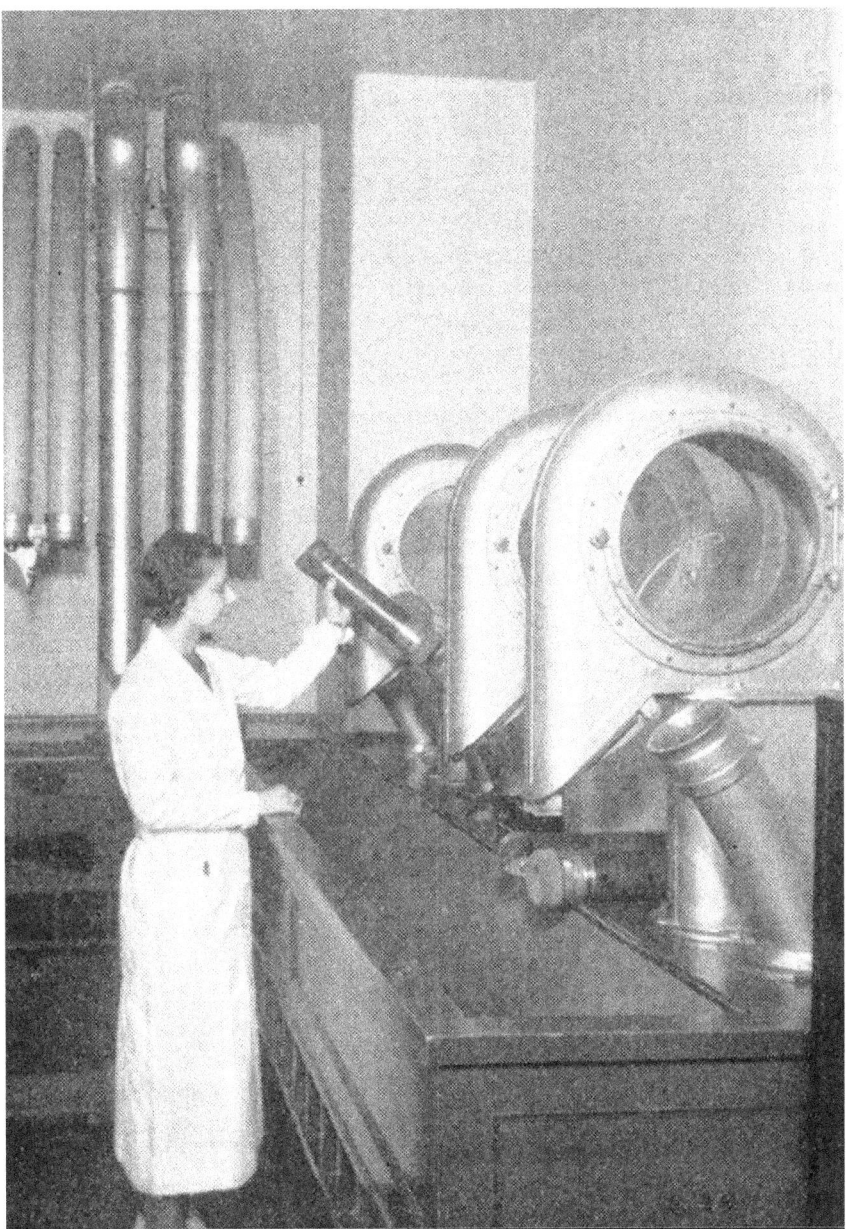

Figure 3.8 Pneumatic tube system for transporting medical records in use at the University of Chicago Clinics and Lying-In Hospital, Chicago, Illinois, USA. Photograph: unknown.

Source: *Modern Hospital* 55, no. 3 (September 1940): 92.

and similar attempts to extract maximum value from nurses' labour were significant for hospital design (Thompson and Goldin 1975).

Stevens introduced his 1918 treatise by highlighting efficiency as the central issue in hospital architecture in a way that left little doubt about the influence of Frederick Winslow Taylor's principles of scientific management (Taylor 1911) on how Stevens perceived the relationship between nursing resources and hospital architecture. He argued "[t]he hospital planner must seek to eliminate here all lost motion or unnecessary work" and that "careful scientific nursing" was one of the principal ways in which the overall productivity or output of the hospital could be enhanced (Stevens 1918: 2). The modifier scientific is somewhat uncertain here, as he does not define what he means. But the wider context indicates that it is the integration with Taylorist scientific management, more than medical science, that was paramount. Even though Stevens always tempered his interest in rational planning with a strong emphasis on the qualitative dimensions of the hospital environment, the implications for hospital employees, of which nurses were a significant proportion, were clear. Henceforth, managers, planners and architects discussed nurses much more explicitly as a resource that must be deployed efficiently.

Some hospital specialists couched focus on the proper use of nursing resources in sympathetic terms, as a concern for the welfare of nurses. In the title of an October 1928 issue of *Modern Hospital*, prominent hospital planner and administrator Jacob J. Golub asked rhetorically, "The Tired Nurse, What Can We Do for Her?" He discussed problems of overwork and the substandard environmental conditions in which nurses performed their duties. Like Stevens, he focused more on how the nurse should be treated and utilised within the hospital system than on the nurse's agency as a carer and decision-maker (Golub 1928).

Writing for the same publication in 1940, Dr Charles F. Wilinsky published an article with the title "Conserving Nurses' Energy". He noted, "the relationship of proper hospital planning to the conservation of energy and the promotion of efficiency have been increasingly recognised" (Wilinsky 1940: 72–4). Wilinsky also highlighted that several of the innovations in hospital bed technology were developed to reduce the burden on nurses. Heavy partitions to provide patient privacy had been phased out and replaced by the much less laborious curtains in open wards. Mechanical jacks had become the norm for raising and lowering the level of the bed and beds were generally raised to make nursing work around the bed less injurious. Hospitals had also introduced various hand trucks and trolleys for delivering food and moving medical equipment such as oxygen tanks. In other words, the nurse of the twentieth century, like the housewife, was the putative beneficiary of a series of labour-saving devices.

In addition to the equipment that reduced motion and unnecessary work, the overall plan of the hospital was the principal way of easing the burden on nurses. Perhaps the single most obvious architectural manifestation of the modern hospital was the preference for the multistorey block. This had several drivers, among them the growing cost of urban land and the shift towards centralised servicing. But the concern to make nursing more efficient and reduce the number of steps taken by a nurse in the course of her shift was also a powerful consideration. Leading hospital architects internationally, such as Jean Walter, Hjalmar Cederström and Arthur Stephenson, all favoured vertically organised hospitals. Stephenson promoted the idea of integration, as opposed to Nightingale's idea of detached hospital planning (Stephenson c. 1955), while Cederström highlighted "intimate cooperation" (Cederström c. 1946: 29–32) as a central objective in his planning for Stockholm's 1,200-bed Södersjukhuset (Southern Hospital), Sweden (Architects: Hjalmar Cederström and Hermann Imhäuser, 1937–1944). In planning the wards Cederström utilised the services of time study engineers and a centralograph – an automated recording device – to ascertain how many patients an individual nurse could efficiently and effectively oversee at any one time (Cederström c. 1946: 29–32).

The value of nursing labour rose as it became more specialised and rationalised in the interwar years. As this happened, other workers gradually assumed some of the responsibilities that had previously fallen to nurses. Hospital architects, planners and managers designed and oversaw rationalised systems of environmental management that were also increasingly mechanical. A growing workforce of maids, cleaners, orderlies and kitchen hands assumed responsibility for many of the most menial housekeeping tasks that had formerly absorbed a great deal of nursing time. As Wilinsky noted, the objective was to free nurses' time so they could focus on their "ever increasing" medical responsibilities (Wilinsky 1940: 73). In the era of the modern hospital, managers deployed nursing resources more carefully, utilising their skills and training in narrower ways.

Architectural historian David Theodore has noted that by 1960, nursing was part of a cybernetic conception of hospital processes in which the activities of the individual nurse and nursing station became nodes in an information network (Theodore 2013). This conception of the nurse as networked producer and recorder of information in a scientifically driven institution was a long way from the older sentimental idea of the nurse as a devoted woman who laboured at the heart of the charitable institution. However, the managerial focus of hospital trade literature from the 1920s, 1930s and 1940s suggests the introduction of computer-aided, systematic modelling of movement as part of hospital planning in the 1960s was not a major departure or innovation in itself. Rather it was the application of new technical tools to a well-developed set of organisational problems. The self-consciously modern hospital of the interwar decades was the premise for the fully realised cybernetic approach of the 1960s. But across the whole period, as Theodore clearly recognises, nurses with a clear sense of their own agency resisted this process of rationalisation and the narrowing of role it implied (Theodore 2013).

In the era of the modern hospital, nurses were more highly trained and educated than before, and the value and cost of their work was more stringently calculated as a result. This specialisation contributed both to the abstraction of their labour and to the ability of nurses to resist and mitigate the implications of that process. The tension between the expanding technical knowledge and capability of nurses and their narrow management and deployment as a resource by the institution was also clearly expressed in the development of hospital nurses' homes between the 1920s and 1950s.

Nurses' homes

Between 1920 and 1950, new hospitals were built to far greater heights than they had been previously. Nevertheless, these tall structures did not incorporate every function. In the Anglophone countries, especially the United States, institutions constructed multistorey nurses' homes behind the main ward buildings or on adjoining sites. Poised somewhere between military barracks and college dormitories, the nurses' homes of this era were a major investment for institutions and a powerful articulation of the gender and work norms that informed the modern hospital and modern medicine.

The central problem for architects who designed nurses' accommodation was navigating the right course between frank institutional efficiency and comforting domesticity. In 1933, Chicago architect Austin Jenkins noted: "No class of workers is more benefited by a complete change in surrounding, when off duty, than institutionally employed nurses" (Jenkins 1933: 67). So while he argued the accommodation building as a whole must be "compact and practical", it should also possess "a quiet, homelike and non-institutional atmosphere" (Jenkins 1933: 70). Architects used wainscoting and other architectural gestures to promote a sense of homeliness and comfort. The overall efficiency of the hospital depended on providing nursing staff with some sense of relief from the institution. Hospital managers and designers, therefore, aimed to accommodate nurses in a way that ensured they received psychological relief and adequate rest, while keeping them physically close to their place of work.

In Australia in the late 1930s, leading hospital architects Leighton Irwin & Company designed a nurses' home for one of the nation's most advanced hospitals, Prince Henry's, Melbourne, Victoria. In an article for the hospital trade publication *Hospital Magazine*, his office defined the problem in very similar terms to North American hospital architects. "The whole character of the building" it noted, "has been determined by its function of providing for nurses' sleeping, playing and living domestically". Their aim was to create an "intimate atmosphere" and "to do the utmost to help nurses feel they are off duty and induce them to relax" (Leighton Irwin & Co. 1941: 12).

The tremendous growth of medical institutions and their rapid change in the interwar period complicated the design of nurses' accommodation. Balancing efficiency in planning with appropriate domestic comfort continued to be a necessity. But successfully achieving that balance was not sufficient for the new nurses' homes connected to larger hospitals in North America. The educational function of major hospitals in the interwar decades made the problem more difficult, as many of the nurses' homes developed in the United States in this period were also schools of nursing. Thus, they combined educational spaces such as demonstration rooms, laboratories, auditoria and libraries with dormitories and living areas. Prominent New York architect Charles Butler designed a school for 478 nurses at New York's Mount Sinai Hospital, Manhattan, New York, USA, in the late 1920s that could easily have been mistaken for a hotel. It contained sixteen floors and a roof terrace with views to both the Hudson and East rivers. In addition to educational spaces and the usual centralised kitchen and cafeteria service, the school contained a variety of specialised utility areas such as shoe polishing and shampoo rooms, as well as significant social and recreational space. The designated recreation room, which seated four hundred using portable seats, also had a wooden dance floor and small stage, and the site included tennis courts (Kohn, Butler and Goldwater 1928; Haywood 1928) (Figure 3.9).

In many ways, the Mount Sinai Hospital nursing school was a great vertical college campus. But the technical sophistication of the building enabled a level of surveillance that would have been unthinkable even at the most paternalistic women's college of the period. S.S. Goldwater, one of the best known North American hospital consultants, described the communication system in *Modern Hospital*:

> The switchboard operator has close at hand and under visual control a bronze, four-position, in-and-out board which, by the use of movable buttons, indicates whether a nurse is in her room, is on duty in the hospital or is elsewhere.... By means of a buzzer system, the telephone operator and office clerk can signal to every room in the building.
> (Kohn, Butler and Goldwater 1928: 65–7)

This was a self-regulating system. The board was "double-faced" and the nurses operated it themselves as they passed through the lobby. But the implication was quite clear. The nurse was responsible to the institution at all times, and information about the nurse was available to the institution via centralised information technology. At work, nurses were expected to observe patients' vital signs using increasingly rigorous methods of recording and documentation. After work, they were expected document and discipline their own movements. But the waning of the classic period of the modern hospital also coincided with a steady decline in the practice of nurses living at the hospital. Between 1962 and 1977, over half the

74 *Knowledge, care and control*

Figure 3.9 Nurses' home, Mount Sinai Hospital, 5th Avenue, Manhattan, New York, USA. Photograph: Wurts Bros., 1931.
Courtesy: Museum of the City of New York, X2010.7.2.4848.

nurses' homes in the United States were either sold or converted to other uses (Elms and Morehead 1977). Living out became the usual practice, and the period when young women negotiated changing professional norms from within the paternalistic setting of the institutions that employed them was clearly over (Nicholson 2000).

Control or controlled?

There is no question that nurses continued to exercise influence on the day-to-day environment of hospitals in the period between 1918 and 1960. But it is equally clear that the modern block hospital with its vertical organisation, its proliferating departments and its focus on data was no longer organised principally around nursing. It was nurse-dependent, but the nurse, or the nursing shift, was now a data point in the system and a human resource problem to be addressed. In the 1960s, this was conceptualised in cybernetic terms. A new breed of hospital managers, consultants and specialist architects in the previous generation had reframed the position of the nurse. They did not, and could not, ignore nursing, but they no longer operated in an institutional environment shaped by the authority of the nurse. This task of reframing the position of the nurse would also apply to every other function of the modern hospital and its accompanying spaces and personnel as it expanded in size, patient number and technological sophistication. As the 1960s approached, the nurse's relationships with the laundry and the kitchen, and with the specialist departments that diagnosed the body internally such as the X-ray department and externally such as physiotherapy, all changed. Within nursing, distinct specialisations began to develop, perhaps none so evident as that of the theatre nurse who assisted in the operating theatre. Instead of general duties, the theatre nurse was expected to develop skills in the various stages of preoperative care, anaesthetics, surgery and recovery. Care and control still remained at the core of what a nurse did, but it was now expert clinical and managerial knowledge that would define their future place in the modern hospital.

Note

1 It was precisely because the nurse was subsequently recognised as the central actor and agent in the pavilion ward that Nightingale became synonymous with that plan form.

References

Adams, Annmarie. *Medicine by Design: The Architect and the Modern Hospital, 1893–1943*. Minneapolis, MN: University of Minnesota Press, 2008.
Babcock, Florence G. "Simplifying Record Keeping in a Teaching Hospital." *Modern Hospital* 30, no. 4 (April 1928): 142–6.
Cederström, Hjalmar. *Södersjukhuset*. Stockholm: Rydahls Boktryckeri A-B, c. 1946.
Edwards & Company. "Modern Hospital Signalling." *Modern Hospital* 33, no. 3 (September 1929): 127.
Elms, R. and J. Morehead. "Will the Real Nurse Please Stand Up: The Stereotype vs the Reality." *Nursing Forum* 16, no. 2 (1977): 121–5.
Fisher, Alison. "Humanist Structures: Bertrand Goldberg Builds for Health Care." In *Bertrand Goldberg: Architecture of Invention*, edited by Zoë Ryan, 130–43. New Haven, CT: Yale University Press, 2011.

Forty, Adrian. "The Modern Hospital in England and France: The Social and Medical Uses of Architecture." In *Buildings and Society: Essays on the Social Development of the Built Environment*, edited by Anthony King, 61–93. London: Routledge, 1980.

Goad, Philip. "Postwar and Polygonal: Special Plans for Australian Architecture 1950–1970." *Cultural Crossroads*, Papers from the Twenty-Sixth Annual Conference of the Society of Architectural Historians, Australia and New Zealand. Auckland, NZ: SAHANZ, 2009, CDROM.

Goldwater, S.S. "A Dark Age in Hospital Planning." *Modern Hospital* 28, no. 3 (March 1927): 50–1.

Golub, Jacob J. "The Tired Nurse, What Can We Do for Her?" *Modern Hospital* 31, no. 4 (October 1928): 77–81.

Group, Thetis M. and Joan I. Roberts. *Nursing, Physician Control and the Medical Monopoly*. Bloomington, IN: Indianapolis University Press, 2001.

Hall, E. Stanley. "Modern Hospital Planning." *Journal of the Royal Institute of British Architects* 42 (6 April 1935): 651–4.

Hayden, Adaline. "Transporting Medical Records." *Modern Hospital* 55, no. 3 (September 1940): 39.

Haywood, A.K. "Providing a Home and School for Four Hundred Nurses." *Modern Hospital* 28, no. 3 (March 1928): 70–4.

Howell, Joel D. *Technology in the Hospital: Transforming Patient Care in the Early Twentieth Century*. Baltimore: Johns Hopkins University Press, 1995.

Hunt, Myron. "Nurses' Stations." *Modern Hospital* 54, no. 3 (March 1940): 65–7.

Jenkins, Austin D. "New Influences at Work in Planning a Nurses' Home." *Modern Hospital* 41, no. 4 (October 1933): 67.

King, Anthony. "Hospital Planning: Revised Thoughts on the Origin of the Pavilion Principle in England." *Medical History* 10, no. 4 (October 1966): 360–73.

Kisacky, Jeanne. *Rise of the Modern Hospital: An Architectural History of Health and Healing, 1870–1940*. Pittsburgh: University of Pittsburgh Press, 2017.

Kohn, Robert D., Charles Butler and S.S. Goldwater. "School of Nursing at Mount Sinai Exemplifies Modern Planning." *Modern Hospital* 30, no. 3 (March 1928): 63–70.

Leighton Irwin & Co. "Housing the Nurses of Prince Henry's Hospital." *Hospital Magazine* (March 1941): 12.

Nicholson, Sally-Anne. "'A Home from Home': The Role of the Nurses' Home in Post-War South Australian History." *Journal of the Historical Society of South Australia* 28 (2000): 70–85.

Nightingale, Florence. *Notes on Nursing: What It Is and What It Is Not*. New York: D. Appleton and Company, 1860.

Nightingale, Florence. *Notes on Hospitals*. London: John W. Parker and Son, 1859.

Nightingale, Florence. *Notes on Hospitals*. London: Longman, Green, Longman, Roberts, and Green, 1863.

Pevsner, Nikolaus. *A History of Building Types*. London: Thames & Hudson, 1976.

Rosenfield, Isadore. *Hospitals: Integrated Design*. New York: Reinhold Publishing Corporation, 1947.

Stephenson, Arthur. "Stephenson-Turner: A Record of the Years 1920–1955." In MS 2235/4 Papers of Arthur George Stephenson, National Library of Australia, Canberra, c. 1955.

Stevens, Edward F. *The American Hospital of the Twentieth Century*. New York: Architectural Record Publishing Company, 1918.
Taylor, Frederick Winslow. *The Principles of Scientific Management*. New York and London: Harper Brothers, 1911.
Teleoptic Corporation. "At Last!" *Modern Hospital* 36, no. 2 (February 1931): 125.
Theodore, David. "'The Fastest Possible Nurse': Architecture, Computers and Post-War Nursing." In *Hospital Life: Theory and Practice from the Medieval to the Modern*, edited by Laurinda Abreu and Sally Sheard, 273–98. Oxford: Peter Lang AG, Internationaler Verlag der Wissenschaften, 2013.
Thompson, John D. and Grace Goldin. *The Hospital: A Social and Architectural History*. New Haven, CT: Yale University Press, 1975.
Verderber, Stephen and David J. Fine. *Healthcare Architecture in an Age of Radical Transformation*. New Haven, CT: Yale University Press, 2000.
Wilinsky, Charles F. "Conserving Nurses' Energy." *Modern Hospital* 54, no. 6 (June 1940): 72–4.

4 Incision and anaesthesia
The operating theatre

Over the course of the twentieth century, the physical spaces in the modern hospital that were devoted to surgery on the human body underwent rapid change. The operating theatre went from being a large space that could accommodate a considerable audience to become an operating suite: a tightly programmed and enclosed group of specialised spaces that contained and supported the operating table at its heart and were dedicated to the strictest levels of hygiene and highest levels of medical, scientific and technical expertise deployed by surgeons and expert nursing staff. This evolution involved significant experimentation, as well as rapid and continual technical and spatial transformation across the first half of the twentieth century.

The origins of the operating theatre lie in the various places that surgical procedures were performed, and spaces for surgery are known as far back as Hellenic and Roman antiquity. But as surgeons often practiced their craft in the patient's own premises, or from the barber-surgeon's shop, specific surgery spaces are a relatively modern invention. "Cutting rooms", as part of a hospital environment in which surgical procedures were carried out, appeared from about 1550, although the rooms were not used exclusively for surgery (Mörgeli 1999: 173). The earliest operating theatres were just that – theatres in which the spectacle of surgery with an interested audience could be performed. The first of these appeared in Padua in 1594, and from the eighteenth century became the primary place surgical knowledge and technique was demonstrated (Figure 4.1). The rise of effective anaesthetics and antiseptics in surgery encouraged the creation of purpose-built operating rooms, ones that could be kept as aseptic as possible. By 1890, it was inconceivable that there would not be a specific space dedicated as an operating room, as "the principle of avoiding wound infections by strict measures became increasingly decisive when equipping, remodelling or building operating rooms" (Mörgeli 1999: 234). The need to be able to wash, disinfect and remove any possibility that dirt might accumulate meant providing non-porous, contiguous surfaced equipment, furniture and spaces. Thus, the modern operating room of 1890 was functional and devoid of ornamentation. Twentieth-century developments in the operating theatre transformed

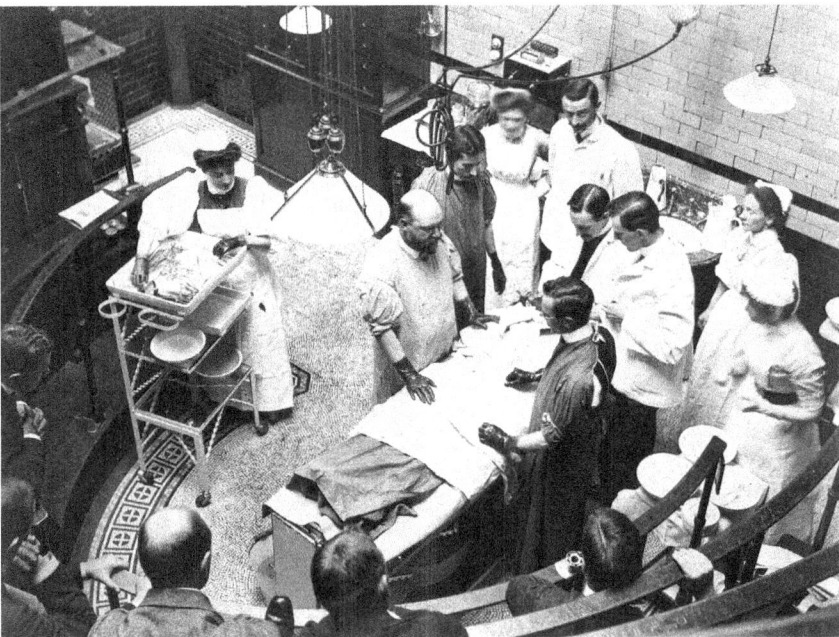

Figure 4.1 Trainees watch Stanley Boyd about to perform surgery in the old operating theatre, Charing Cross Hospital, London, England. Photograph: unknown, 1900.
Courtesy: Wellcome Collection (CC BY).

not only that space (Adams and Schlich 2006), but also drove spatial and servicing changes that profoundly affected the entire hospital.

The requirements for operating on the human body were many and complex. Hygiene and sterile facilities were essential, as were appropriate lighting, the provision and application of anaesthetics, temperature and humidity control, and equipment for operating. These requirements, or at least the architect's interpretation of them, dictated where the operating theatre and its attendant spaces were located within the hospital.

Let there be light

The provision of sufficient light to perform surgical operations was the first element that profoundly affected the position and design of operating theatres. Surgeons needed strong but diffuse light so that shadows would not be cast. From the earliest times, operating theatres were purpose-built: they were lit naturally either through overhead lanterns (skylights) or a combination of north-facing windows (south-facing in the southern hemisphere) and skylights (Figure 4.2). The need for overhead natural lighting

80 *Incision and anaesthesia*

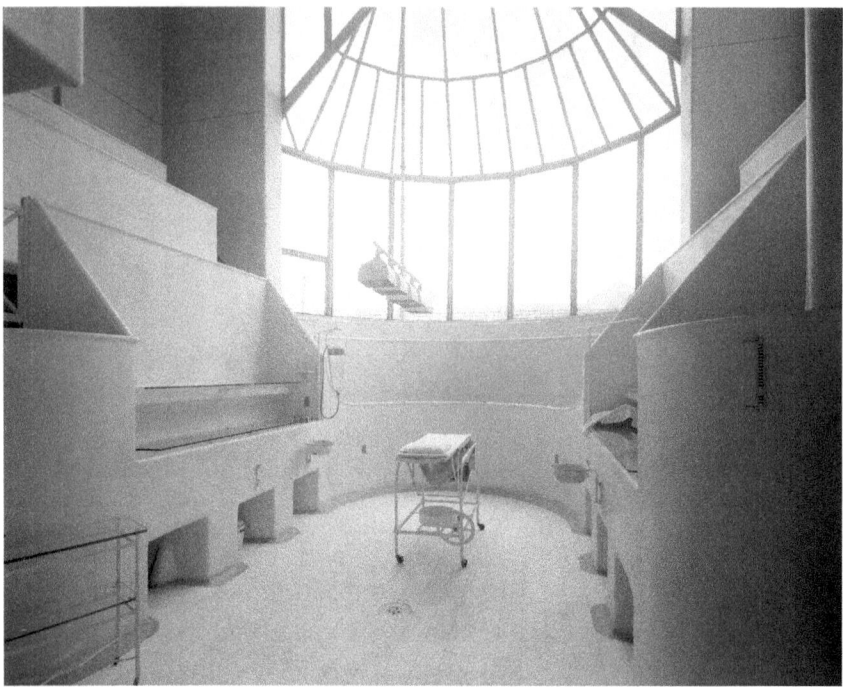

Figure 4.2 Surgical amphitheatre at the Lying-In Hospital, Manhattan, New York, USA. Architect: Robert H. Robertson, 1902. Photograph: Wurts Bros., 1912.
Courtesy: Museum of the City of New York, X2010.7.1.10693.

dictated the location of operating theatres in the modern hospital. They were frequently placed on the top floor of the hospital or in a special pavilion, a place of prestige that persisted until well after natural light was replaced by artificial sources.

The external appearance of hospitals could be profoundly influenced by such functional needs. In the German Hospital in Chicago, Illinois, USA (Architects: Schmidt, Garden & Erikson, 1915), for example, functional needs clashed loudly with expectations of civic decorum. Top lighting the surgical suite resulted in a prominent, steeply angled glazed skylight utterly at odds with the hospital's otherwise polite Beaux-Arts-inflected style. Elsewhere, the expression of function could look thoroughly progressive, as demonstrated by the surgery pavilion at the James M. Jackson Memorial Hospital in Miami, Florida, USA (Architect: Anton Skislewicz, 1934) with its distinctive greenhouse windows to the operating theatres (Skislewicz 1934).

A similar arrangement was evident across the top floor of the high-rise slabs of the Chirurgische Universitätsklinik (University Surgical Clinic) in Tübingen, Germany (Architect: Hans Daiber, 1936), where a brace of four operating rooms were placed, with completely glazed end walls and partly glazed roofs, all facing north. A cross-sectional drawing published in *Moderne Bauformen* in January 1936 shows the logic of such an arrangement ("Die Chirurgische Universitätsklinik in Tübingen" 1936). The operating room could have a higher ceiling because it was at the top of the building and didn't have to align with regular floors. The light that came from the glass roof was diffused by a honeycomb patterned filter (*wabenblende*) before it met a ceiling of translucent glass. If the light was too bright from above, electric roller blinds above the glass ceiling could be drawn across it. The glazing of the external wall was also translucent to obtain an even, diffuse light quality, while intense artificial light could be provided by swivelling and rotating surgical Nissen and Chromofar lamps.

In the late 1930s, the quest for glare-free natural illumination saw the rapid uptake of glass bricks or blocks instead of plate glass, as seen in examples such as the Swedish Hospital, Seattle, Washington, USA (Architects: Smith, Carrol & Johanson, 1937). Glass blocks were seen to have two advantages: their design meant direct sunlight was diffused and the vacuum pocket inside the brick offered an insulating effect that increased the thermal comfort of the operating room (Hickok 1937). But natural light was rarely enough to provide the kind of illumination needed for surgery, and it quickly became standard for natural light to be supplemented or supplanted by artificial light.

Single sources of direct light were problematic in the operating theatre because of the shadows cast as a result, and architects and lighting manufacturers sought to provide alternatives. Most commonly, a bank of lights was arranged in a circular or star-shaped pattern, and either positioned directly above the operating table or embedded into the walls and ceiling (Figure 4.3). Locating the optimum position for these lights was crucial: if the lights were too close, they radiated too much heat and were considered responsible for "spreading dust"; if further away, the illumination was insufficient and did not achieve the desired "shadowless" effect ("Uniform, Shadowless Illumination for Operating Rooms" 1926: 164; "Walls of Glass" 1937). One system advertised in the 1940s that sought to overcome these issues was the Holophane Multiple Controlens Lighting System. It used a bank of lights embedded into an overhead ceiling box, with multiple individual lamps – between fifteen and twenty-one – angled to focus on the operating table which also "gently warm[ed] the area of the incision". Moreover, depending on what was needed for the operation, the system was designed to activate only those lights to the front and side of the surgeon to prevent shadows being cast. It was claimed the Holophane's ceiling-mounted position was "outside the zone of explosion or mechanical hazard" (Holophane 1942: 123).

Artificial illumination had the benefit of providing surgeons with optimal conditions to operate, but the vastly improved intensity of light available had its downside. Brighter lights meant that glare and retinal fatigue

82 *Incision and anaesthesia*

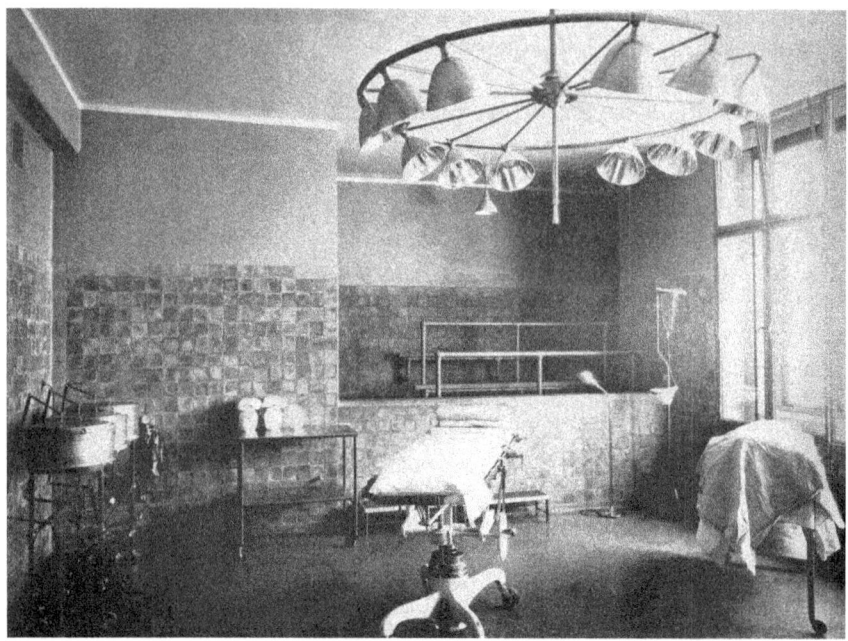

Figure 4.3 This operating room includes green tiles, grey walls and a star-shaped light pendant for optimum surgical lighting conditions. University of Michigan Hospital, Ann Arbor, Michigan, USA. Architect: Albert Kahn, 1925. Photograph: unknown.
Source: *Modern Hospital* 28, no. 5 (May 1927): 92.

(which is the cause of afterimages) became a problem in the operating theatre. As Dr Paluel J. Flagg put it: "The operating room was once large, white and brilliantly illuminated.... The objectionable factor of reflection from intense artificial illumination is generally becoming recognized" (Flagg 1939: 75). Furthermore:

> An intense illumination while revealing the depth of the wound, if reflected from its periphery by white drapes, results in glare and color fatigue. Intense illustration reflected from the white drapes about the field of operation in due time will cause eye strain and headache, with general irritability. To overcome this effect, color of sufficient chroma to absorb the greater part of the reflective rays should be used in the drapes.
>
> (Flagg 1939: 75)

That glare and discomfort might be managed through deliberate use of colours other than white in the operating room was first proposed in

1914 by Harry Sherman, a doctor at St Luke's Hospital in San Francisco, California, USA. Sherman decided to use the complementary colour to red – green – to ameliorate issues he experienced while operating. To test this out, he had one of St Luke's operating theatres painted "bright spinach green", leaving another the usual white. Sherman reported that "no-one who could get into the green room to do an operation ever went into the white room" (Sherman 1914: 181). He initially sought to use sheets and towels of a similar colour, but found the high-temperature laundering they were subject to turned them grey, so instead switched to black linens and scrubs. Green had an advantage over black for drapes as blood could still be easily seen – a potentially important factor in monitoring the patient during the operation. But, as Flagg pointed out, Sherman's description of "bright spinach green" was not specific enough to determine the appropriate shade. To rectify this, Flagg carefully examined the three key issues of illumination – colour, fatigue and reflection. He concluded that "Everest Green", in a dark hue for drapes and a lighter one for walls, was the best colour and helpfully illustrated this in an article for *Architectural Record* (Flagg 1925). As an anaesthetist, Flagg was particularly concerned with the appropriate perception of colour, as it was essential for surgeons and anaesthetists to be able to make "a correct appraisal of the oxygen content of the blood" (Flagg 1939: 78).

Sherman's and Flagg's experiments in the operating theatre were not the only investigations of how colour could be used in the healthcare setting during this period. In 1921, architect William Ludlow began advocating for colour therapy, and Charles Ireland, a doctor at Guy's Hospital, London, England, published *Colour and Cancer* in 1930 (Pantalony 2009). Colour was also promoted as a way to make hospital interiors "strike a friendly note and obviate the coldness of just hard white" ("Hospital Rooms. Planned by Woman Architect" 1938: 27). But the strongly reasoned promotion of a particular colour, green, was highly influential and was adopted rapidly, as underscored by the work of Faber Birren in the 1930s (Pantalony 2009). It became the accepted standard colour for operating theatres and hospitals in general for decades, and remains almost universally used in operating theatre linens and scrubs. Green thus became synonymous with hospital interiors, in reaction to the introduction of better artificial illumination in the operating theatre.

The ideal operating theatre

The quest for the perfect shadow-free operating theatre was the driving force in Carl Erikson's designs for a model operating room, which formed part of an exhibition titled "A Century of Progress" in 1933 (Erikson 1933) (Figure 4.4). Erikson describes the perfect operating theatre as having "the best of working conditions for the surgeons and nurses ... 'room enough', perfect cleanliness, perfect lighting, every mechanical accessory close at

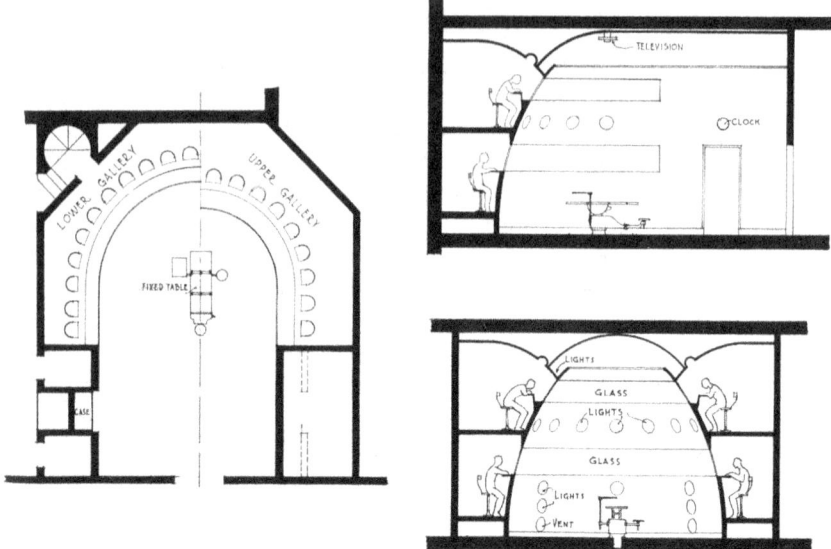

Figure 4.4 Carl Erikson proposed an elliptical paraboloid as the ideal shape for an operating room, with focused lighting, television and the separation of patient and audience. Plan and sectional drawings of Carl Erikson's "Ideal Operating Room" exhibited at the "Century of Progress" exhibition. Delineator: unknown.

Source: *Modern Hospital* 40, no. 6 (June 1933): 87.

hand, and absence of noise and confusion" (Erikson 1933: 87). In a striking departure from the usual design of operating theatres, Erikson proposed a two-storey half-elliptical paraboloid to solve both issues with lighting and the need to house groups of observers separate from the aseptic space of the operating theatre. The shell of the paraboloid was used to separate the "clean" space of the theatre from the observer galleries, and the delivery of services, such as lighting and air handling. Reticulated services such as compressed air, anaesthetic gas and electrical power were to be provided through fixing the operating table in the central position – the natural focus of the paraboloid – allowing for such services to be provided through the table's pedestal.

Erikson provided "bull's-eye" lights in multiple positions, all focused towards the operating table, including lateral, angled and overhead lighting, each of which could be controlled individually. He noted that surgeons were not unanimous in seeing natural light as redundant in operating theatres, "yet surgical nurses will confirm ... that in spite of the large windows and skylights, the surgeons almost invariably request that the artificial light be turned on" (Erikson 1933: 88). Erikson also proposed that a "television" (by this he meant a television camera) could be installed directly overhead, with the enlarged image projected on to the end wall for the benefits of student observers. His ideal operating theatre proposal also included full air conditioning, the need for which we will discuss later.

Erikson's ideal operating theatre foretold the operating theatre of the future: a hermetically sealed aseptic space with an artificially controlled environment. How light, temperature and ventilation were to be provided was carefully considered, as was the means by which other essential services were provided, and the way in which surgical teaching and observation could take place without the physical presence of students in the operating room. The hemispherical or elliptical paraboloid domed operating theatre was not just the stuff of imagination. Multiple examples were realised, including at Lille and Saint-Lô in France and in Sydney, New South Wales, Australia.

The first of these appeared in 1938, when the design for Walter, Cassan & Madeline's Cité Hospitalière de Lille (Lille Hospital Complex), Lille, France, was completed (Figure 4.5). The operating theatre was cylindrical, with a hemispherical-domed ceiling, and the fixed operating table at the focal point in the centre of the room. Spot lights and general lighting were set into the ceiling, and observation galleries ringed the exterior of the dome, physically separate from the space of the theatre. Jean Walter, the architect, had arranged a series of spaces serving the operating room, with a carefully staged sequential entry for the patient that progressed through an arrival point, preparation area and anaesthesia prior to reaching the operating room. As they arrived, patients made an important transition from a hospital gurney to a suspended table or gondola, which then ran on overhead tracks to the operating room. This system included a physical barrier through which only the patient passed, as instead of a door there was only a gondola-shaped slot between the aseptic operation suite and the patient arrival point. This emphasis on sterile separation was also apparent in the pass-through wall openings in the operating room, one for providing surgical instruments to the adjacent – but otherwise unconnected – sterilisation room, and another for removing them. The surgeons, anaesthetists and assistants entered the operating suite through their own series of staging points, which entailed disrobing, washing and showering, dressing in suitable surgical garments, then into the *lavabos* (scrub-up or washroom) for handwashing as the final preparation (Moretti 1951). Such progression from the "infected" to the "disinfected" space of the hospital for clinical staff had been evident in other settings for around forty years (Daws 2017), but the extreme separation demonstrated by the passage of the patient and surgical instruments was not.

In 1940, architects Stephenson & Turner designed a hemispherical-domed operating room on the top floor of the King George V Hospital for Mothers and Babies, in Camperdown, New South Wales, Australia (1939–1941) (Figure 4.6). Like Erikson's design, the shell of the operating room separated viewing platforms from the main space of the operation. In

86 *Incision and anaesthesia*

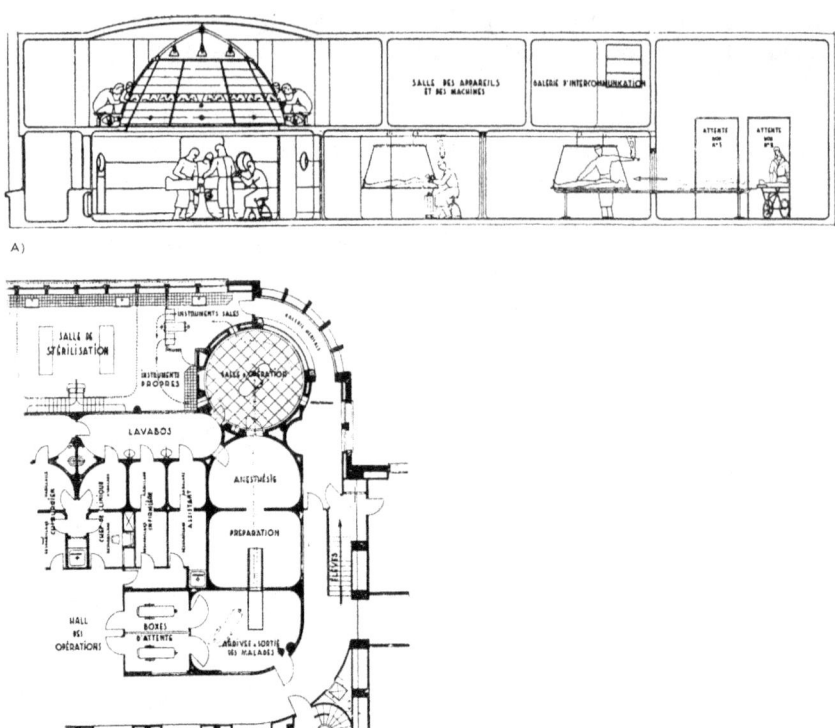

Figure 4.5 Jean Walter's domed operating theatre saw the patient transferred to a gondola and passed through a preparation area and anaesthesis prior to entering the operating room. The operating suite carefully separated the movements of patient, medical staff, equipment and attendants to maintain as sterile a space as possible. Plan and section of the new Cité Hospitalière de Lille (Lille Hospital Complex), Lille, France. Architects: Walter, Cassan & Madeline, 1934–1958. Delineator: unknown.

Source: Moretti, B. Franco. *Ospedali*. Milan: Editore Ulrico Hoepli, 1951: 70.

this instance, the interior shell was polished stainless steel, which allowed for shadowless reflection and for the light to be focused on the operating table. The operating room had no external windows, but brass letters representing the four points of the compass were inlaid into the terrazzo floor. Television was not yet a viable option, but the architects had provided an intercom system in the operating room or labour ward, whereby the surgeon or obstetrician could instruct the medical students located on an external balcony (Stephenson & Turner 1941). Stephenson undoubtedly knew of Erikson's ideal design; the men had met during Stephenson's first

Figure 4.6 Australian architects were inspired by Walter's domed operating theatre, and created versions of their own. Operating theatre at King George V Hospital for Mothers and Babies, Camperdown, New South Wales, Australia. Architects: Stephenson & Turner, 1939–1941. Photograph: unknown, c. 1941.

© Sydney Local Health District, used with permission.

and second trips to the United States in 1927 and 1932–1933 and had maintained correspondence, with Stephenson seeking advice on a number of hospital projects (Stephenson 1932). Stephenson's office also subscribed to *Modern Hospital*. But the direct inspiration came from Jean Walter's Lille design; it was described as "Walter's type operating vaults" (Stephenson & Turner 1941).

At Saint-Lô, in the Normandy region of France, another domed operating theatre was designed by architect Paul Nelson at the Centre Hospitalier Mémorial France États-Unis (France United States Memorial Hospital), designed in 1946–1948 and opened in 1956 (Figure 4.7). Nelson incorporated an elliptical paraboloid operating theatre with dozens of bull's eye lamps, each individually controlled. Nelson's operating room seemed to be Erikson's ideal theatre now realised, some twenty years later, complete with reticulated services provided through the base of the operating table pedestal (Saint-Lô 2006).

88 *Incision and anaesthesia*

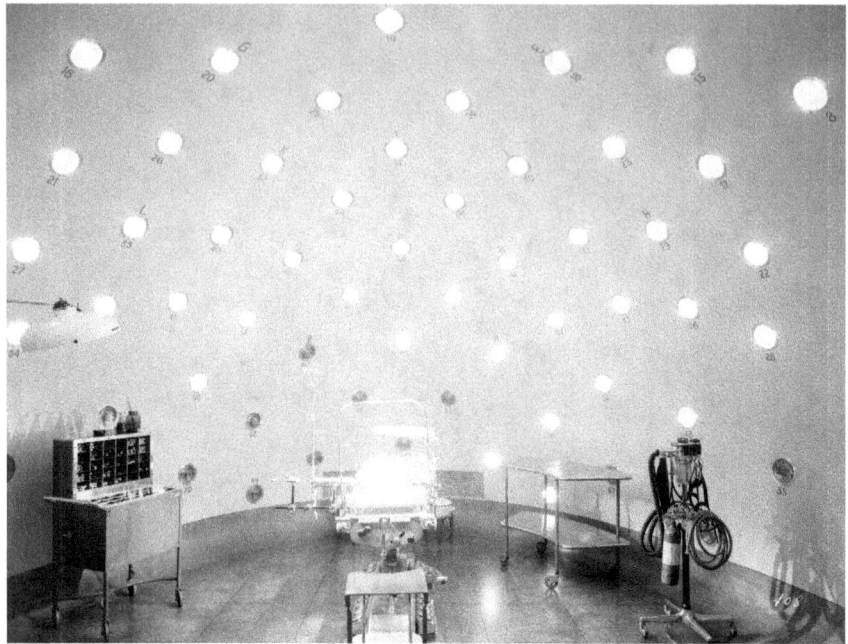

Figure 4.7 To create the perfect shadowless environment, every individual light in the Saint-Lô operating theatre could be individually controlled. Operating theatre at Centre Hospitalier Mémorial France États-Unis (France United States Memorial Hospital), Saint-Lô, France. Architect: Paul Nelson, 1946–1956. Photograph: studio Henri Baranger, 1959.
Courtesy: Conseil dép. de la Manche, arch. dép., 4Fi 20-13-10.

These domed theatres had concentrated on the optimum use of artificial light, excluding all natural light, but some experimental theatres still sought to optimise and focus natural light as best as possible. For the surgical clinic at Saint Ouen, completed around 1938, in the northern outskirts of Paris, architect J. Guy LeNoble created a pair of double-height lozenge-shaped operating theatres, top-lit by skylights and clerestory windows supplemented by a ring of overhead artificial lights above the operating table. Observation galleries, accessible from the floor above, ran around the theatre's rim and allowed observers to look into the operating theatre while separate from it. The operating theatre reflected a concern for providing the most sterile place possible, with an internal metal skin with no sharp angles. All the doors were sliding, with those used by the surgeons operated by a foot pedal. The space could be sterilised at the end of each operation by steam, which was then vented by a fan. The theatre had a glazed ceiling, which completed the closed system, with the lighting and heating above to reduce the possibility of electrical spark. The operating theatres sat within a suite that had clearly defined routes of access, with patients progressing through a separate anaesthetic room before being taken into the operating theatre, and the surgeons passing through a washroom before entering the theatre through a separate door. As in Jean Walter's design, sterilised instruments and materials entered through one door (in this instance shared with the surgeons) and exited as contaminated through another (Moretti 1951). The whole suite sat in its own pavilion, which was connected to the hospital.

The focus on the perfect operating room attracted specific experimental attention in the 1930s and 1940s, with the Walter dome being employed in France and Australia, as well as in England and Scotland (Butler and Erdman 1946; Stevens 1940).[1] Similar domed theatres were still appearing in some new hospitals decades later; a series of six ovoid operating theatres were designed as part of the Copenhagen County Hospital, Glostrup, Denmark (Architects: Martta Ypyä, Ragnar Ypyä & Veikko Malmio, 1959) ("Copenhagen County Hospital" 1959) and another six domed operating theatres formed part of the Ninewells Teaching Hospital, Dundee, Scotland (Architects: Robert Matthew, Johnson-Marshall & Partners, 1970) ("Ninewells Teaching Hospital Dundee" 1968). But circular rooms with double-height spaces to accommodate both dome and observers were inefficient and costly, and apart from these few examples discussed, they did not become standard. Instead, operating theatre design concentrated heavily on realising specific functional needs and essential requirements for what was regarded at the time as best practice surgery.

Pure air: what it is and how to get it

A feature of Erikson's ideal operating theatre proposal was full air conditioning. In part, this was to manage the heat of summer and cold of winter for the comfort of the surgeons, nurses and patients. Thermal comfort was important for this reason, but it was later understood that anaesthetised patients cannot properly thermoregulate (for which they are also at risk in the immediate post-operative period), making temperature control important for maintaining homeostasis in the patient. Architects concentrated on providing clean air, which could be achieved through full air conditioning. Erikson noted that it was impossible to maintain clean air in the operating theatre if there were other potential sources of ventilation that could admit "dirt laden air", such as operable windows. Any windows included, therefore, should be fixed shut to prevent this (Erikson 1933: 88). But there was another pressing reason for the use of air conditioning: it could also be used to control humidity. The use of anaesthetic gases and oxygen meant a real threat of explosion. Architects were at pains to ensure that the material used inside hospitals and the condition of the air did not encourage static electricity to build up and release; controlling humidity was known to reduce the risk of sparks and explosion,

90 Incision and anaesthesia

enabling the safe use of such gases in the operating theatre (Griffin 1953). The very real need for humidity- and temperature-controlled mechanical ventilation (air conditioning) in operating theatres provided the impetus for the eventual air conditioning of the entire hospital.

The operating theatres at the Chirurgische Universitätsklinik (University Surgery Clinic) clearly demonstrated the care with which air handling was managed (Figure 4.8). At the operating room's external edge, there was double glazing with a generous air gap between the two glass layers, whereby warm, moistened air above a low-pressure steam radiator could be recirculated upward, between the gap. This was done by a motorised air conditioning system located in a motor room above the ante room, which had a lower ceiling height than the operating room. The humidified air, along with fresh air drawn from inlets in the upper south wall, was then pumped back into the operating room as fresh air, while the stale air was exhausted by mechanical means at the spandrel level beneath the window. Significantly, this effort was to achieve an idealised state of humidity (between 45 and 55 per cent) and was set to operate automatically, independent of the temperature, season and weather conditions ("Die Chirurgische Universitätsklinik in Tübingen" 1936).

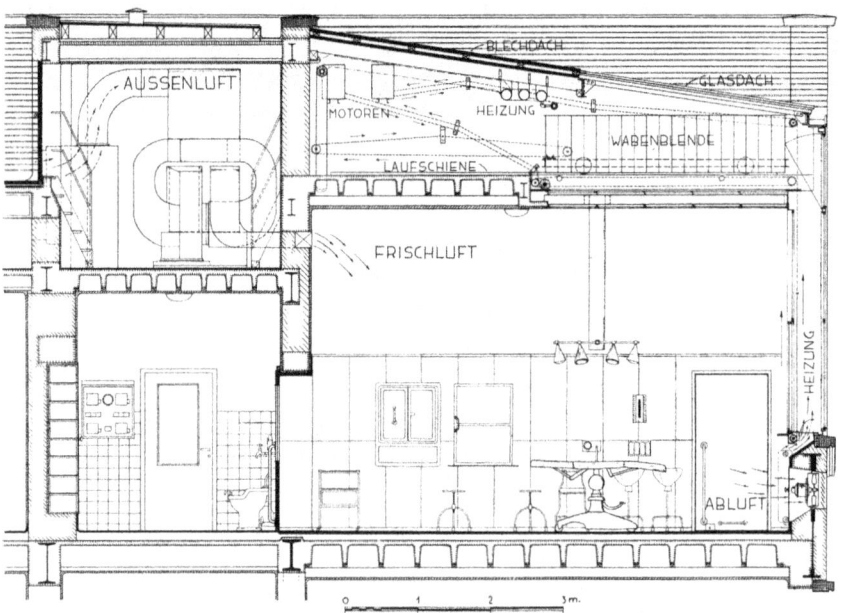

Figure 4.8 Drawing of Chirurgische Universitätsklinik (University Surgical Clinic) in Tübingen, Germany, showing top lighting and air handling. Architect: Hans Daiber, 1936. Delineator: unknown.

Source: "Die Chirurgische Universitätsklinik in Tübingen". *Moderne Bauformen* 35, no. 1 (January 1936): 27.

But it was not enough to just pump air and mediate its relative humidity and temperature. Clean (or pure) air, free of bacterial contaminants, was an essential part of the sterile environment of the operating room. An impetus for the move towards air conditioning, and away from operable windows, was to avoid "dirty" air (that is, air with particulate matter) which was believed to be a mode for the transmission of bacteria. Complete air conditioning for the operating theatre was considered by experts to be "filtered, washed", humidity- and temperature-controlled air that was refreshed (that is, oxygenated) by a minimum number of air changes per hour (Ekland 1938: 80). A.J. Hockett, writing in *Modern Hospital*, advocated independent systems for each operating room, to "avoid odors or bacteria being carried from one room to another" (Hockett 1937). The removal of particulate matter and bacteria from the air supply itself was important, and achieved using a variety of methods, including "purification ... by means of air filters [being] ... baffles coated with a viscous substance" ("Pure Air" 1928: 152). Air was later also sterilised through what was described in the early 1940s as "bactericidal radiant energy", now more commonly understood as ultraviolet radiation. Dr Deryl Hart demonstrated the effectiveness of this method. In reviewing more than eight hundred operations, he concluded that a dramatically reduced number of infections stemmed from operative procedures taking place "in a field of sterile air" (Hart 1940: 14).

Attempts to provide the purest air possible in the operating theatre led to laminar flow clean room systems with high efficiency particulate arrestance (HEPA) filters being adopted (Whitfield 1981: 1). The laminar flow system, first developed in the late 1950s, used the principles of fluid dynamics to create a cone of clean air over a site such as an operating table, so there would be minimal or no mixing of air and therefore contaminants. In 1962, the Lovelace Clinic in Albuquerque, New Mexico, USA, showed initial interest in using clean room systems in the operating theatre, but the first laminar flow surgical suite was installed in Albuquerque's Bataan Hospital in 1966. By 1972, over three hundred laminar flow operating theatres were in use in the United States, and the technology was widely used internationally, including in "Japan, Europe, Australia, Asia and Africa" and "extensively in orthopaedic surgery during hip and joint replacement" (Whitfield 1981: 2). Clean air is a particular concern in orthopaedic operations, as surgical site infections can be difficult or nearly impossible to treat.

The surgical space

Focus on creating a sterile environment for the operating theatre had been a driving force in its design. This was manifest in the concern to reduce the potential for contaminatory cross-traffic by keeping unnecessary personnel from moving through the space of the operating suite. In 1927, Dr Philemon E. Truesdale advocated the use of modern kinematics to promote appropriate traffic management in the operating theatre and deal with problems associated with visiting personnel (Figure 4.9). He was particularly concerned with the position and engagement of those observing operations. The older form of operating theatre, he noted, with a guard rail to separate the audience from the performance of the surgeon, was no longer practical because much of the equipment used during operations required wall-mounted services, presumably suction, electrical or gaseous connections:

> The visiting doctor should not be obliged to negotiate hurdles in order to find his proper place ... nor should he be expected to worm between operating room furniture, covered with sterile linen. There should be a well posted one-way trail for him to follow.
>
> (Truesdale 1927: 85)

The "one-way" path for people and instruments was evident in much thinking about effective operating suites, not only as a traffic control issue, but also as the path between contaminated and sterile spaces. There was an "extreme line of demarcation as to what is sterile and what is unsterile" and the "scrubbed individual should consider the individuals and equipment beyond her sterile field as beds of poison ivy" (Dowler 1935: 42).

Efforts to maintain a sterile environment were understandable and the spatialisation of those practices was embedded into the designs for surgical suites. Operating room procedures and practices from the 1930s contained a number of clear edicts: "Face sterile tables in passing and always turn back to unsterile objects in passing" and "Don't reach over sterile supplies or a sterile table", and theatre staff were exhorted to exaggerate the movement around sterile objects (people and tables) to demonstrate "conscientiousness about steering clear of ... risks" (Dowler 1935: 43). The space required for the operating theatre was therefore not just necessary to accommodate the operating table and attendant surgeon. It also had to include sufficient room for the instrument and supplies tables, items of equipment, surgical and nursing staff and possible observers and the appropriate distances between all these objects and people to minimise contamination of surfaces and patient. In 1931, leading New York hospital administrator S.S. Goldwater described the size requirements thus: "Minimum length and width of room sufficient to permit free circulation of attendants about the operating table and the surgical team (surgeon, operating assistants and anethetist [sic]) without danger of contamination of aseptic field; 320 sq ft" (Goldwater 1931: 66). Some twenty years later, the floor space advocated to fulfil these requirements was similarly substantial: 18 × 15 feet (5.4 × 4.5 metres) or even 18 × 18 feet (5.4 × 5.4 metres) (Butler and Erdman 1946).

It was argued the operating suite of the hospital should be separate from the main building well into the 1950s, ostensibly to minimise traffic through it. Butler and Erdman suggested that, ideally, the unit be housed in a

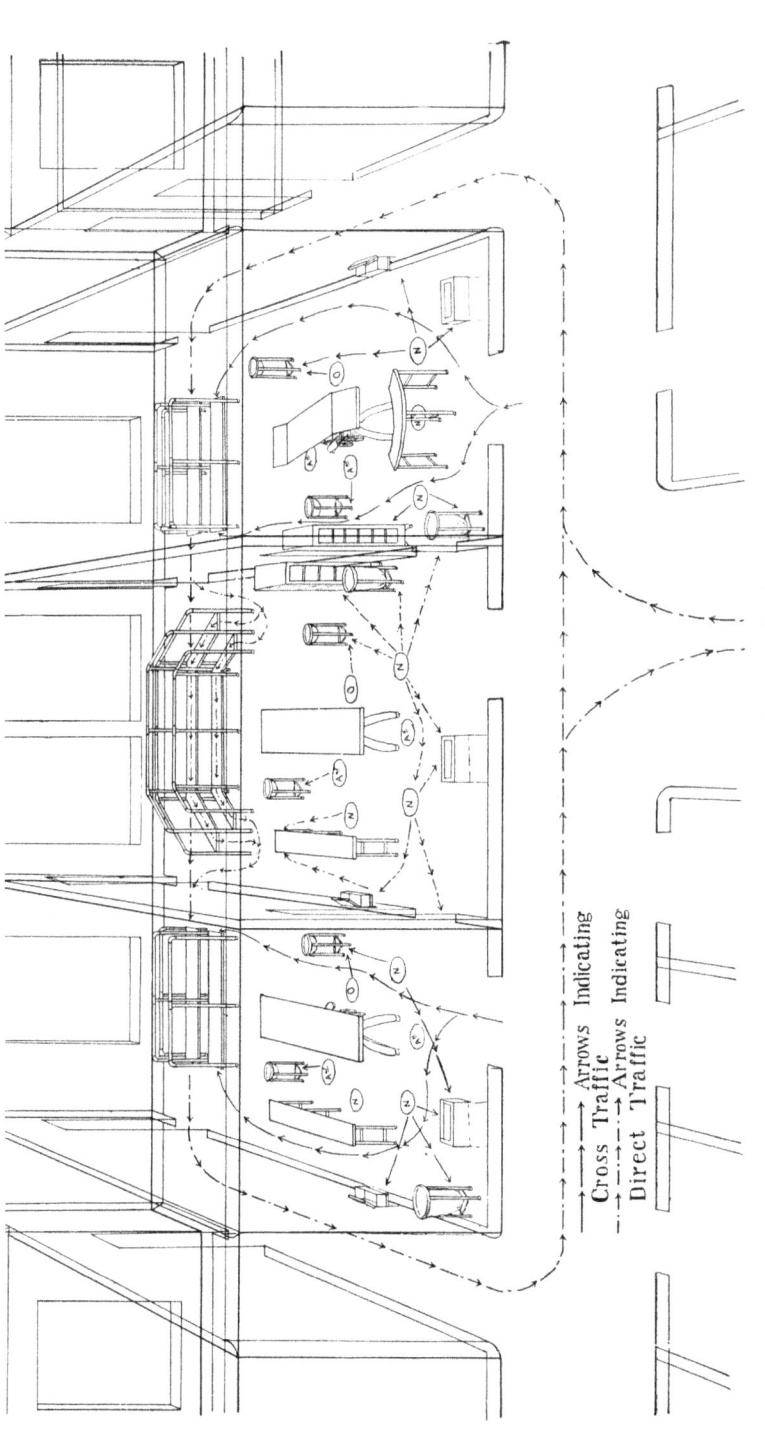

Figure 4.9 The complexity of traffic in operating rooms is clearly demonstrated by this kinetic diagram. Delineator: unknown.
Source: Truesdale, Philemon E. "Regulating Operating Room Traffic". *Modern Hospital* 29, no. 1 (July 1927): 84.

separate surgical pavilion, and if this was not feasible, it should be "isolated from the rest of the hospital as much as possible" (Butler and Erdman 1946: 46). Similar advice was given by the US Public Health Service in 1953 when it advocated a separate wing or floor to allow for such facilities to be "completely isolated from the rest of the hospital" (US Department of Health, Education and Welfare 1953: 62). Such isolation was seen as a means to maintain a sterile environment. The need for natural light had diminished to the point of extinction, meaning there was "no longer any need for skylights or operating-room windows requiring excessive ceiling heights" and the operating theatre could now "be placed anywhere in the building that best suits the plan" (Butler and Erdman 1946: 46).

The set of spatial relationships within the surgical suite was considered as crucial as they had been in the experimental paraboloid theatres. Complex logistical requirements combined with the need for separate circulation pathways meant a great many elements needed to be considered in designing the suite. Where scrub-up rooms, sterilising services for instruments, storage of supplies, pathology laboratories, X-ray, cystoscopic services and anaesthesia spaces were positioned, and which rooms they were close to, was vital. So too was the location of change spaces for the surgeons and nurses, the supervisor's office and patient waiting, preparation and recovery rooms. The difficulty of the architectural task was demonstrated in a rise in explanatory diagrams that mapped movement pathways and relational requirements. In spatial terms, this extreme and necessary attention to the functionalisation of the plan also meant architects needed to develop specialised knowledge of surgical procedures in concert with the increasing advances in surgical techniques and servicing technologies for the operating theatre. The need to attain and deploy such sophisticated logistical knowledge led to the emergence of a niche of highly developed expertise within the architecture profession, and hence the rise of the specialist hospital architect.

During the late 1930s and early 1940s, the diagram as a mechanism of abstraction in urban planning became, as Andrew Shanken has observed, an increasingly common form of persuasion for change based on apparently scientific logic (Shanken 2009). Similarly, mastery of the diagram became a trademark of hospital planners and administrators when it came to planning logistically complex hospital spaces such as the operating suite. A quote from the influential planning pamphlet, *Action for Cities: A Guide for Community Planning* (1943), could be extrapolated to apply not only to planning cities but also to planning departments within the modern hospital:

> Such diagrams are useful for reducing problems of relationships to essentials. They are not plans, but guides to use in working out plans.
> (Action for Cities 1943: 47)

Incision and anaesthesia 95

Important American texts published by the US Public Health Service such as *Design and Construction of General Hospitals* (1953) thus became key sources of such diagrams (Figure 4.10), and in many respects codified them as necessary in describing appropriate spaces for medical procedure – in this case, surgery and the operating suite.

Observation and audience

The practice of medical students observing the operating theatre, essential for teaching and understanding surgical technique, had often meant the design of the operating room needed to accommodate a significant audience. In looking to move away from amphitheatre-style surrounding tiers, the designers of experimental operating theatres sought innovative, often elaborate, ways of allowing surgical procedures to be observed, while

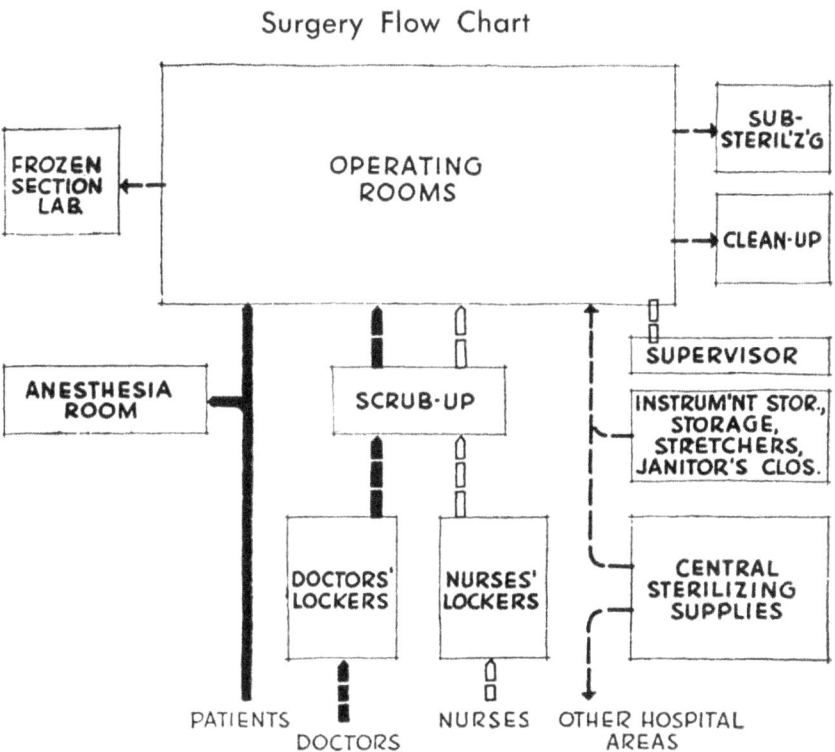

Figure 4.10 It was important to ensure that movement of key actors in operating suites was carefully considered to allow for optimum efficiency and surgical outcomes. Delineator: unknown.

Source: US Department of Health, Education and Welfare: Public Health Service. *Design and Construction of General Hospitals*. New York: F.W. Dodge Corporation, 1953: 65.

separating the observation space from the space of the theatre itself. In some instances, this was achieved by using an angled glass wall to separate observers from the aseptic place of surgery. This meant audience members no longer had put on caps and gowns, and scrub up (Kisacky 2017). Yet, such efforts still required adjacency to the theatre. Therein lay a dilemma. If observers were close enough to easily view surgical processes first hand, they could potentially interfere with the orderly conduct of the operation, heighten the risk of infection and get in the way of staff and equipment. But if their physical distance from the site of the surgery was increased, the observer's capacity to see and understand the details of the operation was diminished.

Carl Erikson's model operating theatre had proposed a solution to this dilemma in the form of "television". This was realised nearly fifteen years later when several American hospitals, working in conjunction with television companies, pioneered the use of closed circuit television to televise surgery for educational purposes (Figure 4.11). In 1947, the first televised surgery was performed by Dr Alfred Blalock at the Johns Hopkins Hospital, Baltimore, Maryland, USA, to an audience of "[s]everal hundred physicians, Baltimore hospital officials, and students" who were located across three rooms more than 60 metres away from the operating room. In another experiment, also in 1947, at New York Hospital–Cornell Medical Center, the audience – a "surgical meeting" – was located some distance away, at the Waldorf-Astoria Hotel. Transmissions were made on a "special frequency", "to prevent private owners of television receiving sets … from picking up the broadcast" (Hague and Crosby 1948: 65).

These early efforts were transmissions in black and white, and took place with the considerable assistance of television broadcasters and manufacturers, such as RCA and CBS, but they still suffered many limitations and were plagued by technical issues. The camera was mounted in a rack above the operating table and its focus fixed before the operation, without the patient and surgical team being present. The camera operator could only guess where the focus point of the camera should be with no capacity to refocus during the operation. Adequate lighting, long the concern for designers of operating theatres, proved to be difficult for televising operations, as well. Colour transmission soon followed and the documentation of the third such event, at St Luke's Hospital in Chicago, Illinois, USA, in late 1949, drew into stark contrast the old and the new: the televised operation was held in a tiered amphitheatre-style operating theatre.

It was Erikson's son, Carl Jr, who profiled the colour television operation in *Modern Hospital* in 1949. Accompanying the article were proposed designs by architects Schmidt, Garden & Erikson for television-equipped operating rooms that incorporated the all-important control room and the new equipment requirements. For all the demands for sterile environments, it is interesting to observe that control desk operators present at the St Luke's operation were not capped and gowned, and the control room in

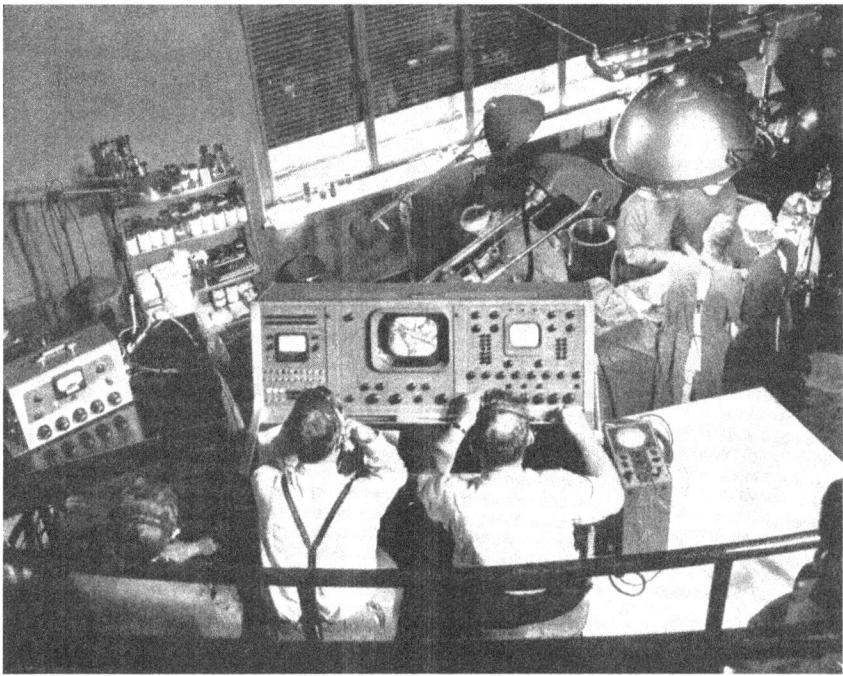

Figure 4.11 A televised surgical session in progress at St Luke's Hospital, Chicago, Illinois, USA. Photograph: unknown, 1949.

Source: St Luke's Hospital. "St Luke's News". Chicago: St Luke's Hospital (December 1949): 4.

Courtesy: Rush University Medical Centre Archives.

the proposed designs opened up from the "surgical corridor" rather than the "open corridor" which the audience would use (Erikson Jr. and Brown 1949: 48–51). The excitement about the new technology was palpable, with stalwarts such as Malcolm MacEachern singing television's praises (Erikson Jr. and Brown 1949). Like the experimental theatre spaces, the prohibitive cost of the television equipment and installation – about $250,000 in today's US dollars – would have put it out of reach for many hospitals, but the potential was significant enough to encourage planning for such technology in the design of new theatres (Hague and Crosby 1948).

Ideas from the theatre

As the operating theatre developed in the twentieth century, it moved from being a naturally lit, functional space to one in which technology was used to progressively solve problems associated with the vulnerable position in which a surgeon and anaesthetist places a patient. Changing technology wrought particular effects, some of which persist to the present day. The adoption of particular shades of green for drapes and walls, for instance, became synonymous with hospital interiors and then extended to institutions in general. The installation of air conditioning (as opposed to just mechanical ventilation) throughout the hospital was driven by the real need for operating theatres to be spark-free, climate-controlled spaces. Solving one problem, such as effective lighting, could lead to others, in this case deep shadows, glare and retinal fatigue, all of which affected the surgeon's ability to operate to their best standard.

The need for a sterile environment encouraged the creative separation of students and observers from the operating theatre. The design of experimental operating theatres sought to solve multiple issues, using physical shape and separation to best advantage, with a series of hemispherical, ovoid and lozenge-shaped theatres proposed and built from the 1930s onwards. Ultimately, these creative propositions were considered redundant, as the operating theatre came to rely more on appropriate artificial lighting and high-performance air conditioning than it did on elaborately shaped theatres and suites to achieve the aseptic space necessary for modern surgical operations.

The success of the twentieth century operating theatre in creating aseptic spaces, leading to better rates of recovery, helped shift the focus of the hospital away from bedside ministrations towards specific expert intervention in dedicated, technologically advanced spaces. The space of the operating theatre offered an increasing capacity for medical treatment to occur *inside* the body, rather than *to* the body. This capacity would soon be supported by an array of technologies that allowed the inside of the body to be seen, understood and diagnosed without physical intervention.

Note

1 The Walter dome is described, but not named, as being used in France and Scotland "but never in the United States" (Butler and Erdman 1946: 49). Edward F. Stevens also notes its use, but not in the United States (Stevens 1940: 83).

References

Action for Cities: A Guide for Community Planning. Chicago, IL: Public Administration Service, 1943.

Adams, Annmarie and Thomas Schlich. "Design for Control: Surgery, Science, and Space at the Royal Victoria Hospital, Montreal, 1893–1956." *Medical History* 50 (2006): 303–34.

Butler, Charles and Addison Erdman. *Hospital Planning*. New York: F.W. Dodge Corporation, 1946.

"Copenhagen County Hospital at Glostrup." Pamphlet reprint of *Ingeniøren International Edition* 3, no. 1 (May 1959).

Daws, Karen. "Framing the Capricious: The Built Response to Infectious Diseases in Victoria between 1850 and 1950." PhD diss., Parkville, Victoria, Australia: University of Melbourne, 2017.

"Die Chirurgische Universitätsklinik in Tübingen." *Moderne Bauformen* 35, no. 1 (January 1936): 27.
Dowler, Marie. "Operating Room Technique: A Step by Step Analysis." *Modern Hospital* 44, no. 6 (June 1935): 42.
Ekland, Herina I. "A Modern Surgery." *Modern Hospital* 50, no. 3 (March 1938): 80.
Erikson, Carl A. "Model Operating Room Is Feature at a Century of Progress." *Modern Hospital* 6, no. 6 (June 1933): 87–90.
Erikson Jr., Carl A. and Robert F. Brown. "EXIT: The Surgical Ampitheater: Enter-Television." *Modern Hospital* 73, no. 6 (December 1949): 48–51.
Flagg, Paleul J. "Color in the Operating Room." *Architectural Record* 57, no. 5 (May 1925): 450–3.
Flagg, Paluel J. "Color in the Operating Field." *Modern Hospital* 52, no. 6 (June 1939): 75–8.
Goldwater, S.S. "Planning the Surgical Facilities." *Modern Hospital* 37, no. 5 (November 1931): 66.
Griffin, Noyce L. "Preventing Fires and Explosions in the Operating Room." *American Journal of Nursing* 53, no. 7 (July 1953): 809–12.
Hague, James E. and Edwin L. Crosby. "Television: Newest Aid in Teaching Surgery." *Modern Hospital* 70, no. 4 (April 1948): 65.
Hart, Deryl. "Sterilization of the Air in the Operating Room by Batericidal Radiant Energy, Results in More Than 800 Operations." *Hospital Magazine* (February 1940): 14.
Hickok, R.N. and H. Florence. "Operating Room, New Style." *Modern Hospital* 49, no. 2 (August 1937): 68.
Hockett, A.J. "Air Conditioning Operating Rooms." *Modern Hospital* 48, no. 5 (May 1937): 83.
Holophane. "Advertisement Lighting for Surgeries Must Be the Best That Science Can Provide." *Modern Hospital* 38, no. 2 (August 1942): 123.
"Hospital Rooms: Planned by Woman Architect." *Sydney Morning Herald* (6 October 1938): 27.
Kisacky, Jeanne. *Rise of the Modern Hospital: An Architectural History of Health and Healing, 1870–1940*. Pittsburgh: University of Pittsburgh Press, 2017.
Moretti, B. Franco. *Ospedali*. Milan: Editore Ulrico Hoepli, 1951.
Mörgeli, Christoph. *The Surgeon's Stage: A History of the Operating Room*. Zurich: Editions Roche, 1999.
"Ninewells Teaching Hospital Dundee." *Modern British Operating Theatres*. Supplement to *Hospital Management* (September 1968): 22–3.
Pantalony, David. "The Colour of Medicine." *Canadian Medical Association Journal* 181, no. 6–7 (September 2009): 402.
"Pure Air: What It Is and How to Get It." *Modern Hospital* 30, no. 5 (May 1928): 152.
Saint-Lô: Centre Hospitalier Mémorial France États-Unis. Saint-Lô, France, 2006.
Shanken, Andrew. *194X: Architecture, Planning and Consumer Culture on the American Home Front*. Minneapolis, MN: University of Minnesota Press, 2009.
Sherman, Harry M. "The Green Operating Room at St Luke's Hospital." *California State Journal of Medicine* 12, no. 5 (May 1914): 181.
Skislewicz, Anton. "An Operating Pavilion Modern in Feeling and Equipment." *Modern Hospital* 43, no. 3 (September 1934): 79.

Stephenson, Arthur. "Correspondence." In Papers of Sir Arthur Stephenson, MS 2072, National Library of Australia, Canberra, Australia, 1932 and 1933.

Stephenson & Turner. "General Description of the Hospital." In *King George V Memorial Hospital for Mothers and Babies*. Sydney, 1941.

Stevens, Edward F. "Newer Trends in Hospital Plans and Equipment." *Hospitals* 14, no. 10 (October 1940): 83.

Truesdale, Philemon E. "Regulating Operating Room Traffic." *Modern Hospital* 29, no. 1 (July 1927): 85.

"Uniform, Shadowless Illumination for Operating Rooms." *Modern Hospital* 27, no. 6 (1926): 164.

US Department of Health, Education and Welfare: Public Health Service. *Design and Construction of General Hospitals*. New York: F.W. Dodge Corporation, 1953.

"Walls of Glass." *Modern Hospital* 48, no. 5 (May 1937): 82.

Whitfield, W.J. "A Brief History of Laminar Flow Clean Room Systems." Proceedings: Institute of Environmental Sciences, Institute of Environmental Sciences Annual Meeting, 1. Los Angeles, CA: Institute of Environmental Sciences, 1981.

5 Treating outside, looking inside
Diagnosis and therapy

In 1930, at the opening of the second International Hygiene Exhibition in Dresden, Germany, one of the highlights contained within architect Wilhelm Kreis's new exhibition building was the life-size transparent glass model of a human being. Since known as the *Gläserner Mensch* or Transparent Man, the glass figure, mounted on a circular podium and with its arms outstretched to the heavens, was indicative of the profound turn in medical and now scientific treatment of the body within the modern hospital (Vogel 1999: 31–61). Not only were the bones visible in Transparent Man, but so were the body's organs (Figure 5.1). The glass figure made the workings of the body available for public view, but, as Christopher Wilk has described, it also:

> suggested that science had unlocked the mysteries of the body, allowing viewers to glimpse its secrets and its workings, and ultimately suggesting that it could be controlled and regulated.
>
> (Wilk 2006: 252)

Previously, most spaces within the hospital had been devoted to providing appropriate amenity for manipulating and treating a patient's visible symptoms and then allowing for repair and convalescence. Developments in the way doctors could literally look inside the body, or even work inside the body with newly developed therapies that required no incision, meant the modern hospital needed new diagnostic, treatment and laboratory spaces to perform these subcutaneous therapies.

Historian of medical technology Audrey B. Davis has also emphasised the increased role of medical instruments in diagnosis and therapy that occurred in the mid- to late-nineteenth century:

> Diagnostic instruments opened up medicine to a greater variety of practitioners by enhancing their basic skills, supplementing their observational abilities, and structuring the diagnostic interview with the patients. Therapeutic devices and machines, such as electric, exercise, and body manipulation tools greatly extended the choice of treatment procedures.
>
> (Davis 1981: 6)

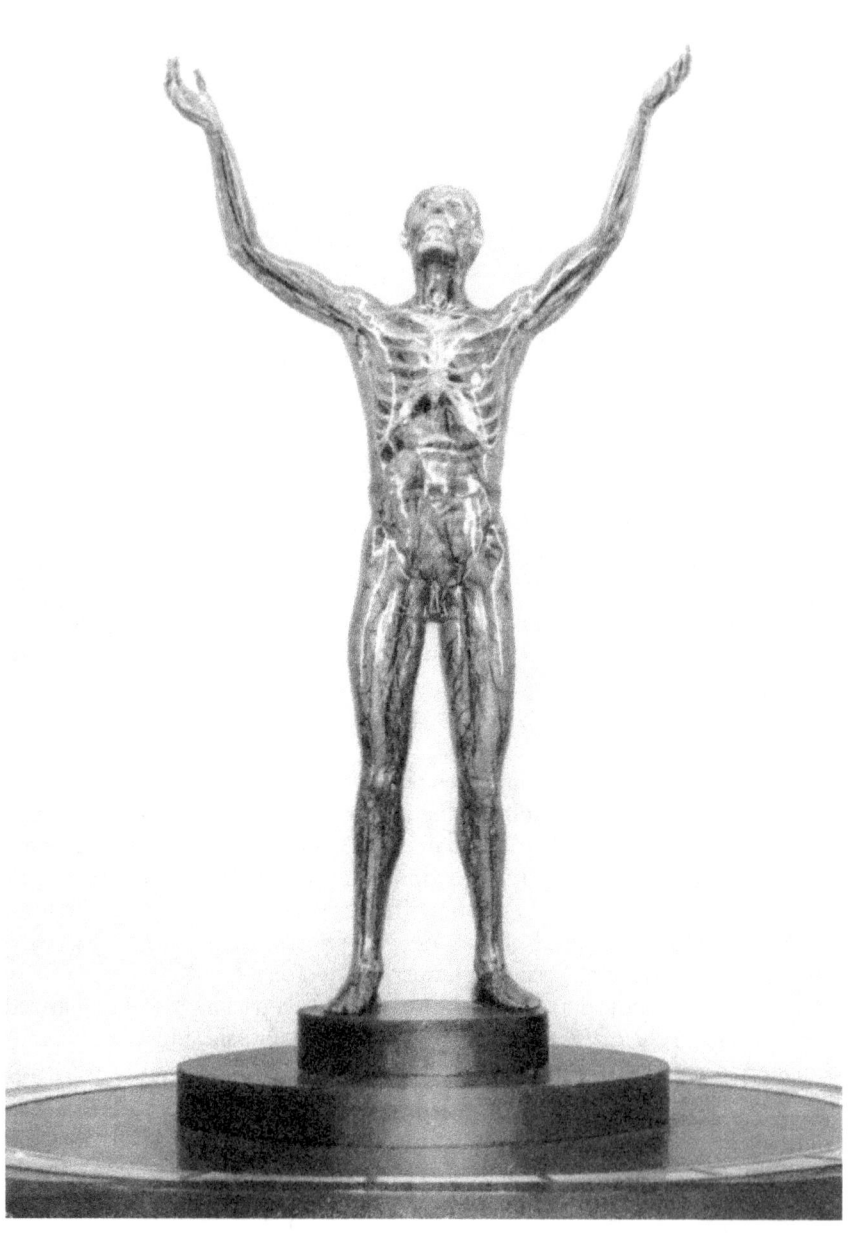

Figure 5.1 Postcard depicting the Gläserner Mensch (Transparent Man). Photograph: unknown, 1930.
Courtesy: Deutsches Hygiene-Museum.

Separate from older methods of diagnosis like the thermometer, stethoscope, cardiac and pulse-related devices and instruments associated with surgery, the instrumentation of diagnosis and non-surgical therapy as it developed in the late nineteenth and early twentieth centuries had, as Davis notes, significant implications. It meant faster and more efficient diagnosis, more effective and alternative treatment choices and the potential to put in place measures to prevent illness (Davis 1981).

External therapies applied to the body did not, of course, disappear from the modern hospital. If anything, they continued to increase, especially with the ongoing fight against tuberculosis and the increasing popularity of heliotherapy within not just the sanatorium but also the general hospital. But diagnosing illness and disease at a fundamental pathological level was now possible and the new techniques of investigation increasingly assumed the power to see inside the body. To support this, laboratories and a range of imaging equipment were added to the modern hospital. As medical historian Stanley Reiser has noted, the subjective evidence of the physician could now be supplemented, and in some cases replaced, by the objective evidence of the laboratory or new medical technology (Reiser 1978). At the same time, whole departments evolved to manage the volume of information generated by the new methods of investigation.

In the 1980s, critic and theorist of the image Allan Sekula argued for the centrality of the photographic archive in articulating illness, madness and criminality in the second half of the nineteenth century, writing:

> The camera [was] integrated into a larger ensemble: a bureaucratic clerical-statistical system of "intelligence". This system can be described as a sophisticated form of the archive. The central artifact of this system is not the camera but the filing cabinet.
>
> (Sekula 1986: 16)

In the 1920s and 1930s, hospitals used cameras and a range of other imaging devices in unprecedented ways. But imaging technology was just one part of a wider apparatus. The ways information was organised and archived were arguably just as important. Photographic archives in modern hospitals thus came to play an important role in statistical and empirical measures of the body and its various states of ill-health, deformity and damage.

As historian of medical technology Joel D. Howell has demonstrated, the decisive period of development in North American hospitals for both this technology and the process of recording and archiving information produced by it, was that between 1900 and 1925. As a result, modern hospitals needed to expand their investigatory and therapeutic ambit, which created a defining architectural challenge. As Howell notes, "the entire hospital had become, by 1925, quite actively and self-consciously based on science" (Howell 1995: 3). Architects, medical people and managers involved in creating new hospital facilities between the 1920s and 1950s simply could not evade the question of what special spaces would be needed for contemporary medical technology such as X-ray machines. Nor could they ignore the problem of how to store the information generated by the new modes of investigation. By the mid-1950s, it was clear that computers would need – spatially – to come to the aid of record keeping and data storage (Reiser 1978). It was the active response to this set of challenges that transformed hospitals in the first half of the twentieth century into institutions of knowledge and places of intensive treatment in addition to their traditional function as places of care. The spaces of therapy and diagnosis began to match and sometimes outgrow the dominance of the ward as the primary space of healing. As the patient's body became more transparent and as the archive of knowledge about patient condition increased, the modern hospital grew in scale and complexity.

Treating outside

During the twentieth century, the range of therapies applied to the exterior of the human body increased in number, and as a result the departments and spaces required in the modern hospital also increased. In broad terms, these "external" therapies included physiotherapy, occupational therapy, hydrotherapy, oxygen therapy and heliotherapy. Many of these therapies were not new, in and of themselves, but they now required increasingly sophisticated machines and/or greater space, contributing to the ever-burgeoning scale of the modern hospital.

Physiotherapy

Physiotherapy generally involves two methods of manipulating the body: first by the patient undertaking repetitive exercise, or doing so with the assistance of others, and second, with the aid of a machine. For the first, where the subject exercised, the physiotherapy frequently involved a gymnasium and booths or rooms for physical massage and, in many cases, the hospital's grounds offered space for "exercise". In Basel's Kantonsspital (Cantonal Hospital) (now Universitätsspital Basel [Basel University Hospital], Switzerland, 1937–1945), gymnastics and physiotherapy occupied a double-height volume with Roman rings, climbing ladders attached to the walls and massage cubicles curtained off from the main space (Moretti 1951) (Figure 5.2). In Bern, Switzerland, at Otto Salvisberg's Loryspital (1925–1926), two gymnasia occupied the top floor, each with its own swimming pool.

The scale and complexity of the machines of physiotherapy, often too large and expensive to be transported to the private home, were housed in hospital departments especially devoted to the various therapies. Part of the innovation and intent behind the increasing sophistication of these

Figure 5.2 Gymnastics and physiotherapy, Kantonsspital (Cantonal Hospital) (now Universitätsspital Basel [Basel University Hospital]), Switzerland. Architects: H. Baur, E. & P. Vischer and Bräuning Leu Dürig, 1939–1945. Photograph: unknown, c. 1945.

Source: Moretti, B. Franco. *Ospedali*. Milan: Editore Ulrico Hoepli, 1951: 261.

machines that worked to correct or ameliorate the body's movement, posture or body shape was that they might begin to take the place of attendants and work more efficiently and with more exact calibration than the human therapist.

As early as 1904, it was recognised that:

> The aim of all these machines is to take the place of the attendant. The partisans of the method assert that machinery can perform with success the part of an attendant in the production of passive, resisted, and duplicate movements, in the application of vibrations, and in a large proportion of the ordinary massage manipulations; that properly adjusted it is more exact than an attendant, makes no mistakes, and, most important of all, affords a precise measurement of the amount of work done.
>
> (Cohen 1904: 133)

106 *Treating outside, looking inside*

Contraptions like the Weigel-Hoffa Correcting Machine for Lateral Curvature or the various Zander Machines for abdominal massage or chest movement were not new developments, but they were large and often only sold in sets (Figure 5.3). Capital expenditure was great, as were the running and maintenance costs (Cohen 1904). The implication of such limitations for private purchase and private use was that the modern hospital took on the responsibility to provide and maintain these various therapies and their accompanying "machinery". Some hospitals even had workshops for brace-making, where individuals were fitted with corrective supports: wearable forms of the physiotherapy machines.

Hydrotherapy

Physiotherapy required large spaces to accommodate free and controlled bodily movement over distances larger than the scale of the bed and specialised machines. In contrast, hydrotherapy involved completely serviced spaces with copious amounts of water. Hydrotherapy in the twentieth

Figure 5.3 Zander Machines for abdominal massage or chest movement were often used in early twentieth century hospitals. Photograph: unknown.
Source: Levertin, Alfred and Gustav Zander. *Dr G. Zander's medico-mechanische Gymnastik: ihre Methode, Bedeutung und Anwendung, nebst Auszügen aus der einschlägigen Litteratur.* Stockholm: Königl. Buchdruckerei, P. A. Norstedt & Söner, 1892.
Courtesy: Tekniska Museet (CC BY 2.0).

century was, largely, a continuation of earlier practices of using water for pain relief and another form of physiotherapy and occupational therapy. In the eighteenth and nineteenth centuries, hydrotherapy had been fashionable as well as popular. It had encouraged a form of health tourism, with the rise of grandiose bathing establishments across the United Kingdom and Europe, generally associated with hot mineral springs like Evian-les-Bains in eastern France and Baden-Baden in southwestern Germany, and it continued a tradition of "taking the waters" that had been popular across cultures, both East and West, since Ancient times (Soroka 2017).

In the twentieth-century modern hospital, facilities such as the Hubbard bath (often used for patients with burns), scotch douche, wet pack table and Sitz bath were commonly installed in areas floored with reinforced concrete to assist drainage and carry the additional weight of water. In the paediatric department of the Cincinnati General Hospital, Ohio, USA, a special burns room was designed and constructed in 1937 under the supervision of Dr Jerry Lavender. It comprised five raised tubs (three large and two small) in various pastel shades with various spray fixtures (Figure 5.4). Complementing these was a specially constructed electric kaleidoscope that

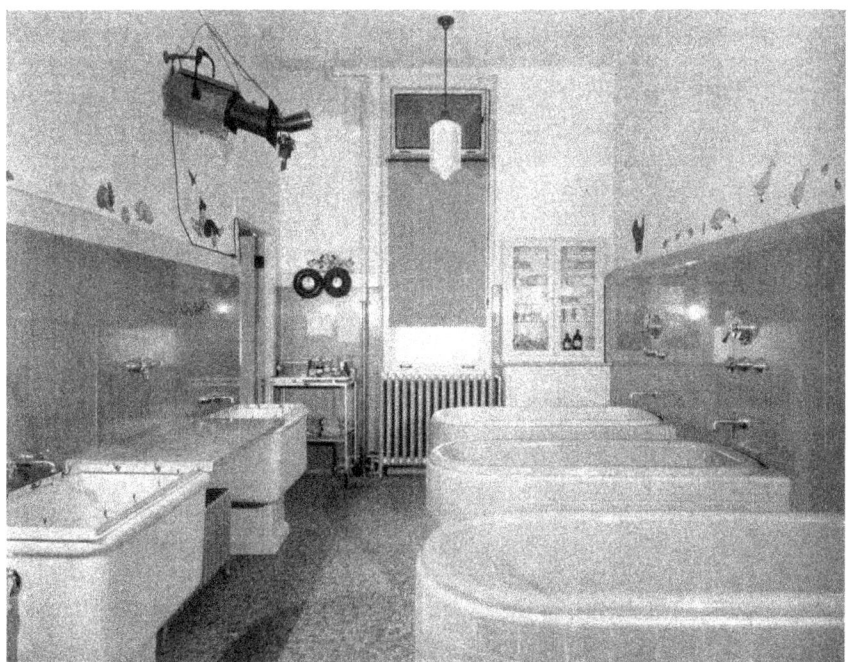

Figure 5.4 Burns room, Cincinnati General Hospital, Cincinnati, Ohio, USA, planned, designed and constructed by dermatologist Dr H. Jerry Lavender, 1937. Photograph: unknown.
Source: *Modern Hospital* 48, no. 2 (February 1937): 56.

projected constantly changing images of coloured designs and patterns on the upper walls and ceiling, providing welcome distraction to the child having daily treatments (which ranged in time from a few minutes to several hours) in the room's tubs ("Balm for the Burned" 1937).

In many hospitals, physiotherapy and hydrotherapy were combined, as they involved the same group of medical specialists. In March 1938, *Modern Hospital* used the example of the 177-bed Passavant Memorial Hospital in Chicago, Illinois, USA, to describe the needs and layout of a typical "physical therapy" department for a general hospital. It consisted of five rooms grouped together, three for electromagnetic and heat ray therapy, and two for hydrotherapy. Of the latter, one room was devoted to underwater exercises with a Hubbard tank (an elevated bath with a narrow section at its middle to allow the therapist to reach the patient, and then wider sections at arms and legs to enable full abduction). Overhead, a crane and sling assisted transfer of the patient to and from the tank. The second hydrotherapy room contained a bed, ultraviolet (UV) lamps and an adjacent arm and leg whirlpool bath accessible either from a stool (for the leg) or a cut-down chair (for the arm and hand).

Spatially, the rooms were unremarkable. But it was significant that the rooms were acknowledged as a specific department, and with that came the corresponding need for accurate records of their use to be kept. "The relative newness of scientifically practiced physical therapy makes accurate records of this specialty extremely valuable". Another important point was made: "To have value in clinical research, the physical therapy department records should conform to the general record system of the hospital" ("Fundamentals in Design for Physical Therapy" 1938: 65). Because of this, the amount of space dedicated to records generally increased in these departments and others, reflecting the greater space allocated to documenting case histories overall. The modern hospital was now not only a place where a patient could be healed efficiently by expert specialists; it was also increasingly a significant repository of health histories and, by extension, critical research data. The modern hospital was becoming a body of knowledge.

Oxygen therapy

One therapy that had gained wide interest in the late eighteenth century involved oxygen. English theologian and chemist Joseph Priestley experimented with purifying air in 1774. His publication *Experiments and Observations on Different Kinds of Air* (1775) noted his personal experience of inhaling oxygen:

> The feeling of it to my lungs was not sensibly different from that of common air; but I fancied that my breast felt peculiarly light and easy for some time afterwards. Who can tell but that, in time, this

pure air may become a fashionable article in luxury. Hitherto only two mice and myself have had the privilege of breathing it.

(Grainge 2004: 489)

Priestley was right. Shortly afterward, the new phenomenon of "oxygen bars" emerged in New York, USA, and Berlin, Germany, where one could pay around $10 for five minutes of oxygen therapy (Grainge 2004). Priestley also suggested there might be medical uses for oxygen therapy, but it wasn't until World War I that progress in the application of oxygen therapy for medical purposes accelerated and became more sophisticated – a development induced largely by the use of poison gas in the battlefields of Europe. In the field, treatment was managed with portable "Haldane equipment" – a pressurised cylinder, pressure regulator, reservoir bag and a tightly fitting mask.[1]

Back in the modern hospital, intermittent oxygen therapy was being used for cases of gas poisoning, trauma, pneumonia, asthma and other cardio-respiratory illnesses. As on the battlefield, mobile equipment was used, and nasal prongs inserted when a mask was not tolerated by the patient. This meant, spatially, oxygen therapy could occur directly at the bed. By 1931, for those patients requiring more freedom around the face and a less intimidating experience of inhalation, the oxygen tent (invented in 1921) was widely used: a collapsible suspended "tent" with a window panel was placed over above the patient and across the bed (Munger 1931). A Heidbrink oxygen tent, for example, could be fitted over the patient in their bed, with the accompanying oxygen tank and motorised equipment contained on a wheeled frame and operated by a single nurse (Figure 5.5). A very few hospitals created entire oxygen rooms for oxygen therapy. For these, existing patient rooms were made airtight by gasketed frames and storm sashes fitted to all doors and windows along with locking devices. To ensure safety, explosion-proof lights were fitted and a nurse's signal switch was installed. Generally, these rooms were created as pairs with a control room and airlock between where staff could modulate oxygen supply, heating and humidity. As architect Carl Erikson wrote in 1936, with the addition of lamps that simulated sunshine, "one could here produce the aridity of the Sahara, the humidity of the Amazonian swamp, the rarefied air of Pikes Peak, the temperature of Aden or of Medicine Hat – truly all weather rooms" (Erikson 1936: 64).

Heliotherapy

At the turn of the twentieth century, as the artificial creation of different environmental conditions became more achievable, medical scientists and clinicians also highlighted the therapeutic value of sunlight and fresh air. This had a clear and distinctive effect on the architecture of the hospital. Heliotherapy is the use of sunlight to ameliorate various skin conditions.

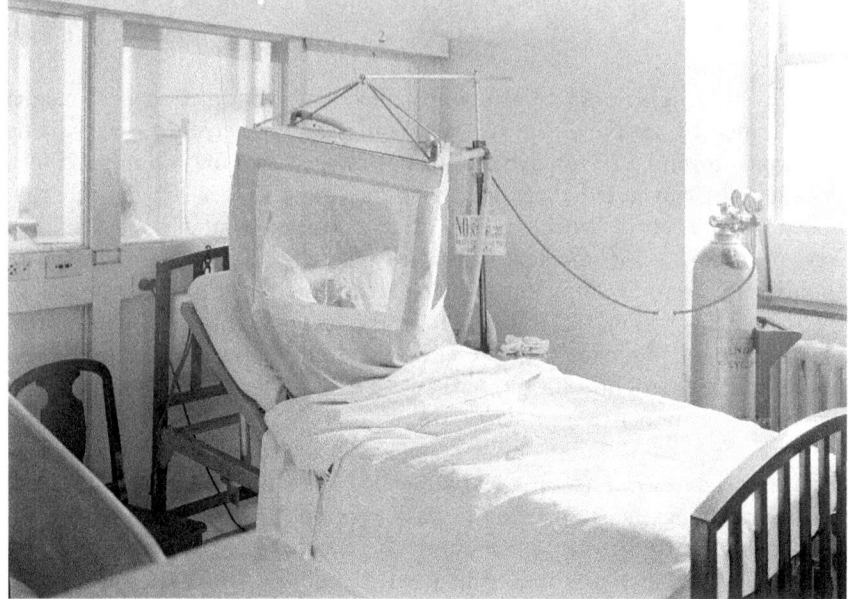

Figure 5.5 An oxygen tent in use, Beth Israel Hospital, Manhattan, New York, USA. Photograph: Samuel H. Gottscho, 1935.
Courtesy: Museum of the City of New York, 88.1.1.3670.

By the end of the eighteenth century and through the nineteenth century, when injured soldiers returned from battle, exposure to sunlight was found to increase recovery time for skin wounds. But it was the 1893 experiments of Danish physician Niels Ryberg Finsen (1860–1904) that formed the main scientific basis for photo- and heliotherapy. In 1903 Finsen won the Nobel Prize for Medicine and Physiology in recognition of his contributions to treating disease, especially skin tuberculosis (lupus vulgaris), with concentrated light radiation. His efforts opened up a range of new avenues for medical science. One of these was taken up by Swiss physician Oskar Bernhard of Samedan, who in 1902, after observing the putrefaction of meat exposed to the sun in alpine conditions, experimented with healing an operation wound by exposure to the sun. Bernhard had already opened his own private clinic in St Moritz, Switzerland, in 1899, and was exploring "sun-baths" for bone and joint tuberculosis. Results were so positive that the application of sunlight (heliotherapy) to tuberculous lesions became not only popular but one of the great determinants of the architectural design of sanatoria and, through their influence, general hospitals.

In 1903, Swiss physician and surgeon Auguste Rollier opened the first clinic for the systematised heliotherapy of surgical tuberculosis at Leysin, near Montreux, Switzerland, where he advocated the general sunbath as opposed to Bernhard's local application of sunlight. Rollier became Europe's most famous and successful heliotherapist, owning, at one point, thirty-six clinics in the Swiss Alps. Despite the discovery of penicillin in 1928 and various antibacterial drugs in the 1930s, it was not until the active take-up of antibiotics after World War II that the use of heliotherapy began to decline. By 1960, its influence had waned and its effect on the architecture of buildings for health had almost entirely disappeared.

In the first fifty years of the twentieth century, however, heliotherapy had a dramatic effect on the architecture of hospitals. As early as 1923, Rollier claimed in his book, *Heliotherapy*:

> the spread of heliotherapy has been rapid and has extended even to the general hospitals of many big cities. Admirable as are these attempts at heliotherapy under difficult conditions, I cannot help thinking that for *treatment* a site in the country would in the long run prove more economical. In towns, the chief use of the sun is for the *prevention* of disease.
>
> (Rollier 1923: 3)

At tuberculosis sanatoria, heliotherapy shaped the construction and internal arrangements of each building. As Rollier described Les Frênes (The Ash Trees) at Leysin, Switzerland, a sanatorium constructed to enable heliotherapy, he noted such facilities needed basic consulting rooms, radiographic and radio-therapeutic departments, rooms for orthopaedics and phototherapy, offices and laboratories, and dining and recreation rooms. For effective heliotherapy, south-facing balconies were required on each floor, open to the sky (making sun treatment possible even at the summer solstice) and large enough to house multiple beds (all on wheels); further, rooftop solaria were needed to maximise sunshine exposure (the solarium could also be used as a children's playground and for patients making their first attempts at walking), and the floors of patient rooms or dormitories were to be at exactly the same level as the balconies, so beds could be wheeled from one to the other smoothly, without any jolting. Beds were to be high and wheeled (for ease of movement) with hard mattresses and movable shades so the patient's head could be shaded in whatever position he or she was in (Rollier 1923). These general principles were applied to almost all sanatoria, then, by extension, to the design of general hospitals.

For general hospitals, broad capacious balconies became common (Figure 5.6), as did the concept of solaria, often defined by lounge spaces or rooms at the fully or near-fully glazed ends of building wings (south ends in the northern hemisphere and north ends in the southern hemisphere). This is demonstrated in examples such as Otto Salvisberg's Loryspital, Bern, Switzerland (1925–1926), Richard Döcker's Krankenhaus Waiblingen (Waiblingen Hospital), Stuttgart, Germany (1926–1928), Stephenson & Meldrum's Mercy Hospital, East Melbourne, Victoria, Australia (1933–1935), the

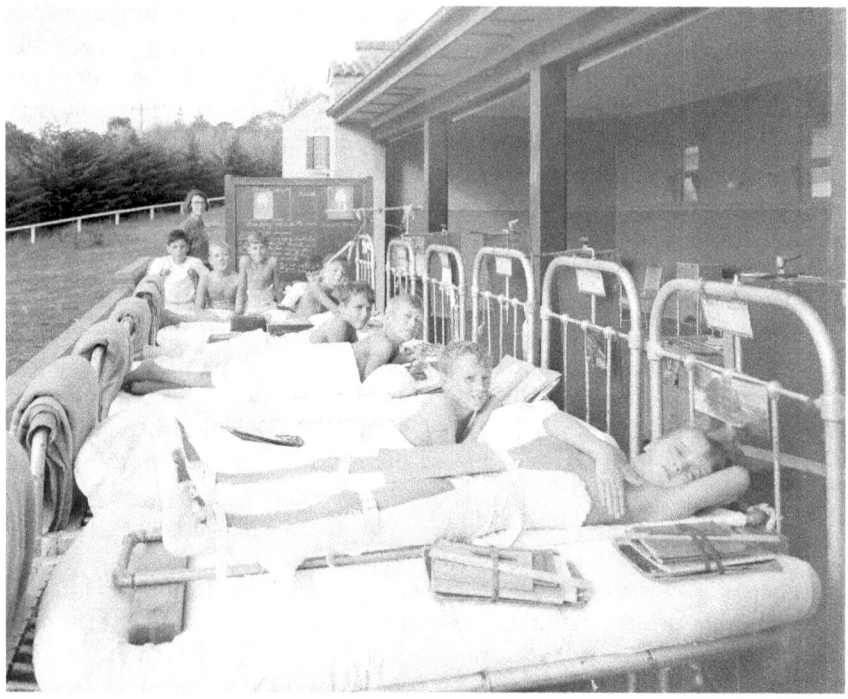

Figure 5.6 School lessons on the sundeck, Frankston Children's Hospital, Frankston, Victoria, Australia. Architects: Stephenson & Meldrum, 1928. Photograph: Lyle Fowler, 1936.

Courtesy: Pictures Collection, State Library of Victoria, H92.20/57.

Meadowbrook Hospital in Long Island, New York, USA (Architect: John Russell Pope & William F. McCulloch, with S.S. Goldwater, 1935), and Hjalmar Cederström and Hermann Imhäuser's Södersjukhuset (Southern Hospital), Stockholm, Sweden (1937–1944). Hospital ward and room design also benefited from this taste for the sun. It was as if the heliotherapeutic benefits of the sun could be generalised as architectural elements and spread across the hospital as a lingua franca of healing. The architectural language of the sanatorium – often modernist in idiom – became in large part the external architectural language of the modern hospital (Campbell 2005).

Phototherapy or artificial solar therapy

The desire for sun all year round also encouraged the development of rooms and machinery devoted to artificial sources of solar radiation, and for treating multiple patients at the same time. This practice was favoured in locations where climatic conditions and hospitals within crowded cities worked against natural forms of heliotherapy. Collaborating in 1895–1896 with Copenhagen Electric Light Works, Niels Finsen's treatment of skin tuberculosis was accelerated by his use of a very powerful carbon arc lamp combined with two optical glass lenses of his own design, which concentrated ultraviolet (UV) rays (or "chemical rays" as they were often described at the time) on the skin for at least two hours a day. The so-called Finsen Lamp was suspended from the ceiling and looked somewhat like an upturned cylindrical gun turret, generally with four, and sometimes more, telescope-like arms which pointed at angles downwards and directed UV light onto reclining patients, who were attended by nurses wearing blue glasses.

Finsen achieved great success with his invention. He founded the Finsen Medical Light Institute of Copenhagen in 1896. The Finsen Lamp was shown with great fanfare at the World Exhibition in Paris in 1900, where it earned a Grand Prix (Mogensen 2001). That same year, the British Queen Alexandria (then Princess of Wales), daughter of Danish King Christian IX, presented a Finsen Lamp to the London Hospital, of which she was president. The hospital proceeded to use the lamp for thirty years (Figure 5.7). In London, Finsen's invention was particularly attractive because of that city's intractable weather. As early as 1902, it was observed:

> Sun treatment has been abandoned at the London Hospital. Among the fogs and clouds and changeable weather of an English climate, sunlight for long is too rare a thing to be counted on, and the necessity of a retreat from the open air to the electric lamps indoors, occurring often even on summer days, has made it impracticable.
>
> (Dickinson 1902: 660)

An observation such as this points to one of the key spatial benefits of artificial solar therapy: it could be performed indoors, at any time and, with more than one machine, with increased numbers of patients.

In October 1924, the Taft Heliotherapy Ward opened at the Cincinnati General Hospital, Ohio, USA (Schwartz 1927). The custom-designed unit was suspended by a cable over pulleys and attached to a counterweight to facilitate raising and lowering the unit of four carbon arc lamps; it could treat thirty patients simultaneously. The incline of the arc lamps could be adjusted to an angle parallel to the plane on which the patients reclined while receiving treatment. The space itself was square in plan, with the patients laid out in a circle around the central focus of the suspended artificial "sun". The practice was widely adopted, including at the New York Hospital–Cornell Medical Center, Manhattan, New York, USA, and manufacturers like Eveready National Carbon Company promoted their "Carbon Arc Solarium Units" on the basis their products were "efficient sources of ultra-violet radiation [that] provide the equivalent of summer sunshine for a large group" (Eveready National Carbon Co. 1932: 117) (Figure 5.8).

114 *Treating outside, looking inside*

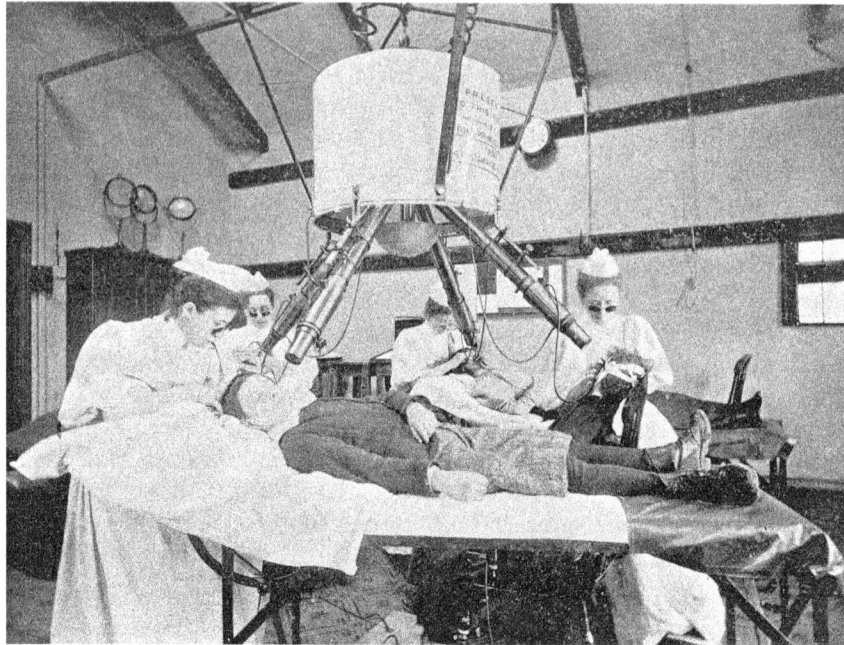

Figure 5.7 The Finsen Lamp, devised for the treating of lupus using ultraviolet rays, presented by Princess Alexandria to the London Hospital, London, England, 1900. Photograph: unknown.
Courtesy: Wellcome Collection, CC BY.

Looking beneath the skin

If many of these therapies acted upon the body externally and their effect was to expand and, in some respects, alter the external appearance of the hospital, there was, in the early twentieth century, a new focus of diagnosis that was internal rather than external. New modes of diagnosis were carried out by "looking" inside the body.

The X-ray or radiography

The most dramatic development was the increasing use of X-ray technology. As J.L. Weatherwax noted in 1927, with the discovery of Roentgen rays (X-rays) in 1895 and radium in 1896, "a new therapeutic agent became available in the field of medicine" (Weatherwax 1927: 52). The role of photography via the X-ray as an aid to internal diagnosis was profound and "another branch was added to the ancient but ever growing tree of medicine – that of radiology" (The Story of X-Rays: Ridiculed First 1938: 16). By the late 1930s, almost every physician, surgeon and dentist relied upon X-rays

Figure 5.8 Advertisement for Carbon Arc Solarium Units produced by the Eveready National Carbon Company Inc.

Source: *Modern Hospital* 38, no. 1 (January 1932): 117.

for diagnosis and prognosis, especially to determine the extent of bone fractures and the condition of teeth. But X-rays could also be used to examine soft tissue and soft tissue organs like the bladder, gall bladder, kidneys, arteries, lungs, liver and body sinuses. It seemed that the whole body could now be read and recorded as a photographic negative known as a radiograph. It was the vision into a new world of diagnosis.

Radiologists and trained technicians were needed to operate X-ray apparatus. There also needed to be rooms to store and develop film, as well as a room or rooms in which to locate the apparatus. In spatial terms, this meant that separate X-ray departments now became standard. In the first decade of the twentieth century, the X-ray room of a large hospital was relatively unsophisticated with the machinery, housed in ornamental cabinets, rattling and crackling as it delivered the high voltage electricity required to produce X-rays (Figure 5.9). The X-ray tube, with a massive football-sized bulb, glowed green as it hung suspended from a complicated device of timber, ebonite and glass. Taking a picture often required an exposure lasting many minutes.

By 1940, X-ray apparatus were more numerous, much larger, more powerful and much faster. They were now located in special X-ray rooms within or attached to the main hospital building. It was essential that a hospital have

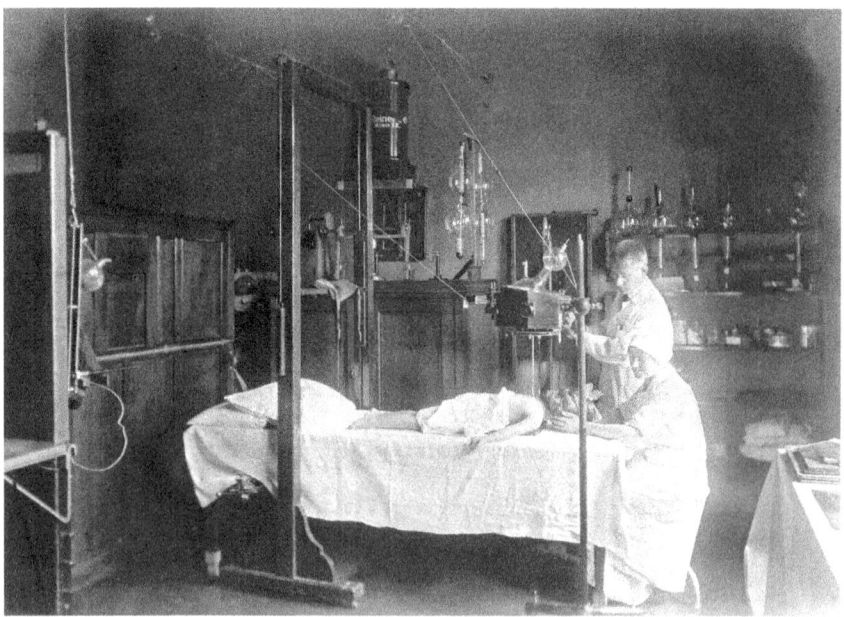

Figure 5.9 A child having an X-ray at the Universitäts-Kinderklinik (University Children's Hospital), Vienna, Austria. Photograph: unknown, 1921.
Courtesy: Wellcome Collection, CC BY.

one or more large radiographic rooms (each of which housed an X-ray machine and examination table), a small room housing the transformer, a processing room (separated from the radiographic room by a light lock), dressing rooms and bathrooms. Developing rooms were key spaces, often planned as a maze so as not to allow any light to enter. An office and viewing room positioned adjacent to the developing room, sometimes called an "interpretation room", was also essential to a radiographic suite. The room would have filing cabinets and a desk, as well as wall-mounted back-lit viewing boxes that had sloping sides for ease of examining the X-ray negatives.

In January 1941, *Hospital Magazine* compared ground floor plans of an old X-ray department (c. 1922) and a new radiography department (1940) designed by architects A. & K. Henderson at the Alfred Hospital in Prahran, Victoria, Australia ("Then and Now" 1941) (Figure 5.10). The main difference over twenty years was that spaces had been consolidated to a single floor and a single department, complete with lead-lined transformer rooms, as opposed to functions like reporting room, museum store (archive) and film store being dispersed. The X-ray department needed to be easily accessible for both inpatients and outpatients, convenient for physicians and, at the same time, not serve as a passage to other sections of the hospital. It also had to enable future development of the hospital.

The use of X-rays in diagnosis created yet more need for record keeping, thus also creating the need for record storage (Figure 5.11). As well as X-rays providing a prime and direct diagnostic aid, the records themselves were proving to be of inestimable value:

> Not only are these records permanent, but also they are perfectly impersonal, being quite independent of the person making the observation, and hence free from the defect of depending on the subjective characteristics of an observer.
>
> (Teasdale 1941: 10)

Companies like Eastman Kodak offered complete service and supply of all equipment needed for X-ray processing darkrooms for both large and small hospitals. They offered to "co-operate in every way with your Hospital Architects" (Kodak 1939). By 1932 the photograph had also become a necessary service (Buerki 1932; Schwarz 1934) and a potent means to diagnose and document on occasions where other methods may not be appropriate. As Eastman Kodak advertised:

> In any instance the photograph gives a clear complete reply. Where words alone can not describe a condition satisfactorily.... Conference, instruction, publication, legal action, all demand specific information – facts which only photographs can give. Hospitals seeking most efficient methods should illustrate their case histories with photographs.
>
> (Eastman Kodak Co. 1934: 103)

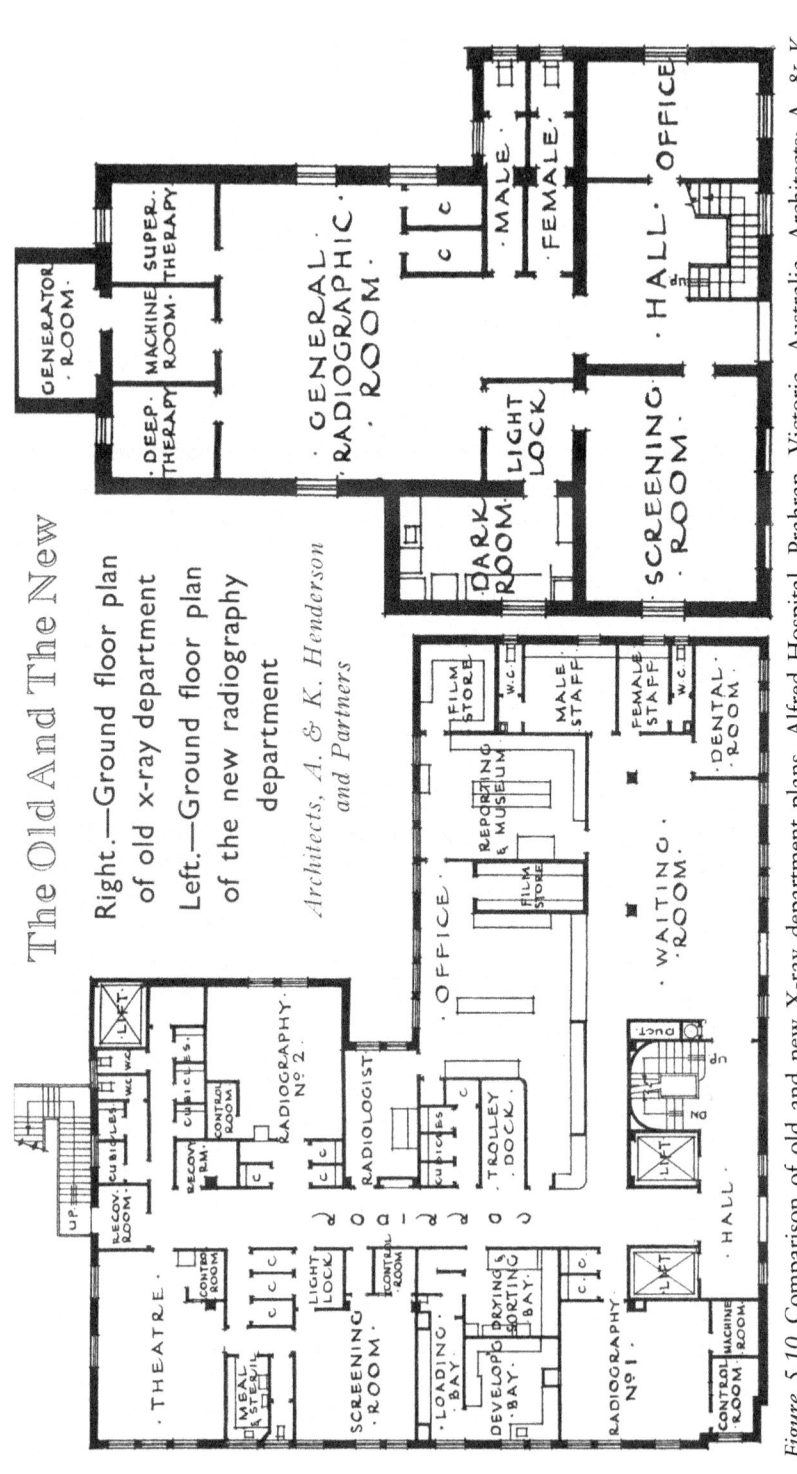

Figure 5.10 Comparison of old and new X-ray department plans, Alfred Hospital, Prahran, Victoria, Australia. Architects: A. & K. Henderson, 1940. Delineator: unknown.

Source: *Hospital Magazine* 4, no. 11 (January 1941): 14.

Figure 5.11 X-ray filing system, Columbia-Presbyterian Medical Center, Manhattan, New York, USA. Architect: James Gamble Rogers, 1928. Photograph: Wurts Bros., 1936.
Courtesy: Museum of the City of New York, X2010.7.2.6717.

In many cases, for a record to be complete, a picture taken before and after treatment was required. This meant more reliable diagnosis and a potential safeguard against litigation, but spatially it also meant these records needed to be protected both for patient security and from fire. Kept records could

120 *Treating outside, looking inside*

also then be matched with results from surgery, pathology, radiology and other clinical branches. In other words, as laboratory science developed, so too the role of the general hospital expanded as a place of potential teaching and research. On one site, there might be hospital beds, operating theatres, radiology and pathology departments, hospital records, laboratories and teaching and research spaces. The hospital had become not only a place for healing, but also a scientific institution. These diagnostic and therapeutic spaces and techniques were markers of the expanded role of the hospital.

Fluoroscopy

While diagnosis or recording using the fixed image of the X-ray negative became common, X-rays also allowed another form of diagnosis. This was fluoroscopy: the ability to look inside the body directly and immediately. In *The American Hospital of the Twentieth Century* (1918), Edward F. Stevens illustrated a vertical fluoroscope (1917), whereby a patient stands behind a complex contraption while X-rays pass through her body. The doctor watches the fluorescent screen in front of the patient to examine her interior in real time. On hand is a nurse, ready with a glass of barium to administer to the patient. The patient drinks the barium mixture, which leaves an opaque coating behind, thus creating an opaque silhouette that allows the doctor to see the stomach, intestines and other body cavities. In this suite, there needed to be a so-called "barium kitchen", which comprised a sink and mixing apparatus as well as a water closet as the barium passed rapidly through the patient's intestines. The procedure produced a live X-ray movie, but these moving picture images were not recorded or stored until after 1956, when videotape playback and recording became available for such images. From the 1950s, fluoroscopes often included X-ray intensifiers and cameras to improve image quality and enable them to be displayed on a remote screen. In the early years and even into the 1940s, the fluoroscope was operated in near darkness, rooms were light-proofed and the radiologist often wore red adaptation goggles (sometimes called dark adaptor goggles).

Radiotherapy

X-rays dramatically improved diagnosis, but they also had a crucial therapeutic function. Radiotherapy or radiation therapy, using ionising radiation via X-rays, was employed to treat cancer and, during the 1920s, tuberculosis. Physician Emil Grubbe (1875–1960) in Chicago used X-rays to treat cancer as early as 1896, but the danger of this form of treatment was not well understood until after World War II, and by 1957, Grubbe had lost his left hand, nose, upper lip and most of the right side of his face ("Pioneer in X-Ray Therapy" 1957). It was often such bitter experience, along with advancing technology, that taught clinicians and hospital planners lessons in safe use and handling of X-rays and radiation therapy.

In the early years, for example, X-ray departments were often located in basements but these were quickly understood to be dangerous because the of extremely high voltages associated with the X-ray machines (Butler and Erdman 1946; Rosenfield 1947). X-ray departments soon came to be generally located above the ground floor for safety and positioned where natural light and ventilation were available. Ideally, they were also located where both inpatients and outpatients could easily access them, so as to avoid the need for two separate X-ray departments and staff. As the dangers of X-rays, whether used for diagnosis or therapy, came to be better understood, the use of lead became common, as its high density could effectively stop gamma rays and X-rays. Patients and staff wore lead aprons and lead gloves for protection, and the walls of X-ray departments were often lined with lead, of varying thicknesses. Because the lead linings were expensive, X-ray departments were often located on outside walls, so only the internal walls needed to be lined. Increasingly, X-ray departments were designed to be carefully protected windowless enclosures that by preference and necessity had to be air conditioned. Using X-rays to look inside and treat the body meant medical reliance on connection to the exterior of buildings decreased. Architectural gestures that once clearly denoted the position and needs of the X-ray apparatus were increasingly reduced to a specific set of controlled conditions that were materially, environmentally and spatially determined.

In 1947, for example, Isadore Rosenfield wrote that it was necessary to shield against the escape of X-rays and the effects of radium to protect people in adjoining spaces. He illustrated this using a chart taken from R.A. Rendich and C.B. Braestrup's "Housing the Expanding X-ray Department" in the nineteenth edition of *The Hospital Yearbook* (Rendich and Braestrup 1941), which gave the specifications for lead protection and the equivalents in concrete. Deep radiation therapy of 400 kilovolts required a minimum of 15 millimetres of lead or a concrete depth of 260 millimetres (Rosenfield 1947). He recommended using solid concrete walls rather than lead where voltages above 40 kv were used, lead for doors and partitions, and with the lead sheets carefully detailed to prevent any gaps through which rays could leak. Lead was also advised for floors unless the thickness of the concrete floor slab gave equivalent levels of protection. This advice to architects is an example of how complex the specifics of designing hospital spaces, with their interaction of equipment, adequate servicing and structural requirements, became during the twentieth century.

The operators of X-ray machines also needed to be protected from exposure to radiation. Radiographers had to be shielded, either by a wall (sometimes with a small viewing window) or in a completely separate and protected control room or booth. Dr G. Failla, a physicist at the Memorial Hospital in Manhattan, New York, USA, developed a novel form of viewing window for this purpose: a leaded glass tank filled with water (Dreher 1946). Other observation strategies included periscopes and mirrors and often, after World War II, microphones for communicating with patients.

Many of the safety-related refinements of planning and fitting out X-ray departments occurred after the regular use of artificially produced radioisotopes for radiotherapy had commenced. These radioisotopes had been enabled by the invention of the nuclear reactor as part of the Manhattan Project during World War II. The subsequent graphic and tragic aftereffects on the human body of the Nagasaki and Hiroshima bombs meant that protective material and spatial practices were rapidly implemented in hospitals and cancer hospitals to ensure protection for both patient and operator.

X-rays revolutionised how patient conditions were diagnosed, but radiation therapy also made use of X-ray technology, relying on radium and the gas that emanated from it – radon gas. Early radiotherapy employed relatively low-voltage X-rays to treat superficial tumours. Significant floor space was needed for this treatment, but as technology evolved to the next generation, much larger volumes were required for effective operation. In the 1940s, hospitals generally allocated a two-storey volume for their new high-voltage X-ray therapy, with the auxiliary aspects of the sophisticated machines accessible from above. X-ray therapeutic departments were therefore sometimes located on an upper floor so they could be accessed from the roof. The machines used 50 million volts or more to treat deep-seated tumours without damaging the skin. These high voltage machines were often extremely large and, in many cases, were suspended from the ceiling to enable movement and complete flexibility. At the Walter Reed Hospital in Washington, DC, USA, for example, the X-ray machine was mounted in a suspended shock-proof tank held aloft in a horseshoe-shaped fork. A tubular extension containing the X-ray tube protruded from the tank. A circular well in the ceiling meant the X-ray machine could be raised and lowered vertically, and it could swivel around the patient who was lying on an elevated bed, allowing the operator to aim the extension at any angle and at any height. All the movements were remotely controlled by a nurse, who then left the room through a motorised lead door and operated the machine from outside, observing through a water tank and lead glass window (Rosenfield 1947).

Each of these ways of looking inside the body had spatial implications for the postwar hospital. New drugs, especially antibiotics, were discovered and applied in the early 1950s, but the need to provide expansive areas for diagnosis and therapy was not radically altered. In most cases, the increasing significance of medical science and imaging technology led to ongoing specialisation of knowledge and the incorporation of expensive cutting-edge equipment. The space needed for storing archives and records did not diminish, either. By the middle of the twentieth century, technologically enabled diagnosis and therapy had become intrinsic to the modern hospital. More than ever, whole departments required dedicated floor space and servicing. Medical equipment evolved and changed across the first half of the twentieth century, but the growing demand for specialised areas continued.

In one sense, the architectural implications of diagnostic and therapeutic intensification in the hospital remained constant from the early decades of the twentieth century right up through the postwar decades. The space needed to house scientifically and technologically enabled diagnosis, and treatment grew. But in another sense, everything changed in parallel to the changing technology and approaches used by the hospital. There was a marked shift in the architectural form of hospitals across the period. This was driven most obviously by the development of more effective and efficient mechanical heating, ventilation and air conditioning, as will be discussed in the next chapter. But fundamental shifts in the hospital form also reflected a changing conception of hospital work, and its relationship to the body of the patient and to human health more generally.

In the interwar decades, many of the most architecturally advanced hospital projects, such as Paul Nelson's unbuilt Lille Hospital, echoed the promise of Transparent Man. Everything aspired to transparency. Great expanses of glazing promised unimpeded visual connections and copious light. But even where such expansive glazing and overt transparency were not central to the architecture, natural light and fresh air were key motifs. The patient was to be bathed in both. In many signal hospital projects of the period, such as the Krankenhaus Waiblingen (Waiblingen Hospital) (1926–1928) near Stuttgart in southwestern Germany, the main building was conceived as a great ocean liner. Terraces provided outdoor areas high up in the hospital close to ward areas, and double- and triple-hung windows and other openings enabled staff to move patients out on to these expansive balconies and terraces.

This expressive, hygienic modernism gave way to a more rigorously controlled functionalism in the 1950s and 1960s as helio-therapeutical ideals were overshadowed by drug therapy and hospitals adopted increasingly rigorous and technologically enabled diagnostic regimes. In that period, it seems that the sealed up black box of the camera was a more apt model for hospital architecture than the ocean liner, hotel or resort. As imaging of the inside of the human body became more and more sophisticated over time, and as diagnosis and treatment took on an increasingly abstract quality, the relationship of the patient to the wider environment of the hospital was likewise abstracted. The connection to the outside diminished and the focus was on finding the most scientifically efficacious ways to understand and treat disease. As such, the individual body of the patient and the natural or normative conception of a salubrious environment lost traction. The operation of the hospital thus became much more machine-like in this period, as complex medical machinery also proliferated.

More sophisticated ways of looking inside the body developed. CT (computed tomography) scans made many X-ray images taken from different

124 *Treating outside, looking inside*

angles to produce cross-sectional images of a body or parts thereof, in effect taking slices through the body, which enabled the viewer to see completely inside the body without actually cutting into it. The principle had been understood and explored as early as the early 1900s, but it was not until 1971 that the first commercially viable scanner using X-ray technology, invented by British electrical engineer Godfrey Hounsfield (1919–2004) in collaboration with South African-American physicist Allan Cormack (1924–1998), became available. It was installed at Atkinson Morley Hospital in Wimbledon, England, where the first successful scan of a cerebral cyst took place. In spatial terms, the surrounding room was not of architectural note – there was an observation room and a room for the scanner and patient – but the machine or scanner was important (Figure 5.12). By 1975, a whole-body scanner had been constructed by Hounsfield, a prototype of what is commonly used today, whereby the whole body, laid horizontal, passes through an X-ray generator that rotates and takes multiple X-rays to form a complete two-dimensional and now, more commonly, a three-dimensional image. This was diagnosis at its most sophisticated, but

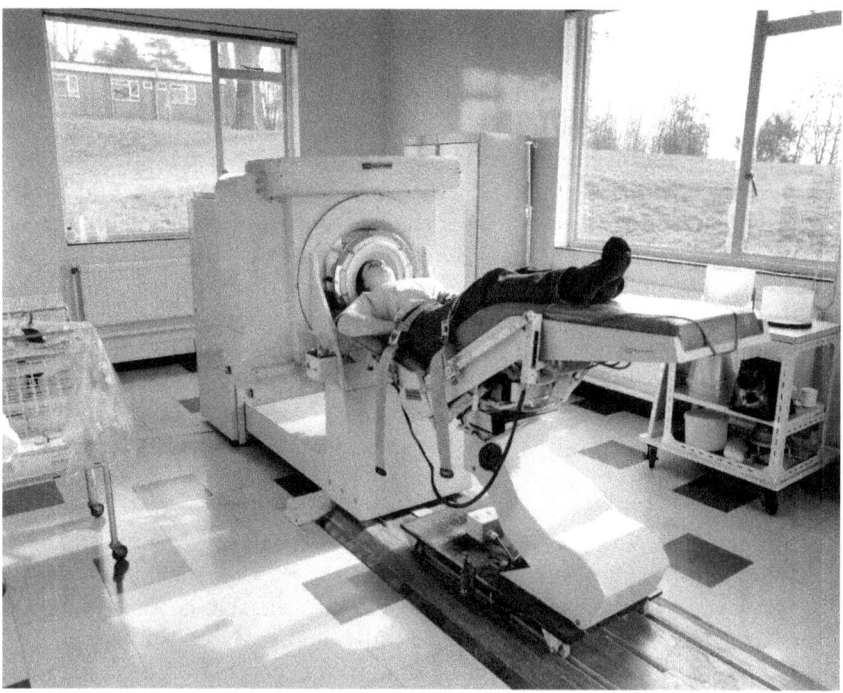

Figure 5.12 CT brain scanner of 1970–1971 in use at Atkinson Morley Hospital, Wimbledon, England. Photograph: unknown, 1980.

Courtesy: SSPL via Getty Images.

it also presaged the idea of preventative medicine. The CT scan (also known as a CAT scan) could be used for screening purposes, to detect coronary artery disease and tumours, instead of the vicarious danger of deadly incision that looking inside the body once had, there was the risk of high-level and too frequent radiation doses. As CT scans can employ a dose 100–1,000 times higher than conventional X-rays, the risk of such scans leading to cancer was much greater.

While CT or CAT scans use harmful X-rays, MRI (magnetic resonance imaging), discovered in 1971, does not. MRI uses magnetic fields, radio waves and field gradients to generate images that essentially map the location of water and fat in the body, and is primarily used for diagnosis. The machine, if large enough, is like a giant tube into which the horizontal body is moved, and it has little spatial implications for the hospital other than need for a room and considerable financial outlay to buy the equipment.

The technology of looking inside was not only for diagnosis and screening for disease and tumours. Perhaps one of the oldest technologies to "see inside" was that used to determine life inside the body itself – in the womb – by listening. And unlike X-rays, the key reason behind its science was that absolutely no harm should be extended to the body being examined. The medical use of diagnostic sonography is another imaging technique using ultrasound waves. It was first used on the human body for medical purposes in the late 1940s, but it was in the early 1960s that Scottish obstetrician Professor Stuart Campbell (b. 1936) pioneered research into the use of ultrasound and obstetrics. The ultrasound uses sound waves with frequencies that humans cannot hear, hence it is markedly more effective than placing one's own ear against the stomach of a pregnant woman. Combined with imaging, a picture of the state of an unborn baby can be detected with the benefit of it being a non-destructive, non-invasive process. The ultrasound is also low-cost and portable. Instead of needing a special room and hugely expensive equipment, the ultrasound and its imaging technology could be brought to the bedside. The hand-held sensor and the digital image had become the "eye" of the doctor or the nurse.

Expertise on the inside and outside

As the ethos of saving lives with science consolidated, a new coterie of paramedical professionals emerged who were able to look inside and outside the body with increasing expertise. As Reiser has noted (Reiser 1978), this increase in medical specialism had been apparent as early as 1900 to Baltimore doctor, William Osler, who had declared of diagnostic and ward laboratories, for example: "They are essential to the proper equipment of the hospital as are the interns. They are to the physician just as the knife and scalpel are to the surgeon" (Osler 1900: 230).

As the "pursuit of a laboratory-based scientific medicine" (Reiser 1978: 141) increased, it was recognised in the United States that all these facilities should be housed under the one roof; that is, a cooperative model of practice that offered an integrated medical service was needed (Reiser 1978). The solution was that the modern hospital should grow and expand its role and scale to encompass all these functions.

Such functions meant new personnel who required laboratory, work and treatment spaces in the modern hospital, which by the early 1960s had made the spatial needs of the modern hospital more complex. On the one hand, X-rays and other imaging techniques led to increased diagnostic accuracy, which, along with preventative screening, meant a patient's time in a hospital bed was reduced. On the other hand, the associated equipment meant specialist spaces were needed within the modern hospital for diagnosis and therapy. The equipment was often very expensive, with high operating and servicing costs, and it required specialist staff to operate and interpret data. In many respects, the expertise of the individual doctor, gained through study and experience, was outsourced to empirically based machines of diagnosis and therapy and the new teams of medical professionals that operated them. The eye, ear and hand of one was replaced by machines and many people – indeed, whole departments.

In 1930, the *Gläserner Mensch* or Transparent Man had made the body explicit for all to see; by the early 1960s, that body could be seen reduced to the thinness of a two-dimensional negative. In a sense, space and the body as a three-dimensional phenomenon or object had been condensed into an image on film or on screen. At the same time, many therapies external to the body – including physiotherapy, occupational therapy and hydrotherapy – remained valid and continued to be used. With the new techniques for looking inside and outside the human body, the significance of the ward and the hospital bed became more acute. As diagnosis became increasingly accurate and exacting, how to determine if a patient was to be allocated a bed became more significant. Pressure increased on hospitals to provide bed space only to those most in need. The modern hospital had changed its overall mission. Now, it was not just a place where the patient should be healed with the utmost efficiency – it had become a place of diagnosis, to take place with equal efficiency and, importantly, new scientific precision.

Note

1 The Haldane equipment was named after Scottish physiologist John Scott Haldane (1860–1936), who advanced the therapeutic administration of oxygen in a series of important papers from 1916 to 1917 and invented the gas mask.

References

"Balm for the Burned." *Modern Hospital* 48, no. 2 (February 1937): 56–7.
Buerki, R.C. "Enhancing the Hospital's Service by a Photographic Unit." *Modern Hospital* 39, no. 1 (July 1932): 85.

Butler, Charles and Addison Erdman. *Hospital Planning*. New York: F.W. Dodge Corporation, 1946.
Campbell, Margaret. "What Tuberculosis Did for Modernism: The Influence of a Curative Environment on Modernist Design and Architecture." *Medical History* 49, no. 4 (October 2005): 463–88.
Cohen, Solomon Solis (ed.). *A System of Physiologic Therapeutics*. Philadelphia: P. Blakiston's Son & Co., 1904.
Davis, Audrey B. *Medicine and Its Technology: An Introduction to the History of Medical Instrumentation*. Westport, CN: Greenwood Press, 1981.
Dickinson, Eveline. "The Finsen Light Treatment for Lupus." *American Journal of Nursing* 2, no. 9 (June 1902): 658–60.
Dreher, Carl. "The Weirdest Danger in the World." *Popular Science* 146, no. 4 (October 1946): 86–90.
Eastman Kodak Company. "Advertisement for Eastman Kodak Company Medical Division." *Modern Hospital* 43, no. 3 (September 1934): 103.
Erikson, Carl A. "Problems the Architect Overcame." *Modern Hospital* 46, no. 4 (April 1936): 64.
Eveready National Carbon Company Inc. "Advertisement for Carbon Arc Solarium Units." *Modern Hospital* 38, no. 1 (January 1932): 117.
"Fundamentals in Design for Physical Therapy." *Modern Hospital* 50, no. 3 (March 1938): 65.
Grainge, C. "Breath of Life: The Evolution of Oxygen Therapy." *Journal of the Royal Society of Medicine* 97, no. 10 (October 2004): 489–93.
Howell, Joel D. *Technology in the Hospital: Transforming Patient Care in the Early Twentieth Century*. Baltimore: Johns Hopkins University Press, 1995.
Kodak (Asia) Pty Ltd. "Advertisement for Kodak (Asia) Pty Ltd." *Hospital Magazine* (November 1939).
Mogensen, Margit. "New Technology for Social Health: The Finsen Lamp at the World Exhibition in Paris 1900." *Icon* 7 (2001): 35–48.
Moretti, B. Franco. *Ospedali*. Milan: Editore Ulrico Hoepli, 1951.
Munger, C.W. "Preventing Oxygen Starvation by New Portable Equipment." *Modern Hospital* 37, no. 6 (December 1931): 140–4.
Osler, William. "Discussion of M.H. Fussell's 'Blood Examination: Its Value to the General Practitioner'." *Journal of the American Medical Association* 35, no. 4 (28 July 1900): 230.
Priestley, Joseph. *Experiments and Observations on Different Kinds of Air*. London: J. Johnson, 1775.
"Pioneer in X-Ray Therapy." *Science* 125, no. 3236 (4 January 1957): 18–19.
Reiser, Stanley Joel. *Medicine and the Reign of Technology*. Cambridge and New York: Cambridge University Press, 1978.
Rendich, R.A. and C.B. Braestrup. "Housing the Expanding X-Ray Department." In *The Hospital Yearbook* (19th edition). Chicago: Modern Hospital Publishing Company, 1941.
Rollier, A. *Heliotherapy*. London: Henry Frowde and Hodder & Stoughton, 1923.
Rosenfield, Isadore. *Hospitals: Integrated Design*. New York: Reinhold Publishing Corporation, 1947.
Schwartz, R. Plato. "Supplying the Equivalent of Sunlight for Treating Chronic Diseases." *Modern Hospital* 28, no. 3 (March 1927): 162–8.

Schwarz, Theodore E. "Biological Photography as a Hospital Service." *Modern Hospital* 43, no. 5 (November 1934): 94–100.
Sekula, Allan. "The Body and the Archive." *October* 39 (Winter 1986): 3–64.
Soroka, Marina. "Therapy versus Pleasure." In Marina Soroka, *The Summer Capitals of Europe, 1814–1919*. London: Routledge, 2017.
Stevens, Edward F. *The American Hospital of the Twentieth Century*. New York: Architectural Record Publishing Company, 1918.
"The Story of X-Rays: Ridiculed First." *Hospital Magazine* (December 1938): 16.
Teasdale, Elvin A. "X-Ray Technology: Its Photographic Basis." *Hospital Magazine* (March 1941): 10.
"Then and Now: Hospital's Pathological: Radiological and Radiotherapy Development." *Hospital Magazine* (January 1941): 12–15.
Vogel, Klaus. "The Transparent Man: Some Comments on the History of a Symbol." In *Manifesting Medicine: Bodies and Machines*, edited by Robert Bud, Bernard Finn and Helmut Trischler, 31–61. Amsterdam: Harwood Academic, 1999.
Weatherwax, J.L. "Is Your X-Ray Machine Efficient?" *Modern Hospital* 29, no. 1 (July 1927): 52.
Wilk, Christopher. "The Healthy Body Culture." In *Modernism, 1914–1939: Designing a New World*, edited by Christopher Wilk. South Kensington: V&A Publications, 2006.

6 Full steam ahead! Servicing the modern hospital

In November 1932, American consulting engineer Alfred Kellogg contributed an article on hospital heating systems to *Architectural Forum*. The piece, titled "Arteries, Veins, Nerves", was accompanied by an evocative image of a seemingly endless subterranean tunnel lined with pipes to the side and above (Kellogg 1932) (Figure 6.1). The analogy Kellogg drew between the workings of the modern hospital and the human body was striking, although he was not the only person to make it during this period. In his 1947 book, *Hospitals: Integrated Design*, American architect Isadore Rosenfield (1893–1980) proposed: "Like internal human organs, the mechanical plant of a building is not visible from the outside, yet it is all important to proper functioning" (Rosenfield 1947: 270). But this evocative analogy between body and hospital tells only half the story of servicing the modern hospital. It was certainly true that the mechanical workings of the modern hospital were, and still are, largely hidden from view, but the modern hospital, as it developed in the 1920s and 1930s, also saw the expressive elements of servicing become powerful motifs demonstrating industrial efficiency and technical proficiency. Massive boiler houses with tall chimneys, entire buildings devoted to hospital laundry and sophisticated delivery ramp systems were strikingly visible and indicated, psychologically and technologically, that the message was "full steam ahead".

The modern hospital relied as much on its mechanical services and capacity for efficiency as it did on the new frontiers of medicine and therapeutic treatment. Indeed, from the eighteenth century as hospitals developed into large-scale building types, they became dependent on central heating and forced ventilation being successfully provided to, first, specific areas and, ultimately, the whole building. As Robert Bruegmann has written, enclosing and servicing an interior atmosphere, especially in a hospital, became a key task of the architect and, increasingly, the responsibility of a newly developed specialist in the building field, the mechanical engineer (Bruegmann 1978). In 1935, Edward F. Stevens (1860–1946) identified "three of the invisible but no less important engineering problems" faced by hospital designers: sound absorption, insulation and heat and air control. He emphasised that all the best planning in the world would be to no avail

130 *Servicing the modern hospital*

Figure 6.1 "Arteries, veins and nerves", opening photograph to the article, "Hospital Heating Systems" by Alfred Kellogg, in *Architectural Forum*. Photograph: Woodhead, c. 1932.
Source: *Architectural Forum* 57, no. 11 (November 1932): 450.

"if the patient is disturbed by the unnecessary noises without and within, or if he suffers the discomfort of uncontrolled heat in summer and lack of humidity in winter" (Stevens 1935: 104).

Large hospitals were often run by government or charitable institutions, but in effect they were large, multifunctional businesses that relied on and demanded the greatest financial and material efficiency so maximum effort could be focused on treating patients and optimising their comfort. Where possible, processes were centralised and mechanised, which supported efficiency along Taylorised lines. Each section contributed its particular expertise to the overall performance of the hospital, as though part of a production line. Reticulated services became intrinsic to the operation of the hospital and the experience of individual patients, and provision of essential services like pure oxygen piped to operating theatres and wards, and wired communication systems, became standard.

The industrial scale of North American hospitals, particularly those that rose as "skyscraper cities" on tight urban sites, coupled with a rapidly industrialising society that surrounded them, encouraged the centralisation of services. Large central boiler houses provided reticulated hot water and steam to the whole hospital complex, industrial dietetic kitchens provided meals and giant laundries provided clean and sterile linen. This central grouping of services enabled the efficient mechanical provision of light, heat, power, laundry, refrigeration and food services, with pipe runs and staff traffic kept to a minimum (Butler and Erdman 1946).

Efficiency was the basis for most arguments in favour of stacked pavilion wards, a form adopted in many hospitals in the 1880s and 1890s – perhaps most famously at the Johns Hopkins Hospital in Baltimore, Maryland, USA (1876–1885) (Thompson and Goldin 1975). The rationale for stacking wards was to decrease the distance between wards without also decreasing patient separation. The vast sites previously required by hospitals to accommodate multiple single-storey pavilion wards could be reduced if wards were stacked one on top of another, and economies could also be achieved in terms of circulation space, ventilation, heating, cleaning and supervision. Such a design meant it was no longer necessary for each ward to have its own set of services for preparation, cleaning and storage. Previously, each ward had virtually been "a hospital in itself" (Thompson and Goldin 1975: 182), but stacking allowed the individual service areas, usually connected to one end of the ward, to be reduced in size and separated from the ward. Stacking also meant adequate ventilation, heat, steam, water and waste pipes could be provided more efficiently.

On constrained central city sites, mechanical services were often located in basements and sub-basements. Boiler rooms, sometimes located alongside the morgue, fuel supply or refrigeration, were placed directly beneath the kitchen and laundry. On larger sites, however, and for very large hospitals, many of these services were each housed in its own building or complex of buildings, separate from the main hospital building. This was due to a number of factors. As hospitals grew in scale and complexity, so too did the range of technical and mechanical services needed to support them. Advanced patient care in the 1920s and 1930s required surroundings that were quiet, odourless and clean. The mechanical means for achieving these aims were inevitably noisy, smelly and somewhat messy. Consequently, where possible, mechanical plant and equipment for major services were discreetly located to the rear and side boundaries of the hospital site, where truck and delivery access might be assured and where noise, smell and waste might be banished from sight and mind. Larger sites also enabled servicing that created noise, smell and waste to be visually and physically removed. In this sense the evolving modern hospital paralleled the planning and development of twentieth-century cities. They produced a growing amount of pollution and waste and required ever more intense servicing, but at the same time these elements were separated from daily life with increasing rigour.

Ventilation: open air or air conditioning?

The influence of Florence Nightingale and her fellow sanitarians in the mid-nineteenth century made the need for fresh air a mantra for hospital development and ushered in the era of the pavilion ward. Ventilation, through openable windows, ceiling vents and proprietary systems like Tobin Tubes, became essential for patient wards. But in the twentieth century, the guaranteed movement of air became a virtual science of design. As the century progressed, concerted efforts were made to increase the amount of floor area in the modern hospital where so-called conditioned air (that is, filtered, temperature-controlled and humidified air) was available. This was perceived as particularly necessary for isolation against infectious diseases, and in areas where surgery was performed, and cadavers and waste were treated. The risk of airborne infection from both without and within the hospital constituted an invisible battleground. Service spaces and containment were key weapons that complemented the surgeon's steady hand. Increased control over ventilation, air movement and air conditioning was integral to this battle. By the early 1950s, such control also had a definitive effect over the form and appearance of the modern hospital.

An interesting conundrum arose as the modern hospital developed in the first four decades of the twentieth century. On the one hand, the ability for beds to be wheeled directly out to balconies (and hence to fresh air) from an individual ward or hospital bedroom was seen as eminently desirable. In many hospitals, this led to the design of generously scaled sliding windows that could double as doorways. On the other hand, openings like these broke the seal that was needed for constant and consistent conditioned air to be delivered. As Gail Cooper has written, there was therefore "tension between the use of open windows or mechanical systems to provide ventilation" (Cooper 1998: 2). But by the 1950s and 1960s, the issue was resolved firmly in favour of conditioned air and almost every major new hospital building was designed and constructed to be hermetically sealed.

An important early development in controlling indoor temperature related not to cooling or heating, but to humidity. Human comfort depends largely on humidity levels, so early mechanical engineers saw the successful regulation of humidity as essential to creating an artificial indoor climate. One of the most important developments in this regard was achieved by New Jersey-born engineer Alfred R. Wolff (1859–1909), who in 1899 successfully combined cooling and dehumidification for the postgraduate dissecting room on the fifth floor of the Cornell Medical College building in New York City, New York, USA. Wolff employed a large ammonia-absorption refrigeration machine supplied by the Carbondale Machine Company, which had a cooling capacity equal to melting fifty tonnes of ice daily (Cooper 1998). The machine, located in the basement, cooled a brine solution contained in pipes that then made their way to the fifth floor. Fresh air was drawn in from above the roof through a cheesecloth filter by fans and forced across a vast arrangement of coils containing the brine solution in the building's attic. It was then blown into the dissecting room. The installation was not aimed primarily at comfort cooling but rather to help preserve cadavers during teaching. The system proved so successful that the college held a graduation ceremony there on one hot and humid day, leaving the door to the postgraduate dissecting room open for the 1,500 people in attendance (Cooper 1998).[1] The spatial implications of Wolff's system were critical. Substantial service space was needed, certainly above and almost always below critical floors where cooling and humidification were required. Over subsequent decades, the desire to control humidity and temperature, and also provide comfort cooling, increased to encompass a far greater area of the hospital. As Cooper emphasises, it was also critical when it was recognised that "both winter humidification and summer dehumidification – was an integral part of the modern heating and ventilation system" (Cooper 1998: 17).

Air conditioning was expensive, however, so uptake was initially slow and confined to areas considered a priority, such as operating theatres, dissecting rooms and morgues. In 1934, an early example of the installation of air conditioning in an operating department appeared in the new semi-private building of Mount Sinai Hospital, New York (Kisacky 2017). "Open air crusaders" (Cooper 1998: 64) and those interested in open-window ventilation did not always condone these technological developments – or indeed the concept of man-made weather that was enthusiastically championed by manufacturers and further developed by individual engineers such as Willis Carrier. A pervasive fear of tuberculosis, the major public health crisis of the early twentieth century in Europe, amplified this reticence about closed systems. In this context, air conditioning that could provide both ventilation and humidification became the goal.

In 1932–1933, American-French architect Paul Nelson (1895–1979) forecast a hermetically sealed envelope for the modern hospital in his unbuilt project for a Cité Hospitalière (Hospital Complex) at Lille, France (Nelson 1933). By 1935, American hospital designers had accepted it was almost inevitable that the hospital envelope of the future would be fully sealed. Edward F. Stevens argued it was "necessary that the use of windows for ventilation be abandoned" for comfortable conditions to be produced within an enclosure, on the grounds that a balanced and stable temperature of 68–71F (20–22C) could be maintained at a reduced cost. "This means that we have resorted to and depend entirely upon mechanical means for all air movements" (Stevens 1935: 105). A benefit of this, Stevens believed, was architects now only needed to consider architectural effect when positioning windows. They could be any size, and only needed to open for cleaning. For operating theatres, he stressed special conditions, especially that a relative humidity at 55 per cent or higher be maintained to limit the danger of sparks making contact with the explosive gases used for anaesthesia. By 1940, in the United States most operating theatres were air conditioned, but a completely air conditioned hospital was uncommon (Munger 1940). Even Stevens admitted that the air conditioning of an entire hospital was "impractical, unnecessary, and economically unsound" (Stevens 1940: 556). After World War II, Isadore Rosenfield noted that complete air conditioning was "slow in coming", but also implicitly indicated its arrival was now regarded as inevitable (Rosenfield 1947: 277). By this time, clearly, air conditioning was considered necessary for a wide range of specialised spaces within the hospital, including operating and delivery rooms, obstetric and paediatric spaces, and in the fluoroscopy and developing rooms of X-ray departments. But its complete acceptance was hindered by cost and clumsy design and fears that airborne bacteria might be recirculated persisted, although return ducts had been eliminated during the 1940s.

As air conditioning technology became more sophisticated, so too did the design of the glazed curtain wall high-rise office building, especially in the United States with such buildings as the United Nations Headquarters (1947–1952) in Manhattan, New York, USA. Contemporary hospital design followed suit and it was natural in many respects that a firm like Skidmore Owings & Merrill, expert in hermetically sealed high-rise office design with buildings like New York's Lever House (1952), should also transform the language of the postwar hospital, with servicing as a key driver. Skidmore Owings & Merrill's dramatic high-rise slab block design for the thousand-bed Fort Hamilton Veterans' Administration Hospital in Brooklyn, New York, USA (1947–1952) was a hybrid model with fully air conditioned operating rooms, recovery rooms and allergy rooms (all of which had fixed glass windows), while the wards and other spaces had openable double-hung sash windows. The hospital's heating and ventilating system was served by electrostatic air filters which delivered tempered outside air to rooms from corridor ceiling ducts and exhausted it by fans ("VA Hospital" 1952). By the late 1950s, Skidmore Owings & Merrill's Northwest Community Hospital (1957–1959) at Arlington Heights, Illinois, USA, had full air conditioning in all its core and service spaces. These were designed as a separate low-rise slab, with provision made for it to be included in the elevated and thickened slab ward block at a later

Servicing the modern hospital 135

time. The complete shift to a fully air conditioned high-rise hospital would become a reality in 1974 with the completion of the 25-storey Bellevue Hospital in Manhattan, New York, USA (Architects: Katz, Waisman, Blumenkranz, Stein & Weber with Pomerance & Breines, 1960–1974). In much the same way that office building planning had shifted from the glazed linear slab to the square planned tower, so too in hospital planning the provision of air conditioning allowed a "fattened" or "thickened" plan, where only the perimeter bed and ward rooms required natural light (Rosenfield 1969) (Figure 6.2). All other spaces and service rooms could rely on artificial light, and this was the case at Bellevue, where, as one historian of building technology has noted:

> supporting functions can be carried on as well if not better in artificial light, patients' rooms are arranged along outside walls, and supporting

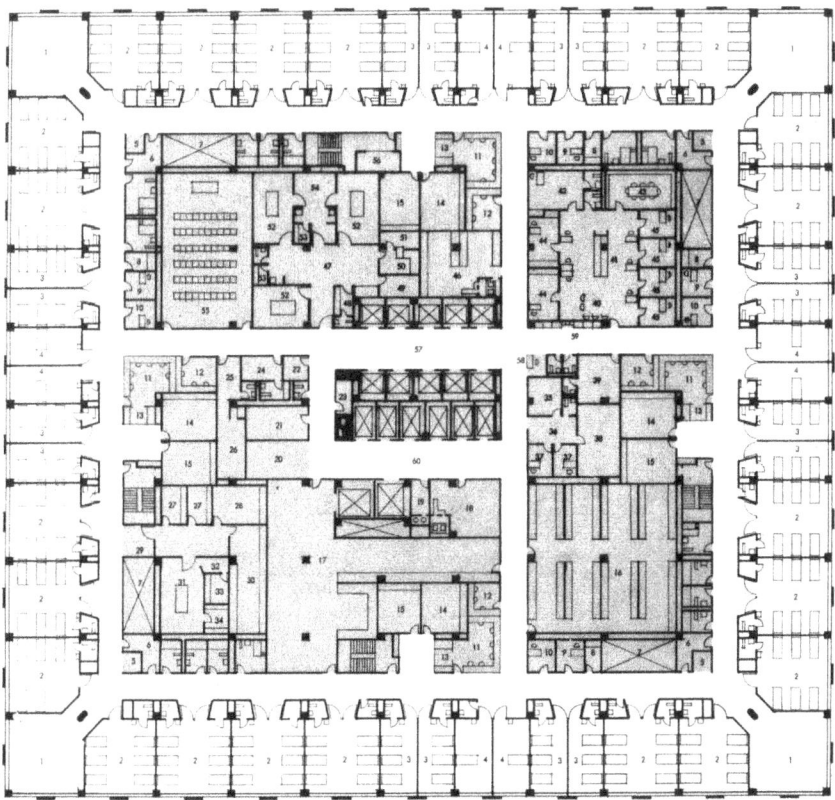

Figure 6.2 Plan of 15th floor, Bellevue Hospital, Manhattan, New York, USA. Architects: Katz, Waisman, Blumenkranz, Stein & Weber with Pomerance & Breines, 1960–1974. Delineator: unknown.
Source: Rosenfield, Isadore. *Hospital Architecture and Beyond.* New York: Van Nostrand Reinhold Company, 1969: 284.

services are located in the central areas of each floor. This deployment sets the need for complete air conditioning, and efficiency of the arrangement justifies the expense.

(Guedes 1979: 216)

North American developments were the global trendsetters in air conditioning the hospital, but other countries slowly took up the habit. In 1955, for example, research undertaken by the Nuffield Provincial Hospitals Trust and the University of Bristol, England, concluded: "Whereas natural ventilation is cheap, mechanical ventilation is costly and lacks flexibility" (Nuffield Provincial Hospitals Trust 1955: 124). The preference for natural ventilation for wards in particular was such that the report further declared: "In fact, mechanical systems are so expensive that they are rarely employed except in special circumstances as, for example, in wards where all the air must be filtered because of atmospheric pollution, or where sealed windows are needed to exclude noise". While it was generally accepted that air conditioning was essential in operating suites, British and European hospitals continued to favour natural ventilation or a hybrid model as late as the early 1960s.

Steam and heat: the boiler house

The completely controlled indoor environment was the ideal and came to be expected in the 1960s modern hospital, but the provision of hot water and high-pressure steam was another essential part of the modern hospital's early twentieth-century story. Hot water and steam was essential for ablution, heating, cooking, laundering, sterilisation and disinfection, all at required temperatures and pressures. Consistent supply was needed twenty-four hours a day, every day of the year. English architect Francis Lorne (1889–1963) indicated in 1933 that each hospital patient required some 900 litres of water each day, half of it hot water, for therapies, treatment and general hygiene (Lorne 1933). To maintain such large volumes of hot water and steam at the required temperature, it was crucial that the length of the pipes to the supply point be kept to a minimum. The boiler house was generally located with other plants for the hospital, which might include generators and air handling and conditioning machinery. This plant could be contained in the main block of the hospital, or, increasingly, in a separate but nearby building.

By 1952, mechanical servicing of the modern hospital had become sophisticated and expensive. The cost of the mechanical and electrical equipment of a hospital alone was approximately one-third the total cost of the building (Rauch 1952), and the subsequent cost of operating and maintaining this equipment was greater than for all other parts of the building. Keeping the systems simple was therefore paramount.

Heating, steam supply and ventilating systems were all closely related to each other, both physically and in functional relationship to the various departments of the hospital. For larger hospitals, as already noted, boiler rooms and laundries were located in separate buildings near the hospital but away from patients' bedrooms. Steam and water pipes could then be run either visibly or in covered conduits or tunnels, which might also double as passages for laundry trucks. But costs dictated that these essential services could not be too distant. How the hospital site was zoned to manage these various requirements was thus of crucial importance. A central position might be desirable, but the potential noise, vibration and exhausts of such plants needed serious consideration if an appropriate environment for patients and staff, conducive to health and healing, was to be maintained. Plants were also large, typically housing at least two, if not more, boiler units (in case one failed) plus associated machinery, pumps and pipes. At least one of these boilers had to be a high-pressure type. Large chimneys were often used to exhaust the boilers, and the prevailing winds needed to be considered when siting the boiler house to ensure smoke and steam blew away from the hospital buildings, not into them.

Thus, boiler houses were usually distinct units within the hospital complex, allowing for acoustic separation, but closely connected to reduce reticulated travel distance, and easily identified by their tall chimneys. In 1936, *Modern Hospital* declared "Power Plants Need Not be Eyesores" and illustrated five examples, claiming that Stevens & Lee's boiler house at Springfield Hospital in Springfield, Massachusetts, USA, "adds much beauty to the whole hospital layout" ("Power Plants Need Not be Eyesores" 1936: 72). It is undeniable that power plants have been celebrated in architecture, and that designers revel in their functional monumentality. Witness the physical importance and monumental rendition of the power plant for Coolidge, Shepley, Bulfinch & Abbott's New York Hospital–Cornell Medical Center, Manhattan, New York, USA (1932) (Figure 6.3), which in scale and sheer capacity might be matched against architecturally feted structures such as Battersea Power Station, Battersea, England (1933) or even Mies van der Rohe's Boiler House at Illinois Institute of Technology in Chicago, Illinois, USA (1945–1950). Its skyscraper form, entirely separate from the main hospital building, constituted a whole city block and contained boiler room, laundry, dynamo room, garage and workshops (Figure 6.4).

By 1946, according to Butler and Erdman, there were generally four principal methods of heating a hospital: hot water radiators, steam, hot air and radiant panel heating (Butler and Erdman 1946). Despite the general need for steam throughout the hospital, the preferred medium for heating in hospitals was pumped hot water, which was more comfortable than steam heating and, when used in radiators, not overly expensive. Hot water pipes embedded into concrete slab floors, ceilings and walls, which then acted as radiant panels, then became the favoured, if more expensive, medium for delivering safe and gentle heat.

Figure 6.3 Rendering for the power plant for the New York Hospital–Cornell Medical Center, Manhattan, New York, USA. Architects: Coolidge, Shepley, Bulfinch & Abbott, 1932. Rendering: Dadmun Company, c. 1932.

Courtesy: Medical Center Archives of New York–Presbyterian/Weill Cornell.

Figure 6.4 The interior of the power plant, New York Hospital–Cornell Medical Center, Manhattan, New York, USA. Architects: Coolidge, Shepley, Bulfinch & Abbott, 1932. Photograph: Edward Beckwith, c. 1930s.
Courtesy: Medical Center Archives of New York–Presbyterian/Weill Cornell.

Internally, supply of hot water and steam had spatial implications. Increased servicing, whether through heating or air conditioning, meant an increased thickening of the space between the ceiling and the floor above. If the hospital's "internal organs" were to be concealed, it meant a corresponding fattening of the hospital's "limbs". As a result, a new form of laminar building section emerged, horizontally and vertically. The plan also thickened to allow for increased servicing, with vertical duct risers needed as well as stairs and elevators.

Laundry: the passage of a sheet

As demands for hygiene increased, the laundry became one of the most important spaces contained within the hospital complex. The best equipment, lighting and ventilation were sought to achieve operational efficiency, and great effort was taken to ensure that there were no "insidious leaks" from uncovered steam pipes, joints, poor window sealing, dirty light bulbs or faulty valves – primarily for cost reasons (Munger 1927: 146). The highly mechanised hospital laundry was critical to the efficient running of the overall organism that was the modern hospital. In 1931, *Modern Hospital* declared: "Linen is one of the hospital's most important tools. Its successful handling is 10 per cent laundry and 90 per cent linen control". At the Children's Memorial Hospital in Chicago, Illinois, USA the new laundry and linen service established in 1931 meant nurses no longer had to make requisitions or count soiled linen, and "[t]heir time and energy are conserved for professional duties" ("A Linen Control System" 1931: 95). Labour was thus becoming increasingly specialised and divided; correspondingly, the spaces designed for such functions also took on specialised features.

An efficient modern hospital had to handle and deliver laundry effectively, and avoid criticism of the linen service from doctors and nurses. Most importantly, patients needed to be satisfied that their most intimate surroundings, the hospital bed, was untainted. Architecture and interiors might be extremely hygienic and even exude a sense of symbolic cleanliness, and the freshness of clean sheets and "fresh crisp uniforms" of hospital personnel complemented this. Immaculate laundry provided comfort to and inspired the confidence of patients, the public and staff (Studebaker 1949).

But achieving this ideal was not simple. In 1949, Glenn R. Studebaker of the US Public Health Service (USPHS) hospital facilities division estimated that the average amount of patient linen circulating was a minimum of four times that actually in use at any one time (Studebaker 1949). This translated as being one set in use, one set at the laundry, one set available for immediate use and one for standby and emergency purposes. Added to this expected daily load of patient linen was another daily load from other sources such as the operating theatre, delivery room, outpatient department and emergency room, not to mention employees' uniforms and the bed and personal linen of nurses and resident doctors and students. As a result, calculating laundry weight became an exacting science based on the average weight of soiled linen per patient per day: a hundred-bed hospital, for example, might therefore generate approximately 2,400 pieces of laundry each day.

The spatial corollary of this demand was that hospitals had to choose whether to operate their own laundry or outsource the task. It was generally thought that it made economic and practical sense for hospitals with more than fifty beds to have an in-house laundry service. If this was the case, the size of the laundry plant was determined by how much flatwork – laundry that could be finished mechanically and didn't require hand ironing – needed to run through the laundry in a seven-hour day. How long it took a sheet to pass through the laundry process therefore became a determining factor in planning (Figure 6.5). Nurses changed patients' beds early in the morning but washing and drying was overseen by laundry staff. Soiled flatwork immediately went to the laundry and was sorted, then placed in washers. After this, it proceeded to tumble dryers, then moved to mechanical flatwork ironers and folders, then in to central linen storage, where

Servicing the modern hospital 141

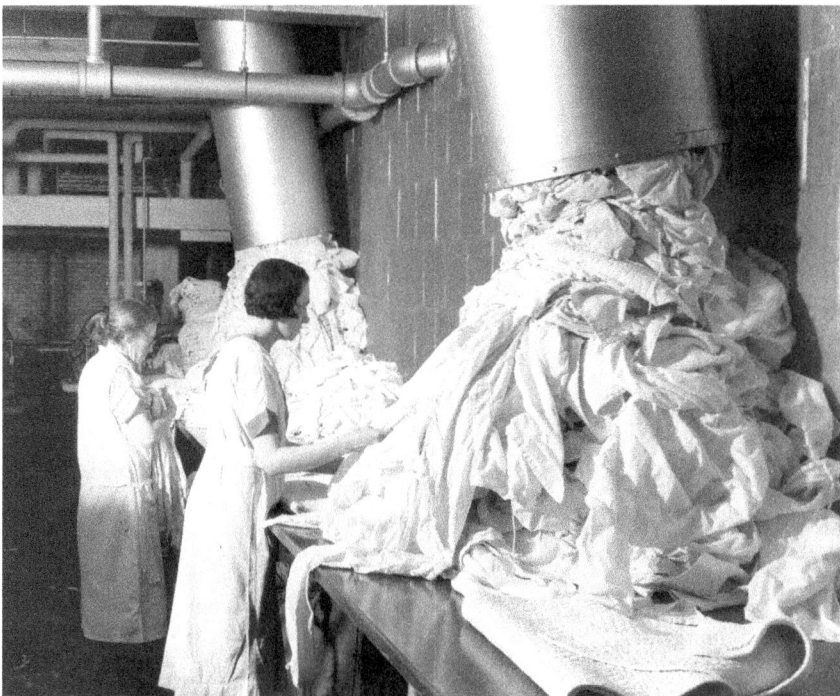

Figure 6.5 Creating order from chaos: workers hand-sort large volumes of linen in the busy in-house laundry and linen department, New York Hospital–Cornell Medical Center, Manhattan, New York, USA. Architects: Coolidge, Shepley, Bulfinch & Abbott, 1932. Photograph: Ewing Galloway, c. 1940s.
Courtesy: Medical Center Archives of New York–Presbyterian/Weill Cornell.

each sheet was sorted and classified like a book in a circulating library. From there, it was delivered back to a patient floor and the bed. This was a mechanised production line at its most sophisticated. The hospital laundry was a miniature factory, and its layout reflected this.

In 1954, the *Annual Report of The Royal Melbourne Hospital* was preceded by a ten-page cover story titled "The Story of a Sheet", which underlined the importance of the sheet to the hospital's operation (Figure 6.6):

> Perhaps you wonder how I, a mere sheet, merit such importance. Let me answer by asking a couple of questions: Can you imagine a hospital without sheets? Can you contemplate anything more comforting to someone who is ill than to be tucked in between a pair of snowy-white sheets?

142 *Servicing the modern hospital*

Figure 6.6 Cover image, "The Story of a Sheet". Artist: unknown.
Source: Royal Melbourne Hospital. "Annual Report, 1953–54". Melbourne: The Royal Melbourne Hospital, 1954: front cover.
Courtesy: The Royal Melbourne Hospital Archives.

But that is only one of my services to patients. Use is found for me in all sorts of ways in many departments of the Hospital. Maybe it will surprise you to learn that no fewer than 156,000 sheets are in use in one year at this Hospital.

So it is that my value rates high in the humanitarian service rendered to patients of The Royal Melbourne Hospital.

This then is the Story of a Sheet.

(Royal Melbourne Hospital 1954: 2)

What followed was a comprehensive photo essay documenting how a sheet was used in casualty, during examination, in the wards, in the operating theatre, during sterilisation and in recovery rooms and X-ray departments. It was also shown in the laundry being mended and washed, dried and pressed, and even being made. The point, clearly, was that even a humble item like a sheet played a key role in the functional and spatial life of the hospital.

Laundry spaces and separate ancillary buildings, as money afforded, were grouped with the boiler and pump room, maintenance shop and garage, with clear traffic routes for soiled and clean laundry to be ferried across the hospital complex. Essential were high ceilings, excellent sound and vibration proofing so the machinery would not disturb patients, dustproof floors and hard-surfaced walls painted for high reflectivity in cream, ivory or white. Floors were partially pitched to allow easy drainage if there were spillages. Window areas were as large as possible, to optimise light and natural ventilation. Ideally, the laundry interior should be a sparkling modernist exemplar. Huge glazed hoods were often installed over the flat-work ironers, and special attention was given to providing enough artificial lighting to maximise productivity, ensure better work quality and reduce the potential for accidents. Assisted extraction ventilation for the ironer, pressers, tumblers and washers removed vapour and heated air, and often a special exhaust equipped with a lint catcher extracted air from the tumbler dryer fans.

In most cases, hospitals had their own dedicated laundry. But in some places efforts were made to consolidate and rationalise laundry services. In postwar New York, for example, alternative laundry locations were proposed, one being for a central laundry to serve all the institutions on Welfare Island (Rosenfield 1947). The Central Laundry (completed 1954) was part of a group of buildings – laundry, fire station and garage – that was then connected by a vehicular ramp to Queensboro Bridge, serving ten hospitals across Welfare (now Roosevelt) and Manhattan islands.

Kitchen: service via the assembly line

A central kitchen was another key element of the efficiently managed modern hospital. In 1946, Butler and Erdman went so far as to state, "the location and layout of the kitchen and related services may become the balancing factor in the success or failure of an institution" (Butler and Erdman 1946: 197). In the same way modern hospital laundries were mechanised and industrialised, hospital kitchens grew to accommodate industrial-scale service that could match the capacity and output of a major hotel or ocean liner. Like the laundries, they became giant machines, which needed optimal positioning. The kitchen had to service not only patients in wards and private rooms, but often also the doctors' dining room, the nurses' cafeteria and the employees' cafeteria, the latter sometimes shared with the public. Kitchens were often placed in dark basements, but many hospital designers made great effort to bring natural light to such basements or, where possible, locate the main kitchen on the ground floor. This allowed lifts and dumbwaiters to be used to vertically service the hospital. Adequate light and air were essential, but so too was proximity to dining rooms, storage and delivery spaces, and elevators. There had to be "garages" for food carts, where they could be stored and cleaned, and also generous scullery spaces for washing dishes and storing the vast range of pots and pans used.

To meet these requirements spatially, hospital kitchens invariably had high ceilings, of one and a half- or double-height volumes, and were often top-lit. In many instances, giant suspended wired glass hoods sat over an orderly series of oven ranges and cooking vats, as in the central kitchen of Walter, Plousey & Cassan's Hôpital Beaujon (Beaujon Hospital) (1932–1935) in Paris, France (Figure 6.7). In an alternative arrangement commonly used in Italian hospitals, giant ventilation stacks, similar to those seen on ocean liners, rose from the floor – a technique also used in the central kitchen in Bohumiz Kozak's Foyers Masaryk (Masaryk Homes) in Prague, Czechoslovakia (1926–40) (Moretti 1951).

After World War II, US hospitals increasingly used frozen food. This was not just because frozen food retained vitamins and looked more appetising than fresh food that had been handled and then cooked, or because it cost slightly less than fresh food. Another key reason was that using frozen food led to considerable savings in waste elimination, time and, significantly, the space required for handling, storage and preparation (Butler and Erdman 1946). As a consequence, sophisticated refrigeration (ideally of the walk-in type) became vital if large modern hospital kitchens were to perform at their most effective. Other developments were aimed at increasing patient satisfaction with their food. Insulated or electrically heated trucks with separate hot and cold compartments were adopted, which saved serving space if tray trucks were used. Everything could be delivered at one time and placed on a tray. This system, in theory, enabled the whole meal to arrive at the patient's bedside at the same time and at the appropriate temperature.

The food service assembly line, like that of the laundry, was designed to be as short as possible. The analogy of the factory process line again came into play in the choice of surfaces and finishes, which had to endure the wear and tear of industrial-style production. Terrazzo or tiled floors, non-slip and impervious to wear, were often supplemented by depressed floors under cooking equipment to reduce the tripping and spilling that sometimes occurred with tile curbs. Glazed brick wainscots or salt-glazed tiles were frequently used, as they were considered more hardwearing

Figure 6.7 Central kitchen, Hôpital Beaujon (Beaujon Hospital), Clichy, Paris, France. Architects: Walter, Plousey & Cassan, 1932–1935. Photograph: unknown, c. 1938.
Courtesy: Archives A.P.-H.P., Structures hospitalières.

than regular ceramic tiles, and columns and wall corners were often protected with heavy bullnose iron guards. Even the main corridors leading from a kitchen sometimes had bumper rails or a stainless-steel wainscot. Acoustic insulation was as essential in hospital kitchens as it was in laundries. Indeed, the need to keep mechanical services in hospitals as quiet as possible was intrinsic to their design. The aim was to silence, as much as possible, the noise of production.

Supply, storage and waste

Efficient systems to store and supply varied implements and equipment were also essential to the modern hospital and were another area that underwent centralisation during this period. Sterile supplies and equipment included linen, dressings, gloves, instruments, syringes and so on, but there were also a great many unsterile supplies and equipment, as well as food, bedding, stationery, linen, clothing and cleaning products. From 1930s to the 1950s, hospitals often spoke of "central supply", and hospital administrators urged architects to provide adequate space for one central storeroom.

These areas were considerable, especially if refrigeration was needed. At the University of Michigan Hospital in Ann Arbor, Michigan, USA in 1934, a root cellar was constructed several years after the hospital had been occupied, to store a seven-month supply of potatoes and other tubers (Dick 1934). Such examples demonstrate the sheer scale of the hospital as an operating organism. In addition to the storage space, sophisticated filing and requisitioning systems were needed and, in larger hospitals, pneumatic tube systems for transporting requisitions. In 1933, British architect Francis Lorne bemoaned the lack of sufficient storage for wheelchairs, stretchers and trolleys in his lengthy article, "Errors in the Technical Equipment and Plant in the Hospital" that appeared in *Nosokomeion* (Lorne 1933). As the modern hospital became a completely networked system, storage became integral to its design.

How goods were delivered to and received by the hospital, and their circulation within it, also had special implications. Like a factory or a major city hotel, a modern hospital needed the capacity and means to transport items to various departments. In 1933, the University Hospitals of Cleveland, Ohio, USA, borrowed techniques from industry by using electrically driven trucks ("Large Hospital Finds Power Truck an Economical Investment" 1933). The hospital consisted of a number of detached buildings, but all were connected by a series of underground tunnels and passages. Before electric trucks, hand trucks were used for all deliveries, which made collecting and delivering soiled linen especially arduous as loads had to be pushed 800 metres up a slight incline. The solution, electric trucks that could be coupled to a train of up to eleven cars, offered considerable savings in effort and time. Similar savings were made in delivering prepared foods from the central kitchens to outlying units and the advent of electrically heated food tray trucks meant food could be kept warm by plugging these in before departure and again at the point of food distribution.

Among the spatial implications of internal mobile delivery were that modern hospital corridors had to be wide enough to take two-way traffic and elevators large enough to take one or more trucks, and the transport network to connect various departments, invariably located beneath the hospital, had to be as simple as possible. And motorised trucks were not just an American initiative. Similar vehicles were used in the Södersjukhuset (Southern Hospital), Stockholm, Sweden (Architects: Hjalmar Cederström and Hermann Imhauser, 1937–1944) and at the Basel Kantonsspital (Cantonal Hospital), Basel, Switzerland (Architect: H. Baur, E. & P. Vischer and Bräuning Leu Dürig, 1939–45). At the Hôpital Beaujon (Beaujon Hospital) in Clichy, France (Architect: Walter, Plousey & Cassan, 1932–1935), motorised trucks were also used to tow what looked like white caravans, but were in fact mobile containers for dead bodies already laid onto a flat stainless-steel gurney ready for discreet travel to the morgue (Figures 6.8 and 6.9).

Of course, the dead and the recuperated patient were not the only products of the hospitals. Modern hospitals also produced an enormous volume of waste. US estimates in the 1950s suggested that each individual in the hospital generated several pounds of refuse per day (US Department of Health, Education and Welfare 1953). To deal with these quantities, many large modern hospitals had their own garbage and refuse incinerators, either as separate structures or in or near the boiler room. For health reasons, it was essential that refuse from the hospital was disposed of swiftly, as in addition to regular garbage it might include items such as infected dressings, discarded surgical specimens and food scraps from patients' dishes, all of which were capable of carrying infection. Reducing offensive odours was also a priority: in more sophisticated and larger hospitals, garbage was sometimes stored in an adjacent cold room over weekends, before being incinerated.

Hospital planners and managers regarded incineration as an efficient and safe method of waste disposal. A specialised field arose in designing incinerators that might minimise odour and smoke, and in 1953, the US Department of Health, Education and Welfare recommended George C. Dunham's *Military Preventative Medicine* (1930, republished 1938, 1940) as a suitable reference text (US Department of Health, Education and Welfare 1953). The boiler room's smokestack was sometimes used for the incinerator, but

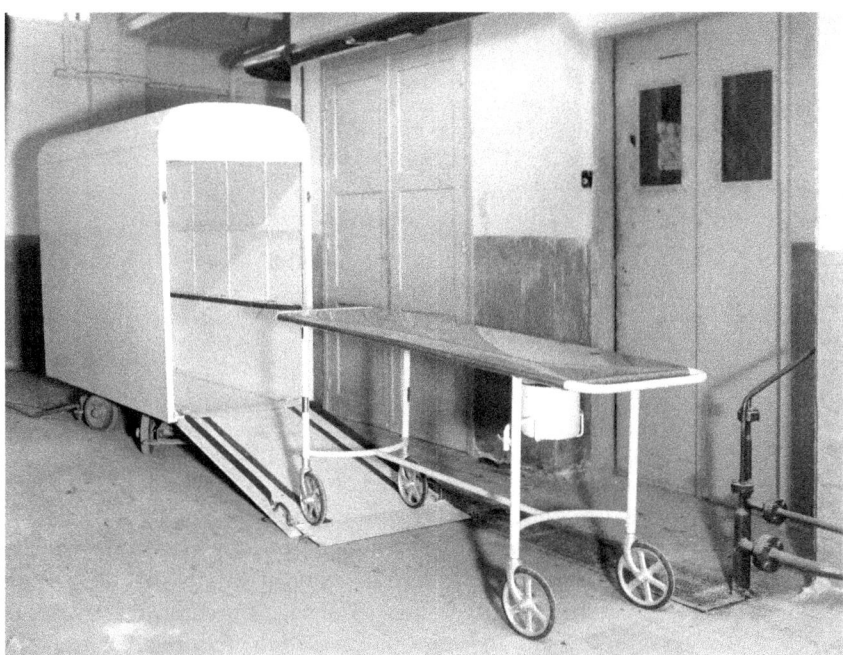

Figure 6.8 Morgue caravan and gurney, Hôpital Beaujon (Beaujon Hospital), Clichy, Paris, France. Architects: Walter, Plousey & Cassan, 1932–1935. Photograph: unknown, c. 1938.

Courtesy: Archives A.P.-H.P., Structures hospitalières.

148 *Servicing the modern hospital*

Figure 6.9 Morgue caravan being towed through the hospital grounds, Hôpital Beaujon (Beaujon Hospital), Clichy, Paris, France. Architects: Walter, Plousey & Cassan, 1932–1935. Photograph: unknown, c. 1938.
Courtesy: Archives A.P.-H.P., Structures hospitalières.

in other instances there were two chimneys, adding visual emphasis to the idea of the hospital as a "factory for healing".

Flexible services: designing for change

During the 1950s, hospitals became larger and ever more sophisticated in their servicing, and were increasingly fully air conditioned and externally sealed. As the cost of servicing these behemoths of efficiency mounted, questions began to arise about where such development might end. Hospital expansion and servicing upgrades became part of the everyday business and operation of the hospital. Was there a way in which hospital design might become predictive of change? And would it be possible to reimagine hospital architecture, so the standard aspiration of the modern hospital – to conceal its servicing beneath its hygienic skin – was replaced by a different ideal? To a degree, this question remains unanswered. But in Canada, one radical solution was proposed and constructed in the 1960s.

Craig, Zeidler & Strong's Health Sciences Centre at McMaster University in Hamilton, Ontario, was designed in 1967 and completed in 1972.

It was one of the first hospitals to be designed to be able to be expanded and reconfigured as needs and hospital technologies changed. It was based around an exposed and expandable steel megastructure contained within glass towers, which also contained stairwells, and was one of the first hospitals to be designed so the wiring, pipes and conduits of its mechanical systems ran between the floors in hidden "interstitial" space (Figure 6.10). There were no interior load bearing walls, which allowed vast expanses of open interior space clear spans of approximately 21 metres – to be planned and changed at will (Zeidler 1974). There was even provision for a fifth floor to be added on the roof that would bring an extra 18,500 square metres of space.

Zeidler's 1960s scheme at McMaster University bears comparison with Paul Nelson's project for the Cité Hospitalière at Lille. Nelson had envisaged a completely flexible, large-scale campus plan, its radical form based largely on a huge, fully air conditioned and hermetically sealed podium. Belgian doctor René Sand, then president of the International Hospital Association, appraised Nelson's design in January 1933, writing:

> The economy of upkeep, time and money represented by your plan is truly remarkable. No less praise is due to its flexibility which will enable any change in the premises, or the use to which they are put, to be effected with the minimum of cost.
>
> The synthesis and technique which you have evolved represent a great step forward for the hospital world.
>
> (Nelson 1933)

Alfred Kellog's 1932 analogy of the hospital as a body with head, trunk and limbs with hidden services had been replaced at McMaster University by a body with hidden services that might grow in all directions. Further, if the

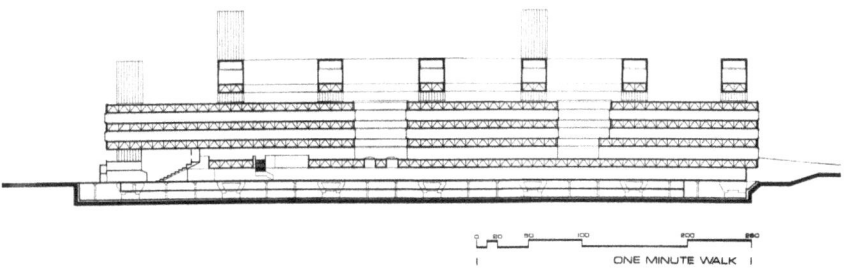

Figure 6.10 Sectional drawing, McMaster University Health Sciences Centre, Hamilton, Ontario, Canada. Architects: Craig, Zeidler & Strong, 1967–1972. Delineator: unknown.

Source: Eberhard Zeidler, *Healing the hospital: McMaster Health Science Centre, its conception and evolution*. The Zeidler Partnership, Toronto, 1974: 33.

design and layout of those service functions like the boiler room, laundry and kitchen had long resembled the spaces of the factory, the entire external image of the hospital had now been transformed by its inner workings. The notion of a completely networked system accompanied by floors of flexible "universal space" that might define the modern hospital was a challenge to prior preconceptions of what a hospital ought to look like. Was the modern hospital a civic landmark? Was it a beacon of modernism? Or, was it, as at McMaster, a neutral but contingent expression of a completely organic machine that might change at will with the individual needs of any given hospital and possess an ability to cope with any unforeseen developments in medical technology and servicing?

By the late 1960s, what constituted an image of progress for the modern hospital had largely been transformed by its inner workings and, for the most part, had thwarted a constant image for the postwar hospital. A state of ongoing physical change, one of ever more alterations and additions, was the new normalcy. It was a far, far cry from the obvious visual markers of an architectural language that had once crowed: "Full steam ahead!"

Note

1 Wolff used his experiences at the Cornell Medical College later in his improved and extended installations at numerous other significant New York buildings such as the New York Stock Exchange (1904), College of the City of New York (1905), Mutual Benefit Life Insurance Company (1906) and the Cleveland Trust Company (1907).

References

Bruegmann, Robert. "Central Heating and Forced Ventilation: Origins and Effects on Architectural Design." *Journal of the Society of Architectural Historians* 37, no. 3 (October 1978): 143–60.
Butler, Charles and Addison Erdman. *Hospital Planning*. New York: F.W. Dodge Corporation, 1946.
Cooper, Gail. *Air-Conditioning America: Engineers and the Controlled Environment, 1900–1960*. Baltimore: Johns Hopkins University Press, 1998.
Dick, F.H. "A Central Storeroom: How Organized and Operated." *Modern Hospital* 43, no. 4 (October 1934): 104.
Dunham, George C. "Military Preventative Medicine." *Army Medical Bulletin* 23 (1930). Carlisle Barracks, PA: US Army Medical Field Service School.
Guedes, Pedro (ed.). *The Macmillan Encyclopaedia of Architecture and Technological Change*. London: Palgrave Macmillan, 1979.
Kellogg, Alfred. "Hospital Heating Systems." *Architectural Forum* (November 1932): 450–70.
Kisacky, Jeanne. *Rise of the Modern Hospital: An Architectural of Health and Healing, 1870–1940*. Pittsburgh: University of Pittsburgh Press, 2017.
"Large Hospital Finds Power Truck an Economical Investment." *Modern Hospital* 41, no. 3 (September 1933): 116.

"A Linen Control System That Saves Time and Money." *Modern Hospital* 37, no. 6 (December 1931): 95.

Lorne, Francis. "Errors in the Technical Equipment and Plant in the Hospital." *Nosokomeion* 4, no. 3 (1933): 522–38.

Moretti, B. Franco. *Ospedali*. Milan: Editore Ulrico Hoepli, 1951.

Munger, Claude W. "Hospital Equipment and Operation, with Special Reference to Laundry, Kitchen and Housekeeping Problems." *Modern Hospital* 29, no. 3 (September 1927): 146.

Munger, Claude W. "New Trends in Hospital Plans and Equipment: Discussion." *Transactions of the American Hospital Association* 42 (1940): 559.

Nelson, Paul. *Cité Hospitalière de Lille*. Paris: Editions Cahiers D'art, 1933.

Nuffield Provincial Hospitals Trust. *Studies in the Functions and Design of Hospitals, the Report of an Investigation Sponsored by the Nuffield Provincial Hospitals Trust and the University of Bristol*. London: Oxford University Press, 1955.

"Power Plants Need Not Be Eyesores." *Modern Hospital* 47, no. 2 (August 1936): 72–3.

Rauch, Maynard. *Heating and Ventilating in the General Hospital*. Washington, DC: US Department of Health, Education and Welfare, Public Health Service, Division of Hospital Facilities, 1952.

Rosenfield, Isadore. *Hospitals: Integrated Design*. New York: Reinhold Publishing Corporation, 1947.

Rosenfield, Isadore. *Hospital Architecture and Beyond*. New York: Van Nostrand Reinhold Co, 1969.

Royal Melbourne Hospital. *1953–54 Annual Report of the Royal Melbourne Hospital*. Melbourne: Royal Melbourne Hospital, 1954.

Stevens, Edward F. "Sound Absorption, Insulation and Air Conditioning of the Modern Hospital." *Nosokomeion* 4, no. 1–2 (1935): 104.

Stevens, Edward F. "New Trends in Hospital Plans and Equipment: Discussion." *Transactions of the American Hospital Association* 42 (1940): 556.

Studebaker, Glenn R. "Planning the Hospital Laundry." *Modern Hospital* 73, no. 5 (November 1949): 118–22.

Thompson, John D. and Grace Goldin. *The Hospital: A Social and Architectural History*. New Haven, CT: Yale University Press, 1975.

US Department of Health, Education and Welfare, Public Health Service. *Design and Construction of General Hospitals*. New York: F.W. Dodge Corporation, 1953.

"VA Hospital: Brooklyn, New York." *Progressive Architecture* 33, no. 7 (July 1952): 63–74.

Zeidler, Eberhard H. *Healing the Hospital: McMaster Health Science Centre: Its Conception and Evolution*. Toronto: Zeidler Partnership, 1974.

7 Health, hygiene and progress
Designing the hospital of tomorrow

The project of the modern hospital reached a defining moment between the early 1930s and the mid-1940s. The cumulative influences of modernisation on how the comprehensive hospital was programmed, planned and serviced were gradually brought together with the political, social and aesthetic aspirations of modernist architecture. Modernisation and modernism coalesced. A group of hospitals in Europe and Australia, designed by the leading international experts in this period, exemplified the synthesis of the various themes of the interwar decades. These hospitals, located in Switzerland, Australia, Sweden and France, brought a resolved aesthetic sophistication to the complexity of the modern hospital. Health, hygiene and progress were given a visible and identifiably modern image.

The reasons why a specific aesthetic aligned with the specialised and diverse functions of the modern hospital are complex. They have a lot to do with the international exchange between architectural specialists in the field, and their knowledge and preparedness to keep up to date with developments in medical research and medical technologies. Much also has to do with health being accepted as a cultural project that might become a legitimate architectural language within the city. At the same time, it was acknowledged that the way the United States and Canada employed advances in building technologies and managed the logistics of servicing at a very large scale within hospital building was superior.

In aesthetics, development of the modern hospital drew not only on the hotel-inspired American block hospital but also on European architectural modernism and its characteristic themes of light and fresh air, hence the constant vacillation between reference to the skyscraper and the ocean liner in the overall form and detail of the buildings. American hospital architects continued to rely on traditional idioms and modes of civic and religious decorum, but elsewhere artistic programmes of murals and sculpture were frequently used to connect hospitals to their social and religious missions. Meanwhile, the actual architecture leaned towards a more pared-back utilitarian and modernist expression.

The evolution of hospital aesthetics parallels the shifting sands of progressive architectural thought in the twentieth century. The mantle moved from the technical ingenuity of the Americas to European formal experiment, and back again, as the devastation and legacy of World War II left its indelible mark. To draw this together, it is instructive follow the travels of a young and aspiring hospital architect from Melbourne, Australia, in the 1920s and 1930s. Arthur Stephenson (1890–1967) undertook documentary expeditions to see the latest in hospital architecture, which meant he witnessed key moments and ideas in hospital design and became a conduit of communication between two rather distinct regions. Stephenson initially used travel to learn and gain understanding and expertise in the field. As his reputation grew, his travel became a means by which he disseminated this expertise and understanding. His firm, Stephenson & Turner, developed into an internationally recognised practice with work across Iraq, Hong Kong, New Zealand and Australia.

Stephenson made his first international trip to study hospitals in 1926. After encouragement from American surgeon and hospital administrator Dr Malcolm T. MacEachern (1881–1956), Stephenson travelled across the United States and Canada for three months visiting hospitals and hospital architects (Stephenson 1926). MacEachern had visited Australia earlier that year and was a key player in the American Hospital Association, one of a number of prominent hospital consultants who'd had a significant influence on the innovations in hospital architecture across North America from the early 1920s. Stephenson described the change from what he called "the conventional traditional hospital" and the "modern conception" of such:

> It was not until the influence of industry became apparent in the United States of America that a changed conception was established in the hospital world ... they saw they had to devise a more economical method. ... In 1920, the first of their institutions was built on this changed concept. Some were built under the direction of men who saw the need for applying business principles to hospitals, and so the hospital consultant was born. Dr MacEachern, Asa A. Bacon, Dr Marcus Kogel, Dr [Sigismund Schulz] Goldwater, are names we must know if we are to study their views of progress.
>
> (Stephenson 1959)

The "business principles" mentioned were the great improvements that had been made in how hospitals were serviced and organised – inspired in part by the industrialisation of processes in laundries and kitchens. Stephenson managed to visit some sixty-four hospitals on his trip, including the Medical College at Albany Hospital, New York, USA (Architects: Berlin & Swern, 1927), University of Michigan Hospital, Ann Arbor, Michigan, USA (Architect: Albert Kahn, c. 1926), the Butterworth Hospital, Grand Rapids, Michigan, USA (Architects: Robinson & Campan, 1925), the much-feted, but soon-to-be-replaced, Chicago Lying-In Hospital, Chicago, Illinois, USA (Architects: Richard E. Schmidt, Garden & Martin, 1915), the Fifth

Avenue Hospital, Manhattan, New York, USA (Architects: York & Sawyer, 1921) (Figure 7.1), the Columbia-Presbyterian Medical Center of Manhattan, New York, USA (Architect: James Gamble Rogers, 1928), the Highland Hospital, Alameda, California, USA (Architect: Henry H. Meyers, 1926), and the Providence Lying-In Hospital, Rhode Island, New England, USA (Architects: Stevens & Lee, 1926), among numerous other hospitals (Stephenson 1927).

The closest business analogy for these hospitals was the hotel, so it is not surprising that many looked to the hotel, not only as a model of servicing and efficiency but also for examples of how to move beyond the aseptic stringency of earlier designs to a more welcoming and attractive place.

Beauty and utility

Twentieth-century hospital design began with the plan, to ensure that all the required facilities, proximities and amenities were provided. As the decade progressed, the plan was not conceived as determined by an aesthetically driven compositional *parti* but increasingly as a diagram necessary to optimise a hospital's functional arrangement. Functional relationships – between clinical services and operations, and in the location and layout of wards – drove the footprints of hospitals and created their essential morphological character. The demise between 1910 and 1920 of the Nightingale pavilion ward as the fundamental unit of hospital planning, whether single storey or, as later, stacked into medium-height towers, in favour of consolidated "block hospitals", profoundly shifted hospital design in size and scale. Nowhere was this more evident than it was in North America.

Another fundamental shift was occurring with how hospitals were perceived and where they were located. In the twentieth century, specialist medical care based within the hospital setting increased apace and the hospital as an institution grew in its importance as a symbol of a healthy and progressive society. Hospitals no longer had to resemble welfare institutions or appear as staid and sober halls of charity and care. Instead, they could present themselves as modern, civic institutions that embraced notions of progress and position. Writing in 1922, Richard E. Schmidt (1865–1959), of well-known Chicago hospital architects Schmidt, Garden & Martin, posited that hospitals now needed to look and feel more like hotels than "the older forms of hospitals which resembled correctional institutions". The patient should be encouraged to have a "proper mental attitude", and they would be happier, with more faith in the treatment they were to receive, "if everything about a hospital is familiar and inviting" rather than designed to be stern, forbiddingly simple or even taciturn. Schmidt advocated that the entrance and reception areas of the hospital should be designed "with as much care as ... the best hotels and residences", replete with moulded architraves, panelling and "delicate furniture" (Schmidt 1922: 252).

Figure 7.1 Fifth Avenue Hospital, Manhattan, New York, USA, was one of the many structures visited by Australian architect Arthur Stephenson in 1926. Architects: York & Sawyer, 1921. Photograph: Irving Underhill, 1922.

Courtesy: Museum of the City of New York, X2010.29.47.

The interiors of hospitals of the era were praised for their "rich furnishings and draperies and period furniture" and some, particularly, appeared to be like "a hotel or ... an exclusive club" (Peterkin 1929: 64–5). When it opened in 1929, the new Passavant Memorial Hospital, part of the Northwestern University campus in Chicago, Illinois, USA, received even higher praise, having "gone one step farther" to suggest "in some respects a home":

> In these days when the psychological importance of environment is so widely recognized and its significance in relation to the sick is acknowledged by all, it is no mean achievement thus to create for Passavant's patients a background that will unfailingly produce a sense of wellbeing.... The physician could have no more valuable aid in his treatment that the attitude of mind encouraged by a gracious and restful environment.
>
> (Peterkin 1929: 65–7)

Beauty, in the architecture of the hospital environment, was coming to be seen as an asset to the health and wellbeing of patients. S.D. Hunter, superintendent of the Washington Hospital in Washington, Pennsylvania, USA, extolled the beauty of his new hospital's interiors in 1928. These was shown through a series of photographs depicting contemporary domestic furniture, including wooden bedsteads, wooden ladder-back chairs, upholstered wing-back armchairs, upholstered ottomans, table lamps, wooden chests of drawers and side tables, and described as "such as might be used in any private home". The illustrated "deluxe" rooms featured fireplaces with decorative mantlepieces and artworks. The author described patients as "unanimous in their praises" of these interiors and fittings. But perhaps his next statement was more interesting:

> We know that the average stay of the patient in this hospital has been shortened two days. Our modern equipment may partly account for part of this, but we feel that the result is largely due to cheerful surroundings.
>
> (Hunter 1928: 60)

The use of home-like furniture in hospitals was particularly prevalent in North American hospitals, as evinced by the numerous advertisements that appeared in the pages of the leading hospital publication, *Modern Hospital*. The relative attractiveness of the environments was promoted as aiding the health and wellbeing of patients, but it is likely that the familiarity of the interiors – in their similarity to hotels and private homes – was also important making it socially acceptable for upper- and middle-class patients to seek medical care at a hospital.

The architects of most North American hospitals were no less concerned with ensuring the exteriors projected a suitable appearance. The exteriors of

North American hospitals of the 1920s and early 1930s depended on the urban context in which they were conceived, and mostly echoed the prevailing civic modes of architectural style. A number utilised polite Beaux-Arts classicism, Commercial Palazzo or Federalist revival styles, with shallow porticoes and other classical elements on plain brick walls, such as the Doctors Hospital, Manhattan, New York, USA, of 1930 (Sloan 1934) or the Women's Hospital in Detroit, Illinois, USA, of 1929 (Architects: Albert Kahn & Associates) (Kahn 1932). The Syracuse Memorial Hospital, Nebraska, USA (Architect: Dwight James Baum, 1927) likewise chose a traditional architectural mode, adopting the Colonial (Georgian) (Folsom and Baum 1927). Gothic Revival was used at the Chicago Lying-In Hospital at the University of Chicago, Illinois, USA (Architects: Schmidt, Garden & Erikson, 1931); in a more reductive form, it was also seen in the Children's Hospital in Cincinnatti, Ohio, USA (Architects: Elzner & Anderson, 1926) (Elzner, Bachmeyer and Pierce 1927). Others used a Spanish Colonial idiom, such as the Highland Hospital (Alameda County Hospital) in Oakland, California, USA, of 1926 (Architect: Henry H. Meyers), which employed pavilion planning, and the Eagleville Sanatorium, West Norriton, Pennsylvania, USA, 1927 (Architects: Simon & Simon) (Simon & Simon 1927). Civic presence was, therefore, considered an essential part of the hospital's dress.

It was the multistoreyed block hospitals that offered the most progressive imagining of the civic institution. As the hospitals got bigger, often occupying a whole city block, they increasingly embraced the style of progressive American high-rise office buildings that were being built at virtually the same time, such as the late example of the Rockefeller Center in Manhattan, New York, USA (1930–1939). This style – skyscraper moderne – celebrated the height of their multistorey blocks with vertical shafts and stylised and reductive decoration. Multiple versions appeared. In Los Angeles, the Spanish idiom was fused with the skyscraper in the Hospital of the Good Samaritan, Los Angeles, California, USA, of 1927 (Architect: Reginald D. Johnson); a reductive classicism was employed by Albert Kahn at the University of Michigan Hospital in Ann Arbor, Michigan, USA (c. 1926); and the neo-Gothic/skyscraper moderne of the New York Hospital–Cornell Medical Center, Manhattan, New York, USA, by Coolidge, Shepley, Bulfinch & Abbott (1932) (Figure 7.2).

One of the first of these was the enormous Columbia-Presbyterian Medical Center of New York complex in Manhattan's Upper West Side, New York, USA (Architect: James Gamble Rogers, 1928). Described as a "colossus", it brought together a series of separate institutions to represent "the intellectual unifying of scientific medicine in all its branches". It was architecturally progressive, within its context, and the hospital's "massive, towering structures" were described as "[a]rchitecturally ... simple, devoid of ornamentation, [and] somewhat austere in appearance" (Peterkin 1928: 55) (Figure 7.3). Yet, the decorative detail was still recognisably Gothic. Elsewhere, it was described as a "Fortress of Health", and it was noted

158 *Health, hygiene and progress*

Figure 7.2 New York Hospital–Cornell Medical Center, Manhattan, New York, USA. Architects: Coolidge, Shepley, Bulfinch & Abbott, 1932. Photograph: William Frange, c. 1930s.
Courtesy: Medical Center Archives of New York–Presbyterian/Weill Cornell.

that modern hospitals "guard the people of their communities" ("A Fortress of Health" 1927: 122). Similar language was used to describe the New York Hospital–Cornell Medical Center, in an item titled "Vast New Medical Centre Guards New York's Health":

> Against the drab background of the city's east side tenements the buildings stand out ... gleaming white with layer upon layer of solariums forming veritable turrets of glass.
>
> (Sloan 1933: 19)

New York Hospital–Cornell Medical Center also employed a reductive Gothic style on a skyscraper idiom of clustered high-rise buildings. The massive Los Angeles County General Hospital, California, USA (Architects: Allied Architects' Association, 1932) and the Harborview Hospital in Seattle, Washington, USA (Architects: Thomas, Grainger & Thomas, 1931), similarly employed a pared-back skyscraper Gothic style, which emphasised the building's verticality, with blocks and wings stepping up over the site towards the apex of the dominant central tower.

There were a very significant number of new hospitals built across North America in the 1920s and into the early 1930s. The innovative way these

Figure 7.3 Columbia-Presbyterian Medical Center, Manhattan, New York, USA, one of the earliest multistoreyed block hospitals, captured the imagination as a "colossus" and a "Fortress of Health". Architect: James Gamble Rogers, 1928. Photograph: Wurts Bros., 1937.
Courtesy: Museum of the City of New York, X2010.7.2.7077.

hospitals were planned, serviced and managed attracted attention worldwide. A whole industry emerged around the design of hospitals: consultants, specialist architects, a professional society – the American Hospital Association – and journals, in particular *Modern Hospital*. All advocated the newest and best in hospital design and management. Arthur Stephenson connected closely to this tightly bound network on his first trip to the United States in 1926, when he absorbed its knowledge, met with its exponents and toured its outputs. Indeed, on his return to Australia he realised these ideas in the Jessie MacPherson wing of the Queen Victoria Hospital, Melbourne, Victoria, of 1928, which was styled in a skyscraper Gothic mode. By the late 1920s, modern hospitals had been transformed into efficient, interconnected systems, the rhetoric around which positioned them as fortresses against disease, civic bastions in which medical care was dispensed within surroundings of beauty.

Stephenson undertook a second international trip in 1932–1933 with the express intention of gaining further knowledge about the latest in hospital design. In a key difference from his first trip, this journey included extensive travels across Europe, which complemented further travels in the United Kingdom and United States. In England, Stephenson encountered works like the Royal Masonic Hospital, London, England (Architects: Sir John Burnet, Tait & Lorne, 1931–1933), then under construction, but British hospital buildings did little to capture his imagination. Stephenson was instead enraptured by the modernist designs that were, by 1932, appearing in multiple European countries – particularly as they related to hospitals and sanatoria. The annals of his trip later appeared in a series of articles for *Modern Hospital* titled "A Tramp Abroad in the Hospital Field", published 1933–1935 (Stephenson 1933a, 1933b, 1933c, 1934a, 1934b, 1935). After arriving in London, he was shepherded across the channel to the Netherlands by the Architectural Association secretary, Francis Yerbury (1885–1970), before travelling on to France, Switzerland, Italy, Austria, Hungary, Germany, Czechoslovakia, Poland, Russia, Finland, Sweden, Denmark and Norway. He described his conclusions thus:

> England and the Continent are lands where tradition holds sway.... It seems that administrative methods have altered little ... but in the planning of hospital departments revolutionary developments have taken place. Some of these are due to the advances of sciences, such as deep therapy and the use of radium, but the greatest development has been in the direction of obtaining more light and air for the patients.
> (Stephenson 1933a: 55–6)

Stephenson added, "American hospitals ... are developed on more advanced lines than those of Europe, and the more modern ones are better planned and better equipped, continental thought is more inspiring in aspects of design".

Stephenson admired the expanses of glass, clean lines, use of colour and functional approach of European modernism. While some of his contemporaries preferred the work of Willem Dudok, Stephenson himself embraced the more radical modernist efforts, including the Mies van der Rohecurated Weissenhof Siedlung in Stuttgart, Germany (1927), the Zonnestraal Santorium (Sunburst Sanatorium), Hilversum, Netherlands (Architects: Jan Duiker & Bernard Bijvoet, 1925–1931) and Alvar Aalto's Paimio Sanatorium, Finland (1928–1932), among a series of lesser-known hospital projects. He was not the first to profile aspects of the new European aesthetic in hospitals to an American audience, or to mention the work in architectural circles, but his was the first sustained treatment of European modernism in *Modern Hospital*. Stephenson's drawing together of the works demonstrated a shift in the design of hospitals that demanded and encouraged attention. Carl Erikson, of Chicago architects Schmidt, Garden & Erikson (discussed in Chapter 4 for his model operating theatre), wrote to Stephenson on reading "A Tramp Abroad" that he was envious of the trip and hoped to "follow in [Stephenson's] distinguished footsteps". He asked for Stephenson's list of telephone numbers to help him on this quest (Erikson 1933). Yet, Stephenson's writings belied the array of work he'd seen and the progressive nature of much of it. His papers show he had intended his article series to also include discussions of Scandinavian and English hospitals, believing the former to display some of the most exciting ideas, but these articles did not make it into print.

The cluster of experts on hospital design evident around the American Hospital Association and *Modern Hospital* had an opposite number in the European group centred around the International Hospital Association (IHA) and its journal, *Nosokomeion*. *Nosokomeion*'s international focus (its editorials were produced in French, English, German and Italian), less regular publication and lack of photographic illustration meant it was less nimble, more ponderous and harder to consume than its American counterpart. As leader of the buildings section of the IHA, Hamburg architect Hermann Distel (1875–1945) was at the locus of this milieu and it was his hospital work that was best known in the United States. Erikson came perilously close to deriding Distel's work in his 1931 article in *Modern Hospital* titled "What Germany Does and What Germany Doesn't". It illustrated a series of hospitals that, externally, were conservative brick buildings showing none of the new aesthetics and forms emerging at that time. Erikson, quite possibly with his tongue firmly in cheek, wrote:

> Distel is strongly influenced by the tendencies that have been evident in German hospital plans of the last forty years. Such a statement sounds as if I were trying to make Distel out to be an old fogy; but the contrary is true.
>
> (Erikson 1931: 75)

Distel's writing, and promotion of his own work, had gained him prominence but not respect. Stephenson, too, on meeting Distel, was dismissive of his hospital designs, describing them as "not so good or so thoughtful", adding he'd "written and talked a lot, but has only built 4 or 5 hospitals" (Stephenson 1932b: 533, 539). Instead, innovations in hospital design were being developed by a new generation of architects who showed greater interest in glass, concrete and steel to express and create healthy environments in which to care for the sick.

Healthy and functional

Stephenson saw a series of hospitals that used modern architecture in a new approach to design. These included Zonnestraal Sanatorium; the Loryspital, Bern, Switzerland (Architect: Otto Salvisberg, 1925–1926); the tuberculosis pavilion of the Stadt Krankenhaus (State Hospital), Vienna, Austria (Architects: Fritz Judtmann & Egon Riss, 1929–1931); Hôpital Beaujon (Beaujon Hospital), Clichy, France (Architects: Walter, Plousey & Cassan, 1932–1935); the Cité Hospitalière de Lille (Lille Hospital Complex), Lille, France (Architects: Jean Walter, with Cassan & Madeline, 1934–1958); the Krankenhaus Waiblingen (Waiblingen Hospital), Stuttgart, Germany (Architect: Richard Döcker, 1926–1928); the Deutsches Rotes Kreuz Kliniken (Red Cross Surgical Hospital), Berlin, Germany (Architect: Otto Bartning, c. 1931); and the Paimio Sanatorium. These buildings were striking in their appearance. They utilised expanses of glass to absorb daylight and sunshine, concrete (or at least the appearance of such), and steel balustrades and window frames. In most cases, large windows or glass doors allowed access to the exterior for patients. At Vienna and Berlin, these opened directly from patients' rooms; at Waiblingen, the patients' beds could be wheeled out on to the balcony (Figure 7.4).

The exteriors of these hospitals were plain, unadorned stretches of wall with the functional expression of structure and services, their prismatic forms punctuated by the practical requirements of balconies and solaria. The buildings often incorporated the latest developments in reinforced concrete construction and were dominated by the long horizontal lines formed by windows and balconies strung across their façades. This gave them articulation without decoration. Unlike the American hospitals of the same period, the European modernist hospitals eschewed any references to traditional styles of architecture: there were no references to the Gothic or Classicism in their form or in their details. The buildings were a reflection of the functional needs of the hospital, oriented to catch the sun and work with the topography, their aesthetic reflecting the desire for clean and efficient spaces focused on patient needs.

The interiors also used a minimalist aesthetic. They avoided decorative details, and used plain unadorned surfaces, hard practical flooring and tubular metal-framed furniture. There was apparently little concern for creating a sense of homely comforts – no fireplaces, overmantles or plush armchairs. Instead, the spaces were practical and unfussy – clean, even clinical. The architectural effect of modernism thus reflected the desired standards of hygiene and asepsis in contemporary medicine, and the progressive care provided within the hospital.

Health, hygiene and progress 163

Figure 7.4 Krankenhaus Waiblingen (Waiblingen Hospital), Stuttgart, Germany. Architect: Richard Döcker, 1926–1928. Photograph: Fotographisches Atelier Ullstein, 1929.
Courtesy: ullstein bild via Getty Images.

These buildings were contemporary to key modernist icons including the Villa Savoye, Poissy, France (Le Corbusier, 1928–1929), the Tugendaht House, Brno, Czechoslovakia (now Czech Republic) (Ludwig Mies van der Rohe, 1928–1930), and the buildings of the Weissenhof Siedlung, Stuttgart, Germany (1927), and used the same visual language. Le Corbusier's inclusion of a handbasin in the entry foyer of his seminal Villa Savoye demonstrated modernist architects' interests in hygiene and cleanliness at this time, as has been highlighted by authors including Mark Wigley (1995), Beatriz Colomina (1997), Nadir Lahiji and D.S. Friedman (1997), Christopher Wilk (2006) and Paul Overy (2007). Margaret Campbell also points to the connections between the treatment of tuberculosis and Le Corbusier's use of sun balconies and flat roofs in his houses (Campbell 2005). Sigfried Giedion's 1929 book *Befreites Wohnen: Licht, Luft, Oeffnung* (*Free Living: Light, Air, Opening*) also encapsulated the interest in fresh air and sunlight as health-giving benefits of the new modernist forms. It has long been argued that the aesthetics of modernism emerged from industrial architecture, but they were also a logical fit to and a logical outcome of the search for an appropriate architecture for hospitals and clinics. They were quickly embraced for this purpose to the point that hospital design was fully entwined with the flowering of modernism in the late 1920s and early 1930s.

Stephenson repeatedly wrote with admiration of the beauty and utility he saw in these modernist works. The Weissenhof Siedlung, he found "very fine, both in design and plan", noting particularly the "glass stair enclosures" (Stephenson 1932a: 208). Zonnestraal, was a beautiful institution, he declared: "From the traditional forms of old building you swing to extreme originality of thought as exemplified in the now famous Zonnestraal Hospital which is constructed almost entirely of glass" (Figure 7.5). He continued that it was "strangely interesting to see all the machinery beautifully kept through the glass walls of the boiler house" (Stephenson c. 1933: 6). He made repeated references in his correspondence to how attractive and useful balconies were, describing Döcker's use of open terraces "an extremely attractive way to build" (Stephenson c. 1933: 27–8). Of the two tuberculosis sanatoria he saw in Finland, he admired the "enormous balconies, where ninety beds were all set in a row without a suggestion of untidiness or a single bed out of alignment" at the Helsinki Sanatorium; and at Paimio noted the "striking features" of extensive windows, placed "so that every fraction of every [ward] room is at some period of the year flooded with sunlight". He highlighted the dining room, with its "glass wall to the southeast 20 feet in height", which was flooded with light and sunshine. Further:

> The inner and outer windows on the corridors and in all living rooms and dining rooms are designed to take flower boxes with a fresh air inlet so arranged that the patients can benefit by the air being introduced over the plants which have, it is claimed, a curative value.
>
> (Stephenson c. 1933: 96–9)

Finally, of the tuberculosis pavilion of the Stadt Krankenhaus in Vienna, Stephenson wrote: "The whole of this hospital is a lesson in beauty of form and colour ... the top solariums are very fine indeed and are operated on enormous pivots from the walls ... all by electric motors" (Stephenson n.d.: 179) (Figure 7.6). The extent to which he highlighted expanses of glass, open balconies and solaria, careful choice of colour and good planning confirms his interest in seeing efficient function and form fused with the curative possibilities of fresh air and sunlight.

Stephenson returned to Australia in 1933, bringing with him first-hand experience of the latest in hospital design. It was immediately translated into his firm's work, first in their Mercy Hospital, East Melbourne, Victoria, Australia (1933–1935), with its plain concrete-rendered walls, open air balconies, triple-hung sash windows wide enough to accommodate patient beds and glassed-in solaria at the ends of the building (Figure 7.7). The building fused fragments and ideas from the European works he so admired, bringing

Figure 7.5 Stephenson admired the "extreme originality of thought" evident in the design of Zonnestraal Sanatorium (Sunburst Sanatorium), Hilversum, Netherlands (Stephenson c. 1933: 6). Architects: Jan Duiker & Bernard Bijvoet, 1925–1931. Photograph: unknown, c. 1930s.

Courtesy: Collection Het Nieuwe Instituut/TENT, o633.

166 *Health, hygiene and progress*

Figure 7.6 For Stephenson, Stadt Krankenhaus (State Hospital), Vienna, Austria, exemplified "a lesson in beauty and form of colour" (Stephenson n.d.: 179). Architects: Fritz Judtmann & Egon Riss, 1929–1931. Photograph: Österreichische Lichtbildstelle, c. 1930.
Courtesy: ÖNB/Wien, L33319C.

modernism to Melbourne, but it also employed the efficient servicing and organisation characteristic of North American hospitals. Stephenson & Meldrum's next hospital, Freemason's Hospital, East Melbourne, Victoria, Australia (1936), followed similar principles, with long ribbon balconies dominating its white façade and projections of walls and roof that were folded to create external stairs and balconies of elegant simplicity. These hospitals were foundation of a reputation for excellence that propelled the firm to international prominence in the field of hospital design.

Stephenson's firm, later Stephenson & Turner, went on to design dozens of Australian hospitals from the mid-1930s. Stephenson's timing was impeccable. His travels meant he'd caught a wave of new ideas in hospital design: on his first trip of the 1920s with the servicing and equipment revolution of the North American hospitals and, on his second, the modernist curative aesthetic of the Europeans. His work in Australia brought together these different approaches and put his firm at the leading edge of hospital design in the late 1930s. This was underscored by the dual effects of the Great Depression and World War II in both Europe and North America, where building virtually ground to halt for more than a decade. In

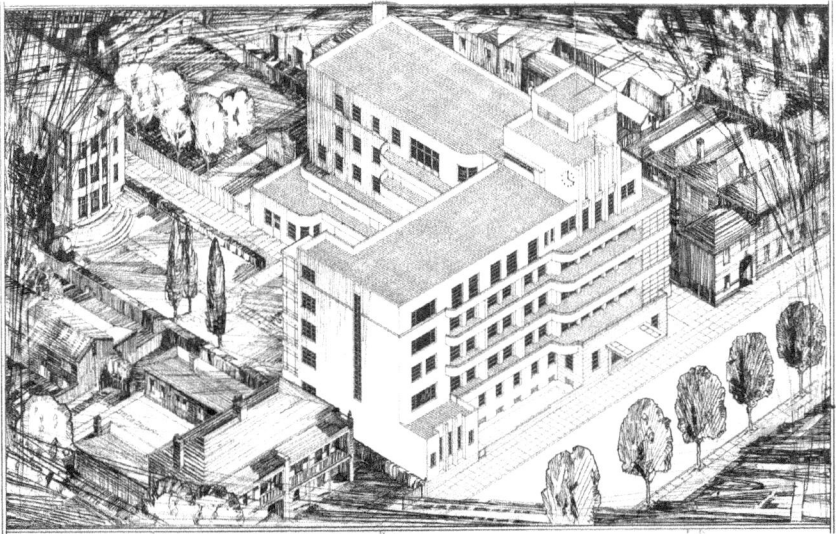

Figure 7.7 Mercy Hospital, East Melbourne, Victoria, Australia. Architects: Stephenson & Meldrum, 1933–1935. Delineator: unknown, c. 1934.
Courtesy: Pictures Collection, State Library of Victoria.

Australia, by contrast, there was a veritable boom in new hospital projects. The firm's leading works included the United Dental Hospital, Sydney, New South Wales, Australia (1936–1941) with its dramatic nine-storey glassed-in circular stair fronting the acute angle of its wedge-shaped plan; the King George V Hospital for Mothers and Babies, Camperdown, New South Wales, Australia (1939–1941), which incorporated Walter-style operating theatres and sweeping balconies across its façades; the Yaralla Military Hospital, Concord, New South Wales, Australia (1940–1942), also with long stretches of balconies and glassed-in solaria; and the huge Royal Melbourne Hospital, Parkville, Victoria, Australia (1936–42). The latter complex, made up of an administrative block, a nurses' home, a medical research institute and a separate laundry and boiler house, was envisaged as only the first in a comprehensive medical cluster of some seven different hospitals, the rest of which were never built. The Royal Melbourne Hospital's imposing boiler house (1945) was an exercise in modernist reductivism. Its mechanical equipment was on show behind a glass wall, just as Stephenson had seen at Zonnestraal, albeit at a much larger scale at the Royal Melbourne Hospital. The firm's projects received international attention, with profiles in *Architectural Review* ("Two Australian Hospitals" 1937), the *Royal Architectural Institute of Canada Journal* ("Royal Prince Alfred Hospital" 1937), *Architectural Forum* ("Hospitals in Australia" and "Dental Clinic" 1946), *Construction moderne* (Derevoge 1947),

Architecture d'aujourd hui ("Hôpital à Melbourne" 1947), and *Architecture française* ("Constructions hospitalières en Australia" and "Royal Melbourne Hospital à Melbourne" 1952). Their reputation also brought international opportunities, with Stephenson & Turner gaining commissions offshore, including for the Wellington Hospital, in New Zealand, in 1937 (not built), where they later established an office. In the late 1950s, Stephenson was invited to contribute designs, along with Walter Gropius/ the Architects Collaborative (TAC), Frank Lloyd Wright, Le Corbusier, Gio Ponti, Alvar Aalto and a number of other leading international architects, to the Kingdom of Iraq (Goad, Wilken and Willis 2004).[1]

The stark difference between hospital architecture in Europe and North America that Stephenson had observed on his travels was only too apparent in the designs for new hospitals profiled in *Modern Hospital* in 1939 to accompany the programme for the American Hospital Association convention, which was being held in Toronto that year immediately after the International Hospital Association convention. A Stevens, Curtin & Mason-designed maternity hospital in Lima, Peru, was profiled – a rather fussy American skyscraper design harking back to designs of the 1920s – against the plain walls and sweeping curved balconies of a modernist sanatorium in Poland, by Mieczyslawa Kozlowskiego. A rather ponderous design employing a reductive Classicism for the Birmingham Hospital (1933–1938) in England by Lanchester & Lodge, was compared to the modernist Tuberculosis Sanatorium at Tervete in Latvia by an uncredited Aleksandrs Klinklāvs. Hermann Distel's traditional design for a military hospital in Hamburg, Germany, was displayed adjacent to the clean lines of the Tuberculosis Clinic in Alexandria, Egypt, then an Italian colony, by Gardella & Martini. Rounding out the profile were the highly modernist designs of Gustaf Birch-Lindgren in Sweden for the Uppsala Sanatorium and uncredited design for the Kantonsspital (Cantonal Hospital) in Lucerne, Switzerland ("AHA Convention Program" 1939).

The influence of modernism as the language of the modern hospital was evident worldwide. In Belgium, the outstanding designers of modernist buildings for healthcare were brothers Gaston Brunfaut, responsible for the specialist cancer hospital for the Institut Jules Bordet in Brussels (1935–1938, with Stanislas Jasinski) and Maxime Brunfaut, who designed the Sanitarium Joseph Lemaire, Tombeek (1936–1938): both exemplified an uncompromising modernist aesthetic of abstraction and functional expression, deploying ramps, balconies, glazed bricks and ship's railings. In Switzerland, modernism's presence was especially strong. Otto Salvisberg's Loryspital, Bern (1925–1926) and Maternity Hospital, Bern (1929–1930) were early and pioneering examples in the idiom. Both featured planar walls, cantilevering reinforced concrete balconies and visually emphatic curved solaria at both ends of a multistorey linear slab. But the later large-scale exemplars in the Swiss setting, which indicated moves towards tempering modernism's sway, were the seven-hundred-bed Kantonsspital (Cantonal Hospital) in Basel

Health, hygiene and progress 169

(Architects: H. Baur, E. & P. Vischer and Bräuning Leu Dürig, 1939–1945) and the Kantonsspital in Zurich (Architects: Haefeli, Moser & Steiger with Dr H. Fietz, associated with Arter & Risch, R. Landolt, Luenenberger & Flückiger, J. Schütz and H. Weideli, 1941–1953). The Basel Kantonsspital comprised two parallel multilevel stripped back linear slabs – one of three levels, the other a nine-level ward block with roof terrace. The hospital's major entry point through the lower level slab was signalled externally by two protruding curved white forms with conical roofs, each housing a lecture hall (Figure 7.8). In Zurich, the slab-like wings of the multistorey hospital spread over a large park-like landscape and responded to the city at its urban edges with an architectural language that, in Swiss fashion, abstracted the Renaissance palazzo into a stretched modern form with expressed square columns, brick pilasters and the thinnest of projecting cornices that even showed timber rafters and eaves lining boards. In 1950, American architect and critic G.E. Kidder Smith said of these hospitals:

> The new Swiss hospitals strive for a humanization of one of architecture's most inhuman forms. Concern for the patient is the genesis of all planning. Sunshine and southerly exposure in all rooms, friendly

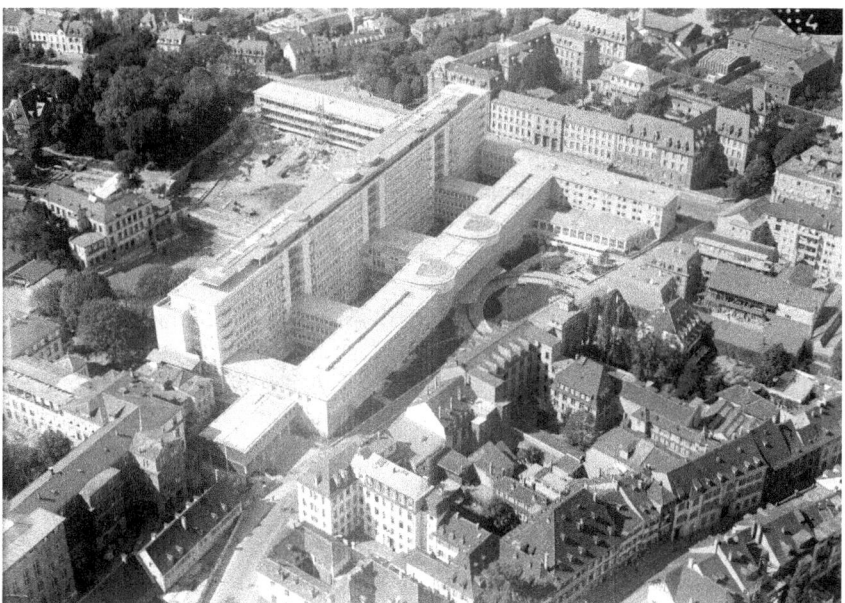

Figure 7.8 Kantonsspital (Cantonal Hospital), Basel, Switzerland. Architects: H. Baur, E. & P. Vischer and Bräuning Leu Dürig, 1939–1945. Photograph: Werner Freidli, 1945.

Courtesy: ETH-Bibliothek Zürich, Bildarchiv/Stiftung Luftbild Schweiz/LBS_H1–008654 (CC BY-SA 4.0).

scale, warm, homelike atmosphere replaced the super sanitation of unrelenting white tile and bare buff walls.... Architecturally, an outstanding characteristic of the new Swiss hospitals in their rejection of the "kitchen and butcher shop" atmosphere which dominated hospitals all over the world, especially those designed under German influence.

(Kidder Smith 1950b: 177)

Outside Europe, there were also pacesetting examples of hospital design that demonstrated a comfortable alliance between the aspirations of health and the aesthetics of modernism. One of the earliest examples of a modernist hospital in South America was German hospital specialist architect Ernst Kopp's German Hospital in Rio de Janeiro, Brazil (1931–1932), a formally planned, severely dressed six-storey structure with unadorned walls, shading balconies and retractable blinds that modulated simple cubic forms (Pawlik 2013).[2] Erich Mendelsohn's design for the Haifa Hospital in Palestine (now Israel) (1938–1940) was a series of plain blocks with balconies and generous expanses of glass – in this case, given the climate, set away from the prevailing sunlight so the building would not overheat ("Hospital at Haifa" 1940). In Japan, the Tokyo Teisin Hospital (Architect: Mamoru Yamada, 1936–1938) was a striking work of rationalist architecture with a white tiled exterior, generous standardised glazing panels and two multilevel ward wings, each terminated by a dramatic zig-zagging concrete ramp.

This is not to say that there were no progressive hospital designs in the United States or the United Kingdom, only that examples were few and far between. Progressive examples included J.B. Harland's inventive polygonal room geometries at the infectious diseases hospitals at Isleworth, Middlesex, England (1938) and Tolworth, London, England (c. 1939). The Tuberculosis Block at the Rochford Hospital, Essex, England (Architect: F. W. Smith, 1938–1939) used a step-fronted V-planned design culminating in a circular solarium that acted as the hinge for the two-storey design, which used extensive amounts of glass (Richardson 1998). A later example was the Poole Sanatorium, Middlesbrough, England (Architects: W. & T.R. Milburn, 1938–1945), which employed a circular solarium and terraces to make the most of the sunlight for patients, and referenced the Dutch modernism of Willem Dudok.

A cluster of progressive designs appeared in New York, all connected to S.S. Goldwater. The Meadowbrook Hospital in Long Island, New York, USA (Architects: John Russell Pope & William F. McCulloch, with S.S. Goldwater, 1935) had long lines of balconies running across its façade capped by large bow-fronted solaria. It echoed the European aesthetic, but was described as "designed in the spirit of the Greek Revival" ("A County Hospital" 1932: 61) and the plain pilasters and cornice indicated a tangible link to the tradition of American hospital designs. The huge Hospital for Chronic Diseases, which occupied much of what became known as

Welfare Island (previously Blackwell's Island, now Roosevelt Island) in New York's East River, New York, USA (Architects: Rosenfield, Butler & Kohn, with York & Sawyer, c. 1938) also had façades dominated by long lines of accessible balconies and circular day rooms (Rosenfield 1937) (Figure 7.9). The multiple ward towers were cranked from their central lobby to make the most of the sunlight and views, using shallow angles, similar to that of Waiblingen. The Lake County Tuberculosis Sanatorium in Waukegan, Illinois, USA (Architects: William A. Ganster and W.L. Pereira in association, 1940) took its inspiration directly from the European sanatoria of a decade or more earlier, complete with metal pipe balustrades and expanses of glass that formed its balconies ("The Lake County Tuberculosis Sanatorium" 1940; Mock 1944; Moretti 1951). The White Plains Hospital, New York, USA (Architects: Schulze & Weaver, c. 1939) similarly took its visual cues from European styling in its box-like forms of brick with minimal embellishment (Schulze 1940).

Figure 7.9 Angles of sunlight and progressive design governed the form of the Hospital for Chronic Diseases, Welfare Island (now Roosevelt Island), New York, USA. Architects: Rosenfield, Butler & Kohn, with York & Sawyer, c. 1938. Photograph: unknown, 1938.

Courtesy: Collection of the Public Design Commission of the City of New York.

172 *Health, hygiene and progress*

The proposed designs profiled in *Modern Hospital* in 1938 attest to the future of hospital design, being multistorey hospitals of considerable size that foretell the postwar modernism that became known as the International Style. A Coolidge, Shepley, Bulfinch & Abbott design for a five-hundred-bed hospital was a tall tower, embellished by bow-fronted balconies that echoed those of Walter, Plousey & Cassan's design for the Hôpital Beaujon (Beaujon Hospital) in Clichy, France, of 1935. The most striking of these was Richard Neutra's design for a five-hundred-bed hospital in an unnamed city in California, USA, which offered individual projecting balconies for each ward. The architecture drew on the latest ideas: "the drawings illustrate the open air character of a modern hospital and the fact that the contemporary architecture, in general, has borrowed significant features from projects designed to serve the sick" ("Hospitals of Tomorrow" 1938: 91) (Figure 7.10).

The subcutaneous age

The "latest ideas" in hospital design touted on the threshold of World War II – patient access to fresh air and sunshine, or the open-air character – would be rendered almost immediately obsolete by the end of the war. Balconies were included for the beneficial influence of sunlight on patients. Its curative effect was particularly noticeable on patients with tuberculosis and

Figure 7.10 Design by Richard Neutra for a five-hundred-bed hospital in an unnamed city in California, USA. Delineator: Richard Neutra.

Source: *Modern Hospital* 51, no. 3 (September 1938): 91.

© Dion Neutra, Architect and Richard and Dion Neutra Papers, Department of Special Collections, Charles E. Young Research Library, UCLA, used with permission.

was an established part of treatment in sanatoria. By the end of the 1930s, the balcony had become mainstream in general hospital design. Architects readily embraced the trend: balconies gave license to create robust forms, were integral to the clean lines of modernism, and were regarded as a key instrument in the treatment of patients. They were the defining element of the progressive aesthetics of the modern hospital.

But the balcony was a device that, while contributing to the care and therapy of patients, could not completely cure them. It was one of a range of therapeutic devices used at the time offering physical treatments that dealt with the body from an external perspective. But their status as effective treatments was soon lost with the arrival of a range of drug therapies, including the development of antibiotics and vaccines. The availability of antibiotic treatment from the mid-1940s and then the introduction of the Salk vaccine for polio in the mid-1950s heralded the subcutaneous age, where physical therapy was diminished in its importance. For a range of diseases, cure, instead of treatment, came within reach.

The rise of pharmaceutical therapies had a profound effect on the design of hospitals and, in particular, on their exterior form. The balcony and solaria were obsolete, remnants of treatment regimes no longer considered necessary. The rise of air conditioning throughout the whole hospital, with its ever-increasing emphasis on pure or filtered air, meant that openable windows were also increasingly seen as obsolete. Why let dirt and pathogens into a hospital through an open window if cleaner air could be provided through air conditioning? The widespread embrace of the "open-air character" for hospitals by the late 1930s proved to be its last flourish, for by the time design and construction of hospitals began again after World War II, the ideal hospital was a hermetically sealed box, proof against the unhygienic conditions of the outside. The treatment of patients, once manifested on or outside the skin of the building, had taken a subcutaneous architectural turn as well.

That didn't mean hospitals that had been substantially designed before the war weren't completed as they had been designed. Hjalmar Cederström and Hermann Imhäuser's enormous Södersjukhuset (Southern Hospital) in Stockholm, Sweden, was completed in 1946, after sixteen years of research and planning by the architect and medical experts (Cederström c. 1946) (Figure 7.11).[3] In 1950, Kidder Smith was enthusiastic, writing, "in both its building and its broad health welfare scope, [it] is certainly one of the most important hospitals of our day, and its effect will be felt wherever new hospitals are built" (Kidder Smith 1950a: 152). It contained forty-four solaria for the benefit of patients (Cederström c. 1946), but these had only subtle expression on the exterior of the building, and there were no balconies. Cederström's design had emerged from 1930s thinking, but the design, with its muted expression and emphasis on the block forms of the hospital, looked forward to the closed forms of the postwar hospital. The design of Södersjukhuset aligned with a series of Scandinavian hospitals, like Jussi Paatela and Uno Ullberg's Turku University Central Hospital

Figure 7.11 Södersjukhuset (Southern Hospital), Stockholm, Sweden. Architects: Hjalmar Cederström and Hermann Imhäuser, 1937–1944. Photograph: unknown, c. 1950s.

Courtesy: Arkitektur – och designcentrum, RKM.1962–101–1431 (CC pdm).

(1934–1937) in Finland (Pesonen 1964), whose architectural aesthetics had relied less on the balcony as an essential element than those hospitals built in warmer climates. Kidder Smith's only hesitation in 1950 with respect to Södersjukhuset was that "it is questionable whether a building as enormous as this does not begin to become inhuman by its very mass, and to so dominate both the patient and the town that its size begins to defeat itself" (Kidder Smith 1950a: 152).

Slabs and podiums, matchboxes and muffins

As the modern hospital was sealed and hermetically enclosed, it lost the last vestiges of function identifiable in its exterior design. As external wall systems intent on a completely hermetic seal were adopted, exterior walls lost permeation and depth. Hospitals became high-rise or low-rise slabs or a combination of the two, and the bulk of hospital design by the early 1960s had become, aesthetically, all but indistinguishable from an office block. This aesthetic shift was not limited to hospitals. Office buildings, international hotels, apartment blocks and university buildings, as well as hospitals, all moved in varying degrees towards a uniform appearance. There was a gradual but steady move from formally designed, inevitably classically composed symmetrical designs – often high-rise and within which functions were expertly contained, dressed externally with an appropriate civic architectural language – to an abstract, slim high-rise slab.

Leading this change in form was the high-rise office building. Two prestigious modernist high-rise slabs – one pre-war, the other postwar – became influential and well-publicised exemplars: the Ministry of Education and Health in Rio de Janeiro, Brazil (Architects: Lucio Costa *et al.*, consultant Le Corbusier, 1936–1943) and the United Nations Headquarters, Manhattan, New York, USA (Architects: Oscar Niemeyer, Le Corbusier, Harrison & Abramowitz *et al.*, 1947–1952) (Deckker 2000; Dudley 1994). Common to both was the notion of repetitive office floors elevated above a public ground plane, where other functions that required differentiated volumes might be accommodated without interrupting the purity of the rectangular slab form. In Rio, the ground level contained a public plaza and a two-storey podium building that had a Roberto Burle-Marx-designed roof garden. In New York, at ground level the UN building had, in addition to the high-rise thirty-nine-storey secretariat, a sculpturally shaped assembly building, a rectangular conference building and, later, a separate library building. In both cases, assumptions were made about the rationality of the slab form: that it provided all workers with equal access to light, air and efficient vertical circulation.

In the hospital setting, this notion of slab plus elaborated ground plane was translated as a high-rise slab of wards (for inpatients) above or beside a collection of buildings at ground level that housed administration, diagnostic, surgical, outpatients and other departments. The most striking example of the new form was Skidmore Owings & Merrill's thousand-bed Fort Hamilton Veterans' Administration Hospital, Brooklyn, New York, USA (1947–1952), designed by Gordon Bunshaft. On a 17-acre (7-hectare) site, a 506-foot (154-metre) long slab of seventeen storeys housed two nursing units of forty beds on each floor, with 95 per cent of beds receiving southern exposure. All other hospital functions were located in attached lower slab blocks. The slab's southern façade had, like that of Rio's Ministry of Education and Health, a permanent form of sunshading. Instead of moveable *brise-soleils* (sun-breakers) as at Rio, a continuous reinforced concrete projecting sunhood shaded each floor. The idea of sunshine as a "healing" agent had largely dissipated following World War II, but vestiges of its influence were still apparent here at Brooklyn. Importantly, too, Skidmore Owings & Merrill's ward slab was not air conditioned: the aluminium-framed windows were openable double-hung sashes on either side of a generous picture window. Skidmore Owings & Merrill's other major hospital design of the period followed the same compositional strategy but on an expanded scale, and was described by the Museum of Modern Art in 1950 as "a precedent-creating plan" ("Skidmore Owings & Merrill"

1950: 16). The New York University–Bellevue Medical Center, New York, USA (1947–1950, design), as originally envisaged, was a series of low, medium and high-rise slabs artfully and symmetrically connected across an 11-acre site from 30th to 34th streets in New York's borough of Manhattan. This constituted a campus or "city" of slabs, separately housing a ward block, administration rooms, a hall of residence, a medical school and a research institute. As in Brooklyn, the ward block slab – of twenty storeys and six hundred beds – had a striking façade leavened by horizontal bands of windows and continuous linear sunhoods. In Brazil, architect Oscar Niemeyer was to reprise his UN Headquarters slab with his 1952 design for the Hospital da Lagoa (Hospital Sul America), Rio de Janeiro (1952–1958). There, in a park setting overlooking botanical gardens and Lagoon Rodrigo de Freitas, the ten-storey slab was held aloft by V-shaped piloti. A detached sculptural ancillary building shaped like the UN General Assembly Building, New York, in plan sat on one side and a detached sculptural lift and stair-core on the other, with one façade facing the sun modulated by vertical aluminium *brise-soleils* and *cobogós* (terracotta block screens), and the other a sheer wall of glass and light blue spandrel panels.

While these examples were stylish and presented a new image of modernity for the modern hospital, there were some flaws, especially in terms of functional efficiency. Jonathan Hughes has noted the shortcomings of some of the early slab hospitals of the United Kingdom, including the Queen Elizabeth II Hospital, Welwyn, England (Architect: C. D. Andrews, North West Metropolitan Regional Hospital Board, 1955–1963) where the T-shaped tower had a high-rise ward slab connected to medical and ancillary services located in a stack that formed the stem of the T. As Hughes writes:

> the hospital was condemned as obsolescent from the start, the vertically layered clinical departments offering poor inter-departmental relationships and little scope for expansion.
>
> (Hughes 2000: 42)

The same issues applied to Altnagelvin Hospital, Londonderry, Northern Ireland (Architects: Yorke, Rosenberg & Mardall, 1949–1960), another slab design, this time L-shaped, that had wards in a twelve-floor slab and diagnostic and treatment facilities in another other eight-level wing and outpatients in a separate single-level ground-floor structure. If these and other designs, despite often occupying large greenfield sites, were not as efficient as they could have been, there was another solution available: the high-rise slab and podium as one combined structure.

Again, the postwar office building appeared to hold the key inspiration. The high-rise slabs of the Ministry of Health and Education and the UN Headquarters had the benefit of large, relatively unconstrained sites, but this was not the case for all new office buildings, where the desire for high-rise repetitive office floors was often negotiated against existing town planning regulations and historic streetscapes. A low-rise podium of two to four storeys could compensate for exceeding height limits. It could also contain different volumes and lessen issues of overshadowing and building bulk. Gordon Bunshaft of Skidmore Owings & Merrill rapidly developed expertise in glazed curtain wall construction for high-rise office buildings, which provided the paradigm of the podium-slab office building – Lever House, Manhattan, New York, USA (1952). This model became favoured for reforming urban typologies such as the hotel and the hospital (Krinsky 1988). Aesthetically, it would be argued as visual counterpoint – a horizontal floating plane juxtaposed against a slender vertical prism. In hospital design, the podium, designed as a horizontally spreading base over which a slab could be located, might contain administration, operating theatres, X-ray and diagnosis departments, outpatient treatment and other ancillary facilities. In many respects, arguments in favour of the podium and slab combination for the modern hospital were far stronger than those in favour of the combination for office buildings.

The podium-slab hospital had already been predicted in the 1930s. In 1932, French-American architect Paul Nelson's unbuilt design for the Cité Hospitalière (Hospital Complex) at Lille comprised two multistorey towers, one cruciform-shaped and the other a tri-radial complex clamped onto a linear slab, both sitting directly above a vast podium of hospital services, diagnostic departments, surgical suites, outpatient departments and ancillary services. Nelson's radical solution was made viable by his proposal to hermetically seal the entire complex and air condition it, to allow occupation of the largely windowless deep floor plan of the podium. This implied an entirely new language for the hospital façade:

> It is therefore, therefore, necessary to have the exterior walls not only highly insulating but hermetically sealed as well, because the "opening window" in air conditioning is not only useless, but a definite obstacle to its proper functioning. The establishment of this fact leads the architect, naturally, to an entirely new conception of the façade.
> (Zervos 1933: xvi)

Nelson proposed an ingenious façade system based on a 490-millimetre-square grid module, whereby the exterior wall comprised a metal frame subdivided into squares into which would be fitted standard panels – opaque, transparent or translucent, according to need, but interchangeable at any moment. The aim was to accommodate flexibility in the available spaces, based on the assumption that developments in medical technology and healthcare would necessitate ongoing change to the building's form and appearance (Nelson 1933).

Though never realised, Nelson's ambitious 1932 scheme forecast not just the fully air conditioned podiums of the late 1950s and early 1960s but also the air conditioning of the tower slabs and their complete sealing. Additionally, air conditioning allowed these high-rise slab plans to be "thickened" as the slab floor plates developed internalised cores of service and ancillary space, surrounded by peripheral ward rooms and served by what came to be known as "racetrack" corridors (Verderber and Fine 2000).

Nelson was able to partly realise his podium and slab ideal after World War II, but without the sophistication of the completely sealed and air-conditioned container. At Saint-Lô in Normandy, France, he designed for the Hôpital Mémorial France-États-Unis (France-United States Memorial Hospital) (1946–1956), a spreading low-rise single-level mat-like podium on the building's entry side that contained outpatient facilities, administration and diagnostic spaces as well as garden courtyards (Saint-Lô 2006). The only protrusions in the podium were box-like elements that protected the dome-shaped operating theatres beneath. The podium was thus potentially flexible, able to adapt to the dynamic conditions of medical and technological change. Facing a rural landscape behind and sitting on the edge and over the top of the podium was the more functionally "stable" eight-storey ward block that was served by a centralised vertical circulation system. All façades were modulated in white square panels, as were the smaller divisions of the floor-to-ceiling windows and their square frames in red (slab 1), blue (slab 2) and yellow (ground level). Fernand Léger's colourful commemorative mosaic mural, located at the hospital's low, friendly scaled entry, gave the entire scheme special distinction. It was arguably the most complete statement on what direction the postwar modern hospital might take: a highly rationalised, efficient machine set in open fields, enhanced by modernist art and carefully tailored landscape design.

Over time, the podium-slab model as a design strategy became extremely common. In the postwar years in the Netherlands, outpatient treatment accelerated as medical specialists moved from home-based clinics to the general hospital. Because of this, hospitals had to cope with both the short-term stay of treatment and outpatient areas and the longer stay of inpatient wards, which encouraged the composite building form (Huijsman 2006; Mens and Wagenaar 2010). The first convincing Dutch example of the type was the Diaconessenhuis (Deaconess House), Eindhoven (Architect: W. F. Lugthart, 1956–1966), while its architecturally most elegant expression could be found at the Leyenburg Ziekenhuis (Leyenburg Hospital) (now the HagaZiekenhuis locatie Leyweg) in The Hague (Architect: K.L. Sijmons, 1971) (Mens and Wagenaar 2010). In Denmark, the podium-slab form of the University Hospital, Odense (Architect: K. Boeck-Hansen, 1957–1967) was the formal complement to Arne Jacobsen's SAS Hotel (1956–1960) in Copenhagen. In Germany, the form was known as the *Breitfuß* (wide feet) (Wagenaar 2013), exemplified best by the thousand-bed Cologne University Hospital (1967–1969) with its sixteen-storey bed tower crowned by a heroic grid of giant beams, which sat above a vast podium that also connected to a huge car park. This was systems thinking writ large. One of the most sophisticated examples was Charité Berlin-Campus Klinikum Benjamin Franklin

(Benjamin Franklin Campus Clinic) (Architects: Arthur Q. Davis, Curtis & Davis, 1955–1958, 1959–1968) in Steglitz, Berlin (Davis 2009) (Figure 7.12). There, set in parkland and close to a river, sitting above a two-level podium are two arrow head-shaped ward blocks that cantilever over the edge of the podium and a third lozenge-shaped block, all connected by pedestrian bridges, and the central lozenge with two courtyards reaching down into the podium proper. This hospital is given its special quality externally by the delicate vertebrae bone-like concrete screen that covers the entire podium façade and hovering lozenge block and the ward blocks that have a faceted window system within an externally expressed lightweight frame. The individuality of the patient room is expressed architecturally, in contrast to the uniformity and indeed monumentality of the decorative and functional screen, a signal of both the hospital's medical expertise and its civic decorum.

In the United States, hospital specialist architect Isadore Rosenfield called this formal development "tombstone on a pad", but also acknowledged the British term "matchbox on a muffin", which had become commonplace in English-speaking hospital design circles (Rosenfield 1969: 29, 46). In French hospital circles, the type was variously known as *socle tour* (tower base), *hôpital arbre* (hospital tree) or *mono-bloc sur galette* (single block on a galette tart), while in Italy, the term *piastra torre* (plate/tower)

Figure 7.12 Charité Berlin-Campus Klinikum Benjamin Franklin (Benjamin Franklin Campus Clinic), Steglitz, Berlin, Germany. Architects: Arthur Q. Davis, Curtis & Davis, 1955–1958, 1959–1968. Photograph: Schöning, 2012.
Courtesy: ullstein bild via Getty Images.

was used (Mens and Wagenaar 2010: 128). British examples included Hull Royal Infirmary, Hull, England (Architects: Yorke, Rosenberg & Mardall, 1957–1965) and Aintree University Hospital (known locally as Fazakerley Hospital), Liverpool, England (Architects: Liverpool Regional Hospital Board, 1965). Another important English example was Wexham Park Hospital, Slough, Buckinghamshire (Architects: Powell & Moya, consultants Llewelyn-Davies, Weeks & Partners, 1955–1966), which reversed the normal placing of wards in the "matchbox". At Wexham, the squat ward tower, containing offices, doctors' flats, libraries and meeting rooms, sat above a greatly extended single-level "muffin" of outpatient and ancillary departments, as well as inpatient ward blocks and courtyards, all connected by architect Philip Powell's idea of "hospital streets" (Rosenfield 1969: 218; Powell 2009: 91). The arrangement defines what English hospital specialist John Weeks described as "indeterminate architecture", an idea that Elain Harwood has argued, "grew out of work on 'duffle-coat' planning, his [Weeks's] name for a large, architecturally expressionless mantle of a building that was serviced and flexible" (Harwood 2015: 289).

The so-called matchbox could also take several forms: a single slab, a T, H or K shape or more than one slab. The latter was seen at one of the most significant European examples of a podium-slab ("matchbox and muffin") hospital, the massive 2,200-bed Allgemeines Krankenhaus der Stadt Wien (AKH) (Vienna General Hospital), Vienna, Austria (1964–1991), Europe's largest hospital and one of the largest in the world, with its two squat nine-storey ward towers over a giant six-level podium.

Hints of change

By the 1960s, the modern hospital seems to have reached an inevitable endpoint in formal and aesthetic terms. New hospitals at the time celebrated the aesthetics of postwar modernity and the logic of efficiency. Hospital architects and planners also increasingly recognised the need to distinguish between long- and short-term patient stays, and aimed to accommodate dynamic conditions of change through addition and alteration. But there were now some new issues. Meeting the growing demand for hospital treatment in the 1960s was a very challenging task. To do so efficiently, and in line with best practice, planners and designers had to reconceive their roles. During the era of the modern hospital, the size of the institutions had grown enormously as varied treatments and services had been integrated into the hospital building. The benefits of this change had to be weighed against the new problems such large buildings created. Because of their size, hospitals constructed in this period usually took between five and ten years to build. This was a long time, especially as in the meantime concerns about the provision of patient-centred rather than medical specialist-centred care re-emerged strongly and caused the hospital environment to be reconsidered. The interior quality of hospitals was rethought, and a renewed sense of the therapeutic potential of interior design challenged some of the norms of the modern hospital. In particular, patient advocates and ultimately hospital decision-makers reconsidered what constituted a humanised interior setting that would maximise patient healing.

As a consequence, in the 1960s some hospital architects began to experiment with bolder schemes, rethinking the modern hospital at every scale, from the bed to the position of the nurse, to the form of the complex and its increasing dimension as a fully fledged campus of urban scale. In Australia, the Sandringham and District Hospital, Sandringham, Victoria (Architects: J.H. Esmond Dorney and G.M. Hirsch, 1957–1964) was a three-storey building of three interlocking polygons (two heptagonal forms and one larger polygon) straddling a conventional cubic block. The planning of the main street-facing polygon was based on the idea of reducing distances between departments with a twelve-sided light court in the middle. The two flanking heptagons each housed twenty-two beds per floor. Each two-bed room was planned with shared bathrooms at each point of the polygon and with a central, circular nurses' station "so that the Sister, from her central location, has full oversight of every patient, with only the width of the corridor between her and patient" ("Sandringham Memorial Hospital" 1961: 40).

A few years later, in 1961, Californian architect Clarence Mayhew, with physician Sidney Garfield, produced for Henry J. Kaiser two conjoined seven-floor circular towers sitting above a three-storey podium for the Kaiser Foundation at Panorama City, Los Angeles, California, USA (1961–1962), where nursing supervision also determined the circular format, achieving what Garfield conceptualised as "circles of service". Described as "perhaps the most unusual looking Kaiser Permanente hospital ever built", it reversed the typical notion of "matchbox and muffin" (Cushing 2016).

Such reasoning also lay behind American architect Bertrand Goldberg's later but more sophisticated resolution of the same idea (Fisher 2011). At the Prentice Women's Hospital in Chicago, Illinois, USA (1969–1975), Goldberg inverted the "matchbox on a muffin" idea by conjoining four circular "muffins" (four twelve-bed units) and placing seven storeys of them above a matchbox-shaped glass-curtain walled podium. The rationale of the extraordinary form of the four-leafed-clover-shaped exposed reinforced concrete tower "sprouting" above the neutral street-scaled podium was to prioritise the nurses' station as the central point of the composition, with lift cores and stair access relegated to secondary positions. A further departure, in terms of aesthetics, was the inclusion of dramatically scaled elliptical windows. For arguably the first time, the image of the urban hospital was now otherworldly, almost space age. Goldberg explored similar design strategies for the four petals on a matchbox at St Joseph's Hospital, Tacoma, Washington, USA (1969–1974) with its ten-bed "villages" clustered around a nursing station, and the much larger and later Providence Hospital at Mobile, Alabama, USA (1982–1987).

These experiments were not copied, but a creeping sense of dissatisfaction with the standard appearance and rationale of the modern hospital became evident in the 1960s, not least because of the apparent hegemony of its typological formation. One of the few architects to directly challenge the entire rationale of the hospital setting – but largely from a technological standpoint – was Chicago-based architect E. Todd Wheeler (1906–1987) of the firm Perkins & Will. Stephen Verderber and David Fine have outlined Wheeler's provocative, and to this date unparalleled, exploration of alternative forms for the modern hospital, labelling his unbuilt designs of the 1960s as "visionary" (Verderber and Fine 2000: 125). Wheeler was ostensibly located as a health specialist within a respected practice, but he was also author of *Hospital Design and Function* (1964) and *Hospital Modernization and Expansion* (1971). He proposed in the latter book a series of extraordinary hospital designs that were described as "tents", "trees", "inverted pyramids" and "bathyspheres" (Verderber and Fine 2000). Each design was deliberately polemical in intent, while aiming to forecast a time when certain ideal conditions were realised in the modern hospital. These included a completely controllable atmospheric environment demonstrated by his "tent" scheme (Wheeler 1971) – a draped double plastic envelope – for hyperbaric medicine; a "tree" hospital (1971) that could grow and expand with prefabricated room units from a permanent central trunk; a massive "inverted pyramid" that could be slotted into an existing dense and perhaps historic urban neighbourhood without compromise to existing urban fabric; and his vast underwater ten-level "bathysphere" hospital, planned to achieve a completely stable, energy efficient environment.

Wheeler's schemes were startling in terms of invention and scale, but limited in application. As Verderber and Fine have noted: "These futuristic hospitals, regrettably, responded primarily to internal technological challenges of the 1960s urban hospital. Therefore, in retrospect they remain virtual follies at best" (Verderber and Fine 2000: 109). Yet Wheeler's proposals were important for their focus on the interior environment of the modern hospital as a starting point for change.

Other architects tended to use their exterior efforts to magnify servicing, technology and its potential flexibility to visually heroic proportions, as at the McMaster University Health Sciences Centre, Hamilton, Ontario, Canada (Architects: Craig, Zeidler & Strong, 1967–1972) and its megastructural expression of circulation and services that visually signalled its apparently obsolescence-proof status (Figure 7.13). Perhaps even more striking in demonstrating how the modern hospital had developed beyond a single entity into the scale of a fully fledged interconnected campus was the Universitätsklinikum (University Hospital), Aachen, Germany (Architects: Weber & Brand, 1972–1982). Here, servicing was again celebrated.

Figure 7.13 McMaster University Health Sciences Centre, Hamilton, Ontario, Canada. Architects: Craig, Zeidler & Strong, 1967–1972. Photograph: Historic Hamilton, 2010.
Courtesy: HistoricHamilton.com.

The vast complex was another high-tech megastructure, and it looked like an elegant oil refinery. But what was different was that the largely six-storey complex spread as a giant grid across the landscape with more than eight landscaped internal courtyards and was accentuated at its periphery by servicing towers that encircled the whole complex as if it were a fortified hill town. Just as Paul Nelson had forecasted in 1932, the modern hospital had become a city.

Notes

1 Stephenson & Turner were asked to design three hospitals, including one at Khademain (1957) and another at Basrah. But only the Southern Base Teaching Hospital in Basrah was completed.
2 Ernst Kopp (1890–1962) was a significant German hospital architect, designing the Neusalz Oder District Hospital, Prussia, Germany (now Nowa Sol, Poland) (1927), Martin Luther Hospital, Berlin, Germany (1929–1931), Protestant Hospital, Gütersloh, Germany (1930–1931), Al Moasset Hospital, Alexandria, Egypt (1932–1936) and University Hospital (five-hundred-bed hospital), Tehran, Iran (1936–1939) all before 1939.
3 Another significant modernist hospital in Sweden was the Karolinska Hospital, Stockholm (Architects: Sven Ahlbom & Carl Westman, 1940).

References

"AHA Convention Program." *Modern Hospital* 53, no. 3 (September 1939): 64–71.

Campbell, Margaret. "What Tuberculosis Did for Modernism: The Influence of a Curative Environment on Modernist Design and Architecture." *Medical History* 49 (2005): 463–88.

Cederström, Hjalmar. *Södersjukhuset*. Stockholm: Rydahls Boktryckeri A-B, c. 1946.

Colomina, Beatriz. "The Medical Body in Modern Architecture." *Daidalos* 64 (June 1997): 60–71.

"Constructions hospitalières en Australia" and "Royal Melbourne Hospital à Melbourne." *Architecture française* 13, no. 127–128 (1952): 54–7.

"A Country Hospital That Will Serve Also as a Health Center." *Modern Hospital* 38, no. 5 (May 1932): 61.

Cushing, Lincoln. "More Kaiser Permanente Hospitals by Clarence Mayhew." Accessed 15 June 2016. https://kaiserpermanentehistory.org/latest/more-kaiser-permanente-hospitals-by-architect-clarence-mayhew/.

Davis, Arthur Q. *It Happened by Design: The Life and Work of Arthur Q. Davis*. Jackson, MS: University Press of Mississippi with The Ogden Museum of Southern Art, University of New Orleans, 2009.

Deckker, Zilah Quezado. *Brazil Built: The Architecture of the Modern Movement in Brazil*. London: E & FN Spon, 2000.

Derevoge, Guy. "Le nouvel hôpital royal de Melbourne (Australie)." *Construction moderne* 63 (June 1947): 823–7.

Dudley, George A. *A Workshop for Peace: Designing the United Nations Headquarters*. New York, NY: MIT Press, 1994.

Elzner, A.O., A.C. Bachmeyer and Elizabeth Pierce. "How the Children's Hospital of Cincinnatti Has Been Planned." *Modern Hospital* 28, no. 3 (March 1927): 83–90.

Erikson, Carl A. "What Germany Does and What Germany Doesn't: Some Comments, Not Too Serious, on Several Recent German Hospital Buildings Designed by H. Distel of Hamburg." *Modern Hospital* 36, no. 4 (April 1931): 73–8.

Erikson, Carl A. "Letter from Carl Erikson to Arthur G. Stephenson." 29 May 1933. In Vol. 65B A.G. Stephenson: Private Correspondence 1934, Box 1, MS2072: Papers of Sir Arthur Stephenson, National Library of Australia, Canberra.

Fisher, Alison. "Humanist Structures: Bertrand Goldberg Builds for Health Care." In *Bertrand Goldberg: Architecture of Invention*, edited by Zoë Ryan, 130–43. New Haven, CT: Yale University Press, 2011.

Folsom, Dwight and Dwight James Baum. "A Unique Achievement: Syracuse Memorial Hospital." *Modern Hospital* 28, no. 4 (April 1927): 71–6.

"A Fortress of Health." *Modern Hospital* 29, no. 5 (November 1927): 122.

Giedion, Sigfried. *Befreites Wohnen: Licht, Luft, Oeffnung*. Zurich and Leipzig: Orell Füssli Verlag, 1929.

Goad, Philip, Rowan Wilken and Julie Willis. *Australian Modern: The Architecture of Stephenson & Turner*. Melbourne: The Miegunyah Press, 2004.

Harwood, Elain. *Space, Hope and Brutalism: English Architecture 1945–1975*. New Haven, CT and London: Paul Mellon Centre for Studies in British Art, Yale University Press in association with Historic England, 2015.

"Hospitals of Tomorrow." *Modern Hospital* 51, no. 3 (September 1938): 90–1.

"Hospital at Haifa, Palestine." *Architect and Building News* (2 February 1940): 139–41.

"Hospitals in Australia" and "Dental Clinic." *Architectural Forum* 85 (December 1946): 109–14.

"Hôpital à Melbourne: Stephenson and Turner, Archts." *Architecture d'aujourd'hui* 18 (November 1947): 52–3.

Hughes, Jonathan. "The 'Matchbox on a Muffin': The Design of Hospitals in the Early NHS." *Medical History* 44 (2000): 21–56.

Huijsman, Robbert. "History and Trends in Dutch Hospital Architecture." In *The Architecture of Hospitals*, edited by Cor Wagenaar, 463–8. Rotterdam: NAi Publishers, 2006.

Hunter, S.D. "Beauty Is Another Asset." *Modern Hospital* 30, no. 4 (April 1928): 55–60.

Kahn, Moritz. "Woman's Hospital Sets a New Goal in Its March of Progress." *Modern Hospital* 39, no. 1 (July 1932): 67–72.

Kidder Smith, G.E. *Sweden Builds: Its Modern Architecture and Land Policy, Background, Development and Contribution*. London: The Architectural Press, 1950 (1950a).

Kidder Smith, G.E. *Switzerland Builds: Its Native and Modern Architecture*. London: The Architectural Press, 1950 (1950b).

Krinsky, Carol Herselle. *Gordon Bunshaft of Skidmore Owings and Merrill*. Cambridge, MA: MIT Press, 1988.

Lahiji, Nadir and D.S. Friedman. "At the Sink: Architecture in Abjection." In *Plumbing: Sounding Modern Architecture*, edited by Nadir Lahiji and D. S. Friedman, 35–60. New York: Princeton Architectural Press, 1997.

"The Lake County Tuberculosis Sanatorium." *Architectural Forum* (September 1940): 146–56.

Mens, Noor and Cor Wagenaar. *Health Care Architecture in the Netherlands*. Rotterdam: NAi Publishers, 2010.

Mock, Elizabeth (ed.). *Built in USA, 1932–1944*. New York: Museum of Modern Art, 1944.

Moretti, B. Franco. *Ospedali*. Milan: Editore Ulrico Hoepli, 1951.

Nelson, Paul. *Cité Hospitalière de Lille*. Paris: Editions Cahiers d'art, 1933.

Overy, Paul. *Light, Air and Openness: Modern Architecture between the Wars*. London: Thames & Hudson, 2007.

Pawlik, Peter R. *From Saarow to Alexandria: Ernst Kopp (1890–1962): The Detours of a Great Hospital Builder*. Herzogenrath, Germany: Murken-Altrogge, 2013.

Pesonen, Niilo. *Suomen sairaaloita; Sjukhus i Finland; Hospitals of Finland*. Helsinki: Werner Söderström Osakeyhtiö, 1964.

Peterkin, Janet. "Manhattan's Colossus of Medical Centers." *Modern Hospital* 31, no. 1 (July 1928): 55–66.

Peterkin, Janet. "Capitalizing Color Appeal by Means of the Interior Decorator's Art." *Modern Hospital* 33, no. 1 (July 1929): 64–5.

Powell, Kenneth. *Powell & Moya: Twentieth Century Architects*. London: RIBA Publishing, 2009.

Richardson, Harriet (ed.). *English Hospitals 1660–1948*. Swindon: Royal Commission on the Historical Monuments of England, 1998.

Rosenfield, Isadore. "The Fruit of Research." *Modern Hospital* 48, no. 3 (March 1937): 58–64.

Rosenfield, Isadore. *Hospital Architecture and Beyond*. New York: Van Nostrand Reinhold Co, 1969.

"Royal Prince Alfred Hospital, Sydney: Mercy Hospital, Melbourne: Freemason's Hospital, Melbourne: Ballarat and District Base Hospital, Victoria." *Royal Architectural Institute of Canada Journal* 14 (November 1937): 233–9.

Saint-Lô: Centre Hospitalier Mémorial France États-Unis. Saint-Lô, France, 2006.

"Sandringham Memorial Hospital." *Foundations* 6 (June 1961): 40.

Schmidt, Richard E. "Modern Hospital Design." *Architectural Forum* 38, no. 6 (December 1922): 252.

Schulze, Leonard. "White Plains: Its Present and Future." *Modern Hospital* 54, no. 6 (June 1940): 64–7.

Simon & Simon. "Porches Feature This Modern Sanatorium." *Modern Hospital* 29, no. 6 (December 1927): 79–82.

"Skidmore Owings & Merrill." *Museum of Modern Art Bulletin* 18, no. 1 (Fall 1950): 16.

Sloan, Raymond P. "Vast New Medical Centre Guards New York's Health." *Modern Hospital* 40, no. 3 (March 1933): 49–56.

Sloan, Raymond P. "A Hospital That Is Known by Its Hotel Air." *Modern Hospital* 42, no. 6 (May 1934): 70–4.

Stephenson, Arthur G. "Letter to Harold D Luxton from Arthur Stephenson." 15 September 1926. In AGS American Letters, Box 48, MS 2072: Papers of Sir Arthur Stephenson, National Library of Australia, Canberra.

Stephenson, Arthur G. "Note Book American Tour." 1927. In Box 1, MS 2235: Papers of Sir Arthur Stephenson, National Library of Australia, Canberra.

Stephenson, Arthur G. "Correspondence." 1932 (1932a). In Social General. Box 1, MS 2235: Papers of Sir Arthur Stephenson National Library of Australia, Canberra.

Stephenson, Arthur G. "Correspondence." 1932 (1932b). In Gen H-II, Box 1, MS 2235: Papers of Sir Arthur Stephenson, National Library of Australia, Canberra.

Stephenson, A.G. "A Tramp Abroad in the Hospital Field." Draft c. 1933. In Box 1, MS2235, Papers of Sir Arthur Stephenson, National Library of Australia, Canberra.

Stephenson, A.G. "A Tramp Abroad in the Hospital Field. Part I: Holland, France Switzerland." *Modern Hospital* 40, no. 5 (May 1933 (1933a)): 55–60.

Stephenson, A.G. "A Tramp Abroad in the Hospital Field. Part II: Italy, Austria, Germany." *Modern Hospital* 41, no. 2 (August 1933 (1933b)): 49–54.

Stephenson, A.G. "A Tramp Abroad in the Hospital Field. Part III." *Modern Hospital* 41, no. 6 (December 1933 (1933c)): 75–80.

Stephenson, A.G. "A Tramp Abroad in the Hospital Field. Part IV: Germany." *Modern Hospital* 43, no. 2 (August 1934 (1934a)): 61–5.

Stephenson, A.G. "A Tramp Abroad in the Hospital Field. Part V: Germany." *Modern Hospital* 43, no. 3 (September 1934 (1934b)): 81–4.

Stephenson, A.G. "A Tramp Abroad in the Hospital Field. Part VI: Germany." *Modern Hospital* 44, no. 1 (January 1935): 74–8.

Stephenson, Arthur G. "Eye Infect Mental TB, Book VI." n.d. In Box 1, MS 2235: Papers of Sir Arthur Stephenson National Library of Australia, Canberra.

Stephenson, Arthur G. "Leadership in Our Sphere as Hospital Architects." 1959. In Travel letters by Sir Arthur Stephenson 1949–64, Box 4, MS 2235: Papers of Sir Arthur Stephenson, National Library of Australia, Canberra.

"Two Australian Hospitals: Stephenson and Meldrum, Architects." *Architectural Review* 81 (February 1937): 51–5.

Verderber, Stephen and David J. Fine. *Healthcare Architecture in an Age of Radical Transformation*. New Haven, CT: Yale University Press, 2000.
Wagenaar, Cor. "The Hospital and the City." In *Healing Architecture*, edited by Christine Nickl-Weller and Hans Nickl, 124–49. Salenstein, Switzerland: Braun Publishing AG, 2013.
Wheeler, E. Todd. *Hospital Design and Function*. New York: McGraw-Hill, 1964.
Wheeler, E. Todd. *Hospital Modernization and Expansion*. New York: McGraw-Hill, 1971.
Wigley, Mark. *White Walls, Designer Dresses*. Boston: MIT Press, 1995.
Wilk, Christopher (ed.). *Modernism, 1914–1939: Designing a New World*. London: V&A Publications, 2006.
Zervos, Christian. "Introduction." In Paul Nelson, *Cité Hospitalière de Lille*, xv–xvii (English version). Paris: Editions Cahiers D'Art, 1933.

8 Health city, healing landscapes and the hospital campus

In 1933, American émigré architect Paul Nelson (1895–1979) published a detailed design for a hospital complex for the City of Lille in northern France under the title *Cité Hospitalière*. Commissioned by the city's new socialist government as part of its ambitious programme of public works, the proposal was unusual for the period in representing both advanced thinking in the hospital field as well as the avant-garde position in architecture. Nelson listed "Directive Ideas" at the beginning of the published design, emphasising that this was more than a hospital in the conventional sense of that term:

> To plan a city of health • To plan a city consecrated to the progress of medical science, teaching and research • To plan a city where the patient will find all the elements necessary for his cure, where the well will be taught to preserve their health and where their person may be respected • To plan a city of production and economy by rationalizing all the movements and needs in a minimum space – To plan a durable city, to construct not only for the present but for the future by assuring the flexibility of the interior and the ease of adaptation in all new needs and scientific discoveries • Rationalization: Group closely all scattered efforts – Reconstruct their out of date buildings in one – Centralize the administration and services – Rationalize.
>
> (Nelson 1933: 4)

Because of the fiercely negative reaction of conservative political forces and local newspapers, the complex was never built, but nevertheless it was a signal project for the modern hospital (Doyle 2016, 2017). It was at once a visionary articulation of the modern aspirations for rational, public-spirited healthcare, and a harbinger of the flawed planning concepts and weak civic design that characterised much hospital development in the postwar decades. Importantly, it highlighted the strong ongoing relationship between urbanistic thought and hospital planning, and the ways in which each could be a proving ground for the other.

Like the most ambitious mega-hospital projects in the United States in the late 1920s and early 1930s, Nelson's Lille project championed vertical organisation as the most efficient strategy for the modern hospital. Like the New York skyscraper hospitals of the period, it also proposed the integration, on a single site, of previously disparate hospital, clinical and teaching functions. Where the city of Lille had been home to ten different hospital buildings in ten separate locations, as well as a medical school, it would now have just one great hospital city (Figure 8.1). Architecturally, however, it differentiated itself from the American skyscraper hospitals through its rigorously abstract language, highlighting space and light rather than mass. It also departed much more fundamentally from tradition than American projects in both its approach to site planning and in the articulation of architectural plan to construction technique. Nelson's project pointed in particular to the potential flexibility of the hospital plan by separating structure from room partitions, and it dematerialised the external wall surface by employing a thin membrane of double glazing rather than an identifiable exterior wall on each of its four multistorey main buildings.

Figure 8.1 General plan for the Cité Hospitalière de Lille (Lille Hospital Complex), Lille, France. Architect: Paul Nelson, 1932–1933. Photograph: Man Ray, 1932.

Source: Centre Pompidou

© MAN RAY TRUST/ADAGP. Copyright Agency, 2018, used with permission. Photo © Centre Pompidou, MNAM-CCI, Dist. RMN-Grand Palais/image Centre Pompidou, MNAM-CCI

In keeping with the architectural avant-garde's conviction that existing cities were at best hopelessly outmoded and at worst diseased and dying, Nelson's conception depended on a clear separation from existing urban fabric. It was to occupy 30 hectares (72 acres) "10 minutes from the centre of Lille. Arrival by an elevated Autostrade [sic]" (Nelson 1933: 1). The Lille project was a gesture of urban reform even as it escaped its host city. Like many pavilion hospitals designed and constructed between the 1870s and the 1910s, it proposed a healthful site away from the noise and dust of the central city. But Nelson's conception of the landscape is far from that cultivated at the park-like Rudolf Virchow Krankenhaus (Rudolf Virchow Hospital), Berlin, Germany (Architect: Ludwig Hoffman, 1898–1906) or its contemporary, the West End Hospital in suburban Charlottenburg, Berlin, Germany (Milburn Jr. 1911). In Nelson's proposal, one would arrive by motorway onto a "vast cruciform terrace from which rise the different buildings". This terrace covered the ground floor, which was to house what Nelson described as all the "intermediate departments" (Nelson 1933: 1). There is an urbanistic double valence to this vision. On the one hand, it is the very model of the city as described by the Spanish philosopher José Ortega y Gasset in 1932 – a clearing that defines itself against the surrounding nature, "a negation of the fields" (Ortega y Gasset 1932: 154; D'Hooghe 2011). On the other hand, it echoes Le Corbusier's dis-urbanised Radiant City. The cruciform terrace creates and defines a hospital city even as it separates itself from Lille and suggests an entirely new set of (anti-) urban forms.

As architectural historian Jonathan Hughes has argued, in several significant ways, the discourse on the modern hospital variously influenced and reflected the development of modernist urbanism (Hughes 1997). The two shared, he suggests, a preoccupation with functional zoning and efficient circulation in particular. But the relationship between the two, as Hughes has emphasised, was far from simple. In many ways, twentieth century urban planning derived its hygienic orientation from hospital planners. Architectural theorist Sven-Olov Wallenstein has argued that this has a long history (Wallenstein 2008). The ideal of the hospital as a hygienic facility, capable of achieving something positive in health terms rather than simply providing accommodation for the sick, underpinned the redevelopment of the Hotel de Dieu in Paris in the 1780s. This idea of hospital as hygiene facility, he argues, became a model for the design and management of modern urban space in general. This powerful explanatory model is compelling at a discursive level. However, the empirical evidence from nineteenth-century hospital development is more equivocal.

The relationship of the hospital to the city is one that vacillates in the nineteenth century between a model of productive and hygienic urban space on the one hand, and a foil to the urban, a kind of peri-urban retreat, on the other. The latter tendency in hospital development derived its relationship to the city in part from models developed for asylums to treat psychiatric patients (Gerlach-Spriggs, Kaufman and Warner 1998). At the end of the nineteenth century, the hospital was, in some instances, a civic institution with a powerful hygienic (and moral) lesson embedded within it, and in others it was a campus or city in itself, designed as a riposte to existing cities and as a model for new urban development. Throughout the twentieth century, this question and this tension was not finally resolved. But what is clear is that the hospital was frequently bound up with the redefinition of urban form and urban space, and Nelson's project is explicit in arguing that Lille's new hospital should perform this function (Hughes 1997; Wallenstein 2008).

The modern hospital as healthcare campus

Neither Nelson's 1932 project nor the Cité Hospitalière realised on the same site for Lille by Jean Walter in 1937 were in fact cities in any real sense. They lack almost all the social characteristics and many of the functions normally regarded as prerequisites for an urban environment. There was no market or shops, no work being performed that was not related to the hospitals and health, and no real sense that people might just go there to see and be with other people, a crucial dimension of urban life. What many major hospitals constructed during this period reflected much more than anything was a highly rationalised, even industrialised, university campus.

University planners and architects in the United States had already evoked the idea of the campus-as-city in the late nineteenth and early twentieth centuries. Architectural historian of the American university campus, Paul Venable Turner, has noted that from around 1900, older references to the collegiate ideal of the "academical village" began to disappear. "Slogans like 'City of Learning' and 'Collegiate City' became common and began to influence the architectural form of the university" (Turner 1984: 167). One of the issues that defined the modern hospital was its embrace of teaching and research as fundamental activities. As such, most of the influential North American hospital projects from the 1920s to the 1940s were either connected to universities or involved collaborations with university partners. Schmidt, Garden & Erikson designed the medically and mechanically advanced but architecturally conservative Chicago Lying-In Hospital on the University of Chicago campus, Chicago, Illinois, USA, in the early 1930s; when completed, it received extensive coverage alongside other clinics and medical buildings at the campus in the *Modern Hospital*. Its buildings were designed in a Collegiate Gothic mode much like the university proper and framed the Janet Ayer Fairbank Cloister, a feature of the overall conception of the hospital and a natural refuge in the midst of a growing hospital and medical school complex (Peterkin 1933) (Figure 8.2).

Cleveland's University Hospitals campus, Cleveland, Ohio, USA, consolidated on a single site in the early 1930s, was a denser configuration than the University of Chicago. Its University Circle neighbourhood included a

Figure 8.2 The collegiate Gothic form of the Chicago Lying-In Hospital, Chicago, Illinois, USA, complemented its university surroundings. Architects: Schmidt, Garden & Erikson, 1931. Photograph: Capes Photo, c. 1931.

Courtesy: University of Chicago Photographic Archive, apf2–01524, Special Collections Research Center, University of Chicago Library.

spacious configuration of parkways and museums and the amalgamated Case Western Reserve University. As such, the environs of the hospital were campus-like. There was an obvious effort to maintain green, open spaces on and around the hospital buildings. It was also one of the first major hospitals in which planners highlighted the use of space between buildings for car parking in promotional copy about the institution. The campus ideal was thus somewhat compromised by the needs of the automobile, though contemporary planners did not necessarily see it that way ("The Hospitals of the Western Reserve University" 1931).

In Europe, the situation was somewhat different. The university was not presumed to be outside or separate from city and town like the American college campus. Universities were part of the fabric of everyday urban life, and had been for many centuries. But American campus planning ideas spread in the early twentieth century and influential hospital designers such as Edward F. Stevens promoted an approach to the hospital site that drew on his admiration for the great European pavilion hospitals, such as Berlin's Virchow, as well as on his understanding of the advantages of American-style campus planning on greenfield sites. As European hospitals were modernised and as they sought new sites on the periphery of towns and cities, lessons of site selection and modification from the campus ideal were adopted and adapted, often joining with established site planning traditions connected with the villa and formal garden (Stevens 1918).

Two significant European hospital projects initiated in the mid-1930s – one in Brescia in northern Italy and the other in Colmar in Alsace in eastern France – adopted a campus approach to site planning. Both fused deeply traditional institutional and planning norms with the scientific promise of the modern hospital.

The old hospital in Brescia occupied a Neoclassical building in the centre of the city. But in 1930, hospital administrators decided to relocate and modernise the city's main hospital in a new 1,430-bed facility. A young local engineer, Angelo Bordoni (1891–1957), designed the new hospital, the Nuovo Ospedale Maggiore di Brescia (New Major Hospital, Brescia), on a site 3 kilometres from the historic centre of the town. Organised along a circular perimeter pathway, the site plan was an extraordinary cellular conception. The plan was highly abstract and photographs of the model indicated that this was to be Italy's most architecturally advanced medical institution in the 1930s. B. Franco Moretti's compendium of hospital projects, *Ospedali*, first published in 1935, even used the site plan as its cover graphic (Moretti 1951). The ostensible rationale for the whole Brescia plan was to ensure discrete systems of circulation for people and materials, preventing interference of one with the other, while also minimising distances between different departments in the institution. However, as realised and as experienced in three dimensions, the hospital campus maintained a deep connection to traditional models. At the centre of the plan was a grand hexagonal plaza containing a church, harking back to early modern hospital plans in Italy in which each bed enjoyed an uninterrupted view of a hospital chapel and its altar. One historian of the site, Paolo Ventura, has also described the detailing and ornamentation of the new Brescia Hospital as maintaining artisanal technologies (Ventura 2017). It was both self-consciously modern and yet still sought forms of institutional validity through traditional material and spatial arrangements (Moretti 1951) (Figure 8.3).

Like many projects of the period, the construction of Brescia's new hospital was interrupted by World War II, and it was not completed until 1953. By that time, it looked much less dramatically modern than it had in the early plans of the mid-1930s. While highly abstract and putatively rationalistic in its planning, it exhibited an obvious concern with civic decorum and traditional symbolic meaning. But it nevertheless still highlighted a number of key themes of the modern hospital's relationship to the host city. It was constructed on the periphery and consolidated disparate

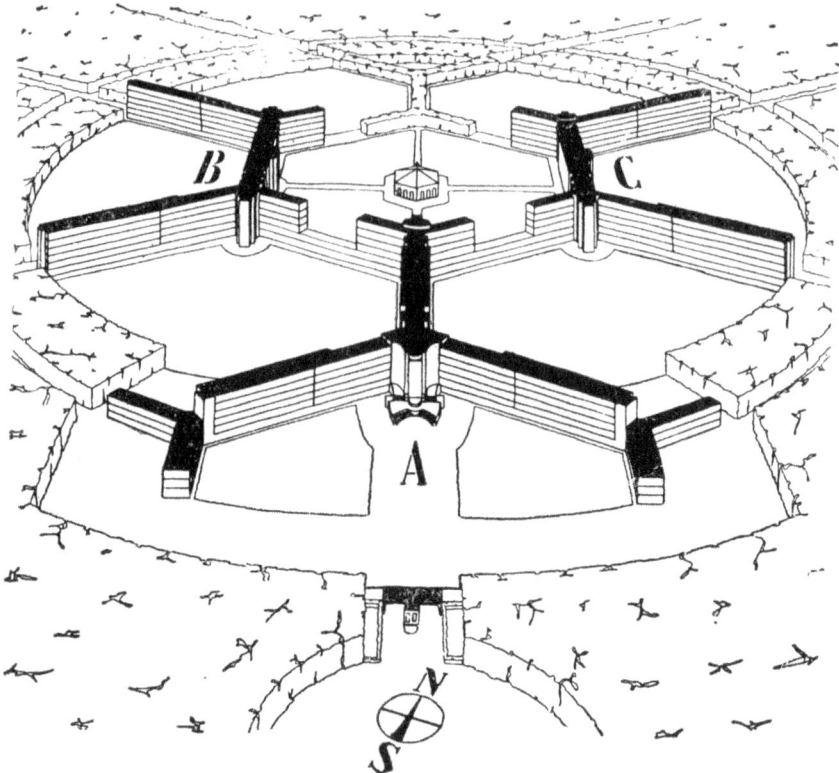

Figure 8.3 Nuovo Ospedale Maggiore di Brescia (New Major Hospital), Brescia, Italy. Architect: Angelo Bordoni, 1930–1953. Delineator: unknown.

Source: Moretti, B. Franco. *Ospedali*. Milan: Editore Ulrico Hoepli, 1951: 26.

clinical, teaching and research functions into a single campus entity, a health city of sorts. It was a graphic symbol of urban modernity, but it also remained a place apart, a walled entity with its own civic and institutional character (Ventura 2017).

The new 740-bed Hôpital Louis Pasteur (Louis Pasteur Hospital) (1935–1937) in Colmar, designed by Swiss architect William (Willy) Vetter (1902–1985), was also widely published in the specialist hospital literature in the 1930s and sits alongside other French projects such as those by Jean Walter (1883–1957) at Beaujon (1932–1935) and Lille (1934–1937), and Nelson's completed postwar hospital in Saint-Lô, France, the Centre Hospitalier Mémorial France États-Unis (France United States Memorial Hospital) (1946–1956), as one of the most architecturally significant modern hospital projects in France. After some years of planning and project publicity,

Health city, landscapes, the hospital campus 195

construction got underway in 1936, around the same time as the new Brescia hospital. As in Brescia, the Colmar project exhibited a form of mixed or hybrid modernism. That is, it did not forcefully proclaim an avant-garde position like Nelson's unbuilt project for Lille, but instead reflected the influence of a number of strongly modern characteristics in its planning and construction. The main inpatient departments, including maternity, the surgical suite and most of the wards, were consolidated in a large single block as in most other major modern hospitals of the period; the entire complex was constructed in reinforced concrete and an effort was made to create large column-free spaces to support flexibility in use; and the south elevation was characterised by a stepped façade that enabled access to wide terraces. Yet in a number of other ways, the hospital was traditional in its form and layout (de la Riviere 1931; Moretti 1951).

This moderation between tradition and modernity was nowhere more evident than in the site plan of the new Colmar hospital. On the one hand, its site plan was a formally striking, graphic gesture like those at Brescia and Nelson's T-shaped conception for Lille. But it was also spatially generous and traditionally landscaped more like a pavilion-plan hospital (Figure 8.4). The complex addressed the street formally, but the main ward building was set well back from the perimeter of the site and cut diagonally across it in order to optimise climatic orientation for the main ward building. The site plan also prioritised vehicular access and circulation, a characteristic of the modern hospital, but still maintained a strong sense of formal axiality. Included, too, were a chapel and nurses' garden reflecting

Figure 8.4 Hôpital Louis Pasteur (Louis Pasteur Hospital), Colmar, France. Architect: William (Willy) Vetter, 1935–1937. Photograph: unknown.
Source: Moretti, B. Franco. *Ospedali*. Milan: Editore Ulrico Hoepli, 1951: 262.

older institutional priorities. The new hospital was situated outside the old city on an 11-hectare greenfield site. But Vetter favoured a more traditional approach to civic design than that which Nelson had prescribed and that which other prominent modern hospital designers would favour in following decades. Visitors all entered through a formal gateway and the administration building, morgue, staff accommodation, laboratories, kitchens and laundry buildings defined the boundary of the site on either side of the entrance, in effect creating a walled refuge inside the institution.

Nevertheless, using covered walkways, Vetter also created a clever functional diagram that reflected the favoured model of modern hospital planners, who used the modern industrial enterprise as inspiration. Supplies such as food and clean laundry would enter one side, and waste and finished products would exit from the other. Separated from the main block were isolated buildings for dermatology, infectious diseases and tuberculosis, and, in between, a large formally landscaped area of open space. In other words, the site plan incorporated medically advanced thinking and was underpinned by an ethos of industrial efficiency. Moreover, the buildings themselves were constructed using the most advanced structural systems of the day derived directly from the work of Vetter's former employer and idol, the French architect and specialist in reinforced concrete construction Auguste Perret (1874–1954). At the same time, the effect of these modern approaches to hospital planning, construction and operations was tempered by the employment of more traditional markers of environmental quality and institutional identity (French Ministry of Culture 2014).

At Brescia, and especially at Colmar, the impact of the discourse on the modern hospital was clearly evident at the scale of the site plan. But, as with so much modern architecture that is outside the canon of modernism, these hospitals also evoked older planning patterns and formal strategies. The ideal of the "health city" promised a new dispensation: total environments dedicated to hygienic treatment and the aspiration of a healthy society. Yet the idea that they were cities was little more than boosterish rhetoric, a reference to the expanded scale at which such places were planned in the 1930s and 1940s. In reality, most of the truly advanced hospital projects completed during this period were essentially entirely new campuses.

Fortresses of health: the skyscraper hospitals

For small and middle-sized cities with ambitions to improve their healthcare systems – places such as Lille, Colmar and Brescia – a new health campus on a peripheral site was an obvious response to the challenges of site selection and conceptualisation in the middle decades of the twentieth century. The same was true of the campus-based teaching hospitals in North America. But for general hospitals at the centre of the biggest cities – New York City, for example, or Paris – such an approach was not necessarily viable. New York architects Butler & Kohn in association with York & Sawyer designed the Hospital for Chronic Diseases (later Goldwater Memorial Hospital) on Welfare Island (now Roosevelt Island), New York, USA during the 1930s. The patients accommodated there in subsequent decades enjoyed expansive views over the East River and back to Manhattan, and the modern buildings were laid out as a campus, with generous provision for open space. But a small island with limited road access, none of it from the Manhattan side, was not a workable location for the city's major acute care and teaching hospitals. For New York's most prominent medical institutions, Manhattan was the only realistic option (Bluestone 1938).

In the late 1920s, the firm of Coolidge, Shepley, Bulfinch & Abbott (CSBA) designed a grand health complex on the Upper East Side of Manhattan for the newly amalgamated institution, the New York Hospital–Cornell Medical Center (1932), composed of five former hospitals and the Cornell Medical School (Robinson 1933; "The Designing Procedure" 1933; "The Structure and Equipment of the New York Hospital" 1933). The architecture firm and its predecessors – Henry Hobson Richardson; Shepley, Rutan & Coolidge; and Coolidge & Shattuck – had a comprehensive portfolio of public and institutional projects dating back to the 1870s, including a masterplan and the design of the inner quadrangle for Stanford University in Palo Alto, California, USA (1891) (Heskell 1999; Turner 1984). In the 1900s and 1910s, the firm designed a series of medical schools, including the austerely Neoclassical Harvard Medical School grouping. In the 1920s, this established pedigree was brought together in the design of medical schools and other campus work with an evolving expertise in hospital buildings, and the firm created two of the most medically advanced complexes of the period, Cleveland's University Hospitals campus (1921–1929) – in fact a series of related projects for Case Western Reserve University – and the Vanderbilt University Medical School, Nashville, Tennessee, USA (1926). The latter, as with Cleveland, was an integrated campus of acute care hospitals and a medical school (Heskell 1999; "The Hospitals of Western Reserve University" 1931).

But the New York Hospital–Cornell Medical Center was their most ambitious and representative project of the period. It spread over four existing city blocks, two of them consolidated into a single block for the main building group, and one critic described it at the time, predictably perhaps, as "almost a city within itself" (Heskell 1999: 57). Certainly, the main buildings dwarfed those on neighbouring blocks and the whole project rivalled the gargantuan scale of the contemporaneous Rockefeller Center development (1930–1939) in midtown Manhattan. Yet, where that project depended on a series of streets and plazas for its identity and its ultimate success as a major civic place, the new hospital complex broke up the massive built volumes with a set of spaces that were much less urban in character. The firm's historian has described the original main entrance along 68th Street as "a large front lawn", and the eastern edge of the site along the East River frontage featured an arcaded, sunken garden and series of "courts of grass and trees" (Heskell 1999: 57). Project information and publicity also highlighted the presence of tennis courts on the site for the recreational use of staff. In other words, the site was more campus-like than city-like, despite its great verticality, tight configuration and densely organised functional programme. Nevertheless, it was physically distinct from anything found on an existing university or college campus. The towering power-house chimney stack on 70th Street, for example, rose almost as high as the central structure, announcing a great industrial presence. As with the hospital sites at Brescia and Colmar, the New York hospital was uncertain in its modernity and in its relationship to the city. Even as it monumentalised its industrial presence and medical capacity, the hospital's architects were careful to highlight the presence of green, open space and the benefits of a college-like atmosphere in the library and recreational areas (Sloan 1933).

The new scale at which hospitals developed their facilities in the 1920s and 1930s challenged existing building or institutional typologies, giving rise to a wide variety of analogies to describe the modern hospital. Advertisements in *Modern Hospital* referred to "Cathedrals of Healing" and "Citadels of Health". In the early 1930s, the Metropolitan Life Insurance Company produced an advertisement with the heading "A Fortress of Health" ("A Fortress of Health" 1927). The accompanying picture was a perspective drawing of the recently completed New York Columbia-Presbyterian Medical Center, New York, USA (1928) designed by architect James Gamble Rogers (1867–1947). Advertisements, publicity and editorial content about the hospital in many different publications characterised it as a colossus and as a great fortress of health. A 1928 profile in *Modern Hospital* evoked its presence as follows: "Rising Above the banks of the Hudson River at Washington Heights, Manhattan's highest point, now stand the massive, towering structures of New York's new medical centre, dominating the local landscape" (Peterkin 1928: 55). In the same year, the architects themselves described it as "a great and grim fortress, benign in purpose, raised high and strong against the assaults of disease" (Betsky 1994: 217).

The new medical centre, which combined the Presbyterian Hospital, Columbia University Medical School and several smaller institutions – including the new Harkness Intermediate Hospital – into one great complex, was the product of nearly two decades of planning and opened in 1928. Its position on the cliffs above the Hudson River made the complex highly visible and amplified its fortress-like quality. In his study of Rogers' work, architectural historian and critic Aaron Betsky variously characterised the medical centre as "an abstract composition of blocks" and a "thrusting mountain range" and suggested that "it resembled a condensation of the 'virtual city-in-itself', or an integrated city-mountain range into which designers like Raymond Hood, Harvey Wiley Corbett, and

Hugh Ferriss only dreamed of transforming Manhattan" (Betsky 1994: 218–19). But even in this great complex of buildings, a seemingly self-conscious exercise in making New York sublime, there was acknowledgement that a more conventional campus ideal should also inform the site planning for a contemporary hospital. Separating the main buildings were a series of private courtyards for the use of staff and patients, which, as at the other great Manhattan hospital of the period, were not overtly urban in character. More generally, the hospital was not an obvious precursor for the automobile-friendly, functionally oriented site plans that would become prominent between the 1950s and 1970s. Planning for vehicular circulation was evident in the ambulance and service courts, but these were spatially modest and self-effacing in the context of the overall site plan.

New York was thus home to the two most dramatic skyscraper hospitals, the literal high points of vertical organisation in the modern hospital. But many institutions around the world embraced the skyscraper form for their hospitals in the following years. The Walter, Plousey & Cassan-designed Hôpital Beaujon (Beaujon Hospital) in suburban Clichy in Paris, France (1932–1935) and the Los Angeles County General Hospital, Los Angeles, California, USA (Arch: Allied Architects' Association, 1932) – the general hospital that gave the long-running soap opera its name and was featured in its opening titles sequence – followed directly after the New York skyscraper hospitals. These were twelve- to fourteen-storey structures in big cities with intense land uses. But they were also both situated in urban contexts not nearly as built-up as their New York predecessors. At both hospitals, the process of vehicular arrival and circulation was innovative for the period and central to the site planning process. At the Hôpital Beaujon, vehicles arrived via a ramp that led to an entry point a level above the ground plane. This separation drew on ideas pioneered at railway stations such as Grand Central Terminal in New York where taxi pickup was separated from other vehicles and pedestrian circulation. The New York firm of Skidmore Owings & Merrill later developed this idea for its Veterans' Administration Hospital in Fort Hamilton, Brooklyn, New York, USA (1947–1952), where the internal road system on the hospital site indicated that most visitors and patients were expected to arrive by private car or taxi (Figure 8.5). It was a model later used almost universally at airports, as well as at many suburban shopping malls developed in North America in the 1960s.

Los Angles was the city where the concept of "drive-in" was invented. In the 1920s, and 1930s Angelenos gradually came to expect that they could not only drive to their destination – shops, restaurants, schools and hospitals – but that they could take their vehicles onto the site where those places were located and, in many cases, park them there too (Longstreth 1997, 1999). At the L.A. County General Hospital, the arrival sequence presumed private automobility and the site accommodated several parallel systems of circulation: one for doctors, one for visitors and another for service vehicles. While most of the 1,600 or so beds in the hospital were

Figure 8.5 Vehicular arrival at the Fort Hamilton Veterans' Administration Hospital, Brooklyn, New York, USA. Architects: Skidmore Owings & Merrill, 1947–1952. Photograph: unknown, c. 1950s.

Courtesy: Gordon Bunshaft architectural drawings and papers, 1909–1990, Department of Drawings & Archives, Avery Architectural and Fine Arts Library, Columbia University.

contained in the prominent main tower, a series of tunnels serviced the sprawling 56-acre site, allowing meals, linen and other supplies to be moved around with as little interruption as possible to the movement of medical staff and patients.

The process of rationalisation of movement in the modern hospital did not inevitably put institutions such as L.A. County General Hospital in conflict with ideas of architectural decorum, nor indeed did they cancel out the pursuit of environmental quality at the site. Rather the L.A. hospital had a distinguished programme of artworks that underlined its civic mission and exhibited a highly sophisticated approach to site planning. Located on the city's east side, the whole complex was a kind of constructed landscape, a series of interlocking terraced blocks that rose up from the hillside to form a base for the tall towers above. Moreover, postcard illustrations and photographs from the 1930s and 1940s highlight the richness of the plantings and the care with which the terraced areas were landscaped. While the social circumstances of its evolution and later management militated against the protection and development of these qualities, there is little question that the hospital was an attempt to marry a highly rationalised and efficient model of healthcare with well-designed, stimulating landscaped environs. When it opened, in other words, L.A.'s largest hospital was far from the inhumane, denatured institution that later critics would associate with this and other tall block hospitals (Figure 8.6).

Two projects by German émigré architect Erich Mendelsohn (1887–1953) in the British Mandate for Palestine in the 1930s arguably surpassed L.A. County General Hospital in their integration of landscape and building: the Hadassah University Medical Centre (1934–1939) on Mount Scopus in East Jerusalem; and the Government Hospital at Haifa (1938–1940). Mendelsohn's concept for the dramatic Mount Scopus site was a typically powerful graphic gesture, with the long, narrow main building inscribed along a ridgeline. It was the skyscraper hospital laid down on its side. The Haifa project was less topographically dramatic but was also highly sensitive to the wider environment. It was constructed on the site of an old Carmelite convent and the site plan preserved many of the old trees – eucalyptus, tamarisk, mimosa, palm, olive and jacaranda – that had been cultivated there. The main ward block was a thin slab organised along a single-loaded corridor, and the contemporary descriptions of the project highlighted the consideration given to prevailing sea breezes, the careful solar orientation of the main buildings and the extensive use of insulation and protective balconies. The care taken to landscape the site also underlined the ongoing interest of modern hospital architects in the qualitative experience of patients and hospital staff, not just a narrow programmatic rationality ("Jerusalem's New and Modern Medical Centre" 1939; "Hospital at Haifa" 1940).

Mendelsohn's hospitals in Palestine (now Israel) were developed on exceptional sites and have enjoyed a prominent reputation among hospital

202 *Health city, landscapes, the hospital campus*

Figure 8.6 Postcard depicting the Los Angeles County General Hospital, Los Angeles, California, USA. Architects: Allied Architects' Association, 1932. Artist: unknown.
Courtesy: Boston Public Library: Tichnor Brothers Collection.

projects because of the architect's international fame as a protean figure in the modern movement. But while Mendelsohn was on record as a great admirer of James Gamble Rogers' Columbia-Presbyterian Medical Center and designed three widely published hospital projects himself – the two projects in Palestine as well as the Maimonides Health Center in San Francisco, California, USA (1946–1950) – he was never a hospital specialist. That is, he was not part of the group of hospital experts closely aligned with the International Hospital Association or the specialist hospital journals, *Nosokomeion* or *Modern Hospital*. Because of this, the projects were not central to the evolving tradition of the modern hospital and its discourse in the 1940s and did not decisively influence the direction of hospital site planning.

Rationalised landscapes for health

A group of major hospital projects completed in the early and mid-1940s are much more representative of the direction of the modern hospital – especially the way buildings were disposed to city and site – than Mendelsohn's projects. Sweden's Södersjukhuset (Southern Hospital), Stockholm

(1937–1944), designed by Hjalmar Cederström and Hermann Imhäuser; the Kantonsspital (Cantonal Hospital), Basel, Switzerland (1939–1945) by Hermann Baur, E & P Vischer and Bräuning Leu Dürig; and the Royal Melbourne Hospital, Parkville, Victoria, Australia (1936–1942) by Australian hospital specialists Stephenson & Turner represent the full development of the rationalised landscape for health. While the projects differ architecturally in several significant ways, each of these hospitals turned away from the exaggerated verticality of some of the interwar skyscraper hospitals and highlighted instead a preference for linked slab blocks. In this they presaged the development of the classic postwar modernist housing projects. But instead of large aprons of grass and pedestrian pathways separating the main buildings, the hospitals focused on how to accommodate, as efficiently as possible, a system of vehicular circulation for servicing the institutions. This did not necessarily completely displace soft landscaping, at least not in the first instance, but systems of circulation were prioritised with these new institutions so as to underpin their productivity.

When completed in 1944, Södersjukhuset was the most thoroughly realised example of a hospital that brought together the philosophy of the International Hospital Association and the direction of modern architecture. It was based on social planning, international collaboration, breadth of social mission and a functional plan as the generator of overall form. Swedish medical and political leaders arrived at their decision to build the hospital in light of a thorough regional planning process that attempted to carefully project the health needs of the population (Cederström 1932). Writing about the hospital, Hjalmar Cederström (1880–1953) also highlighted the scope of international and interdisciplinary cooperation that underpinned the hospital's realisation, including the involvement of German hospital expert Dr Wilhelm C.F. Alter (1875–1943), editor of *Nosokomeion* for most of the 1930s and a leading figure in the international hospital movement (Cederström c. 1946). Breadth in the scope of the hospital's mission was also central to Södersjukhuset. It was a place dedicated to building social capital and a good society, in addition to delivering acute healthcare and building knowledge in the field of medical science.

The new medical complex was situated on a bluff overlooking Årstavijen cove on Lake Mälaren. Consequently, most wards enjoyed an expansive natural outlook. But the site plan for the hospital dedicated an unprecedented amount of space between buildings to vehicular circulation (Figure 8.7).

Ambulance arrival was separated from the main driveway and coal deliveries were likewise given a separate service road. Some meandering pathways typical of older hospitals were indicated on the south, or lake, side of the main block in the plan, but in stark contrast to Mendelsohn's plans or those for the L.A. County General Hospital from a few years earlier, there was no overt reference to landscaping or plantings. The detailed booklet released in 1946 to celebrate the opening of the complex and share

204 *Health city, landscapes, the hospital campus*

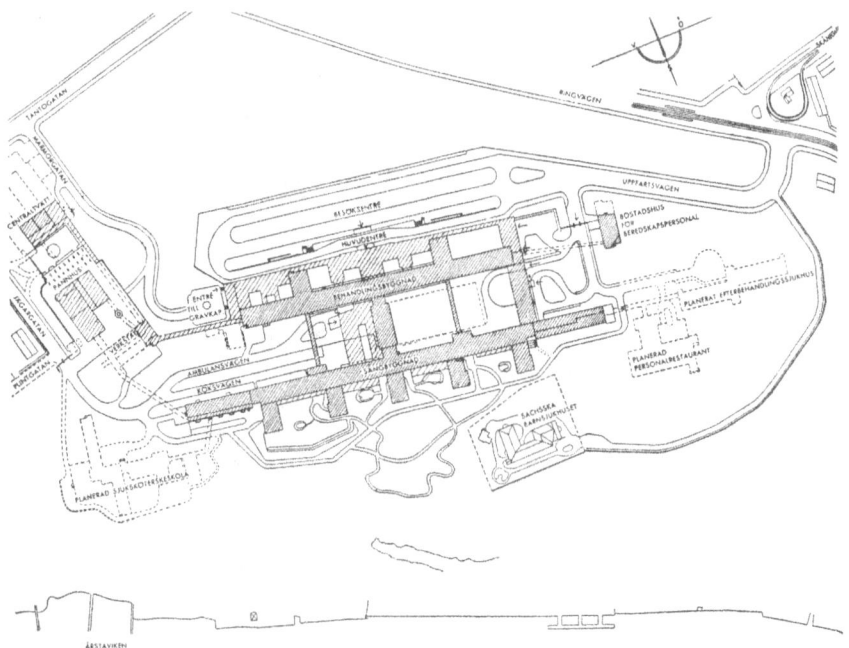

Figure 8.7 Site plan of Södersjukhuset (Southern Hospital), Stockholm, Sweden. Architects: Hjalmar Cederström and Hermann Imhäuser, 1937–1944. Delineator: unknown.

Source: Cederström, Hjalmar. *Södersjukhuset*. Stockholm: Rydahls Boktryckeri A-B, c. 1946: 18.

knowledge of the planning and construction process with international specialists in the field likewise made no reference to natural landscaping (Cederström c. 1946).

The disappearance of careful landscaping from hospital sites in this period was by no means inevitable, as the very carefully presented Kantonsspital in Basel attests. This project incorporated a clever circulation system for motorised arrival and servicing – the programmatic trend of the period. It also provided open-air terraces at the top of the building – the key architectural motif for modern healthcare in the 1930s and 1940s. And yet, even in its relatively dense urban context, the use of long, thin slab blocks that were also very tall for Basel enabled the institution and their architects to dedicate a very significant portion of the site to landscaped gardens and grounds. Even as the institution grew over the decades, most of this space was protected from building development. The hospital's architects and managers showed that a functional orientation to hospital output and rational procedures could be married with a qualitative focus on the hospital environment. They also balanced the somewhat traditional sense that the hospital was a kind of campus, providing respite from the city even with its overtly urban orientation (Gmur and Vacchini 2004).

The Royal Melbourne Hospital (RMH) constructed a new eight-hundred-bed hospital facility designed by hospital specialists Stephenson & Turner, which was also completed during World War II and was used by the US military before reverting to civilian use at the end of the conflict. Almost as far away in distance as one could be from Södersjukhuset and the Kantonsspital Basel, the Australian hospital nevertheless shared many characteristics with its Swedish and Swiss contemporaries. Like those contemporaries, it was a distinctive product of the international discourse on the modern hospital and was touted as Australia's most modern just as Stockholm's new hospital was proclaimed as Sweden's most modern. The RMH was close to the heart of the metropolitan system as a whole, again similar to Södersjukhuset, but at the periphery of the densely developed central city grid plan. And, just as the Södersjukuset provided patients with pleasant outlooks softened by nature so the RMH offered its patients expansive prospects over nearby parkland and university grounds. But, as at Södersjukhuset, the hospital site was imagined as a functional diagram supporting a productive system of healthcare. In terms of site planning and the treatment of the ground plane, both of these hospitals were more like modern industrial facilities than hospitals of the previous generation.

During the design and construction phases of the new RMH, the institution had already reconceived the nature of its work in industrial terms. In its 1937–1938 annual report, the hospital published a diagram that enumerated and graphically represented the "throughput" of the hospital, noting that eight hundred thousand meals had been served during the year, that they had conducted over ten thousand operations, consumed forty-two thousand gallons of milk and laundered almost two million items. The diagram showed an ambulance arriving on one side while on the other an upright figure strides away one of "6,477 cases discharged". Meanwhile, towards the back of the building depicted in the diagram, a truck delivers a portion of the 4,000 tonnes of coal and coke used by the hospital in that year (Royal Melbourne Hospital 1938). The frankly utilitarian focus on quantity of hospital output and the scale of operation was an increasingly obvious characteristic of hospital publicity and self-presentation in the years immediately before and after World War II.

This changing picture of the hospital ultimately also changed the architecture of the hospital, including in particular the site planning and the landscaping of the grounds. The verdant and healthful surroundings that typified the ideal of the pavilion hospital were replaced by a more machine-like conception, one that also made more space for the machinery of hospital operations and its mechanised transportation systems. At RMH, much of this was buried from view. The hospital contained an extensive system of tunnels and the hospital's power plant, for example, was linked to two neighbouring hospitals built in the 1950s.

In a speculative proposal for RMH, the architects also conceived it as part of a comprehensive medical "city" like the New York Hospital–Cornell Medical Center, which they cited as part of the proposal (Figure 8.8). The "hospital-city" idea envisaged multiple specialised hospitals, flanking the existing but brand new RMH buildings, across a huge swathe of land. The new health city required extensive demolition of existing terrace housing – inferred at this time as containers and incubators of disease and misery – into a place which offered "[b]etter doctors, better nurses, better health workers, better babies, more certain relief from disease, in short – longer life" (Grover and Imhotep 1944b: 8). The site plan showed the series of new hospitals, and associated housing, placed on the site with generous spaces in between, to allow for the maximum amount of sunlight, yet

Figure 8.8 Stephenson & Turner publicly proposed plans to create a large hospital precinct, consisting of multiple specialist hospitals and the existing Royal Melbourne Hospital. Melbourne Medical Centre, proposal. Architects: Stephenson & Turner, c. 1944. Delineator: unknown, 1944.

Source: Grover, Dorothy and "Imhotep". "A Great University Medical Centre for Melbourne: Full Details of a Far-Sighted Plan to Safeguard Posterity's Health". *Argus*, 14 October 1944: 8.

serviced by roads and paths that knitted the site together. The spaciousness had a clear purpose: "the Melbourne Hospital ... should be surrounded by adequate open space, not only for beautification purposes, but to act as a buffer to noise" (Grover and Imhotep 1944a: 8). The drawings suggest tennis courts and treed borders to the street edges. But amenity was more than just space:

> Provision must be made, too, for ... centralising of the power station, laundry and stores departments, while a recreational centre comprising hall, cinema and library would also be a necessary adjunct, likewise a shopping centre for resident staff.
> (Grover and Imhotep 1944a: 8)

This was a vision that conceived the hospital and its grounds as "not only a comprehensive plan for medical facilities and training but a complete community devoted to providing the best in healthcare" (Willis 2010: 612).

A similarly expansive health city was also conceived for Sydney, Australia in the same period. Nicknamed "Schlinktown" after its key proponent, the gynaecologist and hospital administrator (Sir) Herbert Schlink (1883–1962), the Royal Prince Alfred Hospital plan (1946) was likewise only realised in part over the ensuing decades and not as the coordinated architecturally coherent "city" proponents envisaged. Like many of the ambitious modernisation plans of the immediate postwar era, a combination of political intransigence and a lack of resources slowed the realisation of Australia's hospital-cities just as they had prevented the construction of Nelson's ambitious project for Lille in the 1930s (Schlinck 1946; Teale 1988).

It took three decades or more after Nelson's unbuilt Lille project for hospital planners and designers to standardise and rationalise the hospital completely, including at the whole-of-site scale. But, by the time this had been achieved – in the 1960s in the wealthiest countries with the biggest healthcare budgets – technical rationality and engineering-based solutions had inspired a counter-reaction. Like the reaction to modernist urban redevelopment, critics of the modern hospital pointed to a dispiriting institutionality and inhumane quality in modern hospital facilities. Critics of the modern hospital have derided institutions built between the 1920s and 1960s as monolithic, techno-centric and environmentally obtuse (Wagenaar 2006). One of the more persistent criticisms is that hospital architects were narrowly functionalist in approach and consequently underrated the significance of the subjective experience of patients, including the perception of their external surroundings. Such critics have noted in particular the gradual diminution of healing gardens, well-landscaped grounds and any sense of contact with nature. Landscape historian Anne Bourke has written that the grounds of modern hospitals became "superfluous ... except as places for the movement of people and cars" (Bourke 2012: 1016). Marcus and Sachs went further still, suggesting that the technical servicing and professional specialisation fostered in the modern hospital severed the "lingering belief in the mind-body connection" and undercut the rationale for healing gardens and natural places for refuge in hospitals (Marcus and Sachs 2014: 9). In other words, the long-standing connection between hospital design and the salutary quality of nature was lost or under-valued in this period. In more recent times, the growing influence of evidence-based design has inspired a revival of some of these lost or ignored aspects of the hospital (Marcus and Sachs 2014; Verderber and Fine 2000).

While the renewed focus on the landscape quality of hospital buildings and grounds has been a welcome trend, critics of the modern hospital writing from a landscape perspective, or a indeed from a patient-centred perspective, have tended to overlook three important factors about the design of modern hospitals. First, they tend to overstate the antipathy of modernist hospital designers to soft landscaping and the salutary quality of gardens. Through careful siting adjacent to parkland and natural areas, and by the design of courtyard spaces, open terraces and wide balconies, many interwar and mid-century hospital designers underlined their interest in providing patients and staff with pleasant and healthful surroundings, even if these gestures were more modest in their scope than late nineteenth- and early twentieth-century predecessors. In other words, the environmental determinism that was at the centre of architectural and urban reform circa 1900 was included in, even smuggled into, the rational hospital of the mid-twentieth century in a surprisingly rich variety of ways.

Perhaps the reason why contemporary critics of the great modern hospitals have not recognised the qualities of those hospitals' external spaces and those between buildings is that in many, if not most, of these places the intensification of the site, the ageing of infrastructure and the careless treatment of exterior spaces undermined their environmental qualities within a few short decades of opening. This was a direct consequence of the success of the medical activities of those institutions. Growing public trust and demand for hospital attendance produced a need for ever more accommodation, and the success of professional development encouraged by the interaction of medical specialists in these institutions, created the impetus for new clinics and research facilities. New buildings were usually introduced expediently, and the overall clarity of the original site plans was obscured by this process. "In-between" and "leftover" spaces were often reappropriated for service functions, car parking and storage, and so the functionality of the institution tended to be prioritised ahead of environmental quality for patients and staff. While this was the result, it was not the design intent of either the institutions or their architects.

Second, the great modern hospitals developed in the decades between the 1920s and 1960s were not as consistently functionalist in their approach to site and environment as is sometimes imagined by critics. Even those leading practitioners such as Hjalmar Cederström, Jean Walter and Australian architect Arthur G. Stephenson (1890–1967), who all adopted broadly modernist idioms, frequently expressed a strong interest in the subjective experience of the patient and the salutary quality of nature. Important modern hospitals in Europe in the 1930s and 1940s were very frequently organised on generous campus plans that referred to long-standing traditions in site planning even as they employed contemporary architectural idioms and fundamentally modernised the hospital's overall mission and facilities.

Third, even where modern hospital planning and design exhibited no overt interest in landscape or the salutary qualities of the natural environment, account needs to be taken of the obvious hygienic environmentalism that was prevalent in the period. The last line of Paul Nelson's "Directive Ideas" for his Lille project reads as follows: "Construction in height: Brightness – Large open spaces: Parks, air, light – Above the tenth floor no more humidity, dust, flies – Increase in light, pure air" (Nelson 1933). What critics of the modern hospital have not acknowledged was that the process of abstraction in modernism was not purely visual and formal. It also applied to the lighting, tempering and hygienic management of buildings. Air, light and water were thus abstracted from their natural condition and made part of more rigorously designed systems. Architects and their hospital administrator clients did not regard this process as unnatural or anti-natural, but rather as a better-managed and systematised nature. Moreover, while Paul Nelson made fairly extravagant claims about the air conditioning system in his proposed Lille hospital, for example, it actually took another quarter century before effective, centralised air conditioning would become part of the normal planning for hospitals. Because of this, through much of the period there was an ongoing focus on connecting patients to the outside and to the air and light available there (Overy 2007).

The movement from the park-like setting of Berlin's Virchow Hospital to the vehicular-focused planning of Skidmore Owings & Merrill's Veterans' Administration Hospital in Brooklyn, New York, USA (1947–1952) was not inexorable or total. But it is, nevertheless, difficult to evade the conclusion that the model of site planning developed in the era of the modern hospital encouraged a detachment of the hospital from the sense of civic presence and institutional decorum that it had presumed in the early twentieth century. This was most pronounced in the 1960s, when the second wave of rationalisation in hospital planning encouraged a turn towards cybernetics and a belief that complete control of the internal environment could and should be the central concern of hospital planners and designers. The quality of external spaces certainly suffered as a consequence and almost certainly, in some instances, the patient experience in the ward suffered with it. But rather than scold hospital architects and managers of this period for their apparent insensitivity to the salutary quality of soft landscaping and the outdoor environment, it is important to understand how they addressed the relative positions of patient, systems of treatment and care and the wider conception of city and nature. Certainly, the degree to which natural systems – what environmental planners and landscape architects sometimes call ecosystem services today – were abstracted and rationalised is to be regretted. And one might also regret the somewhat unchecked influence of private automobiles in shaping the siting and situation of many twentieth-century hospitals, and the degrading influence this had upon them. Nevertheless, there is little doubt that the efforts of those deeply involved in the work of hospital design were sincere in their commitment to the quality, amenity and functioning of the modern hospital.

Architects such as Stephenson and Cederström spent decades attempting to understand how to improve the efficiency and performance of hospitals as healthcare facilities. They collaborated with medical leaders, and both insisted upon and in turn produced evidence for how to design and build hospitals more efficaciously. They certainly made errors and may have paid insufficient attention to the impact of the setting and the outside landscape on patient and staff welfare. But the low quality of some external environments of hospitals from this period are often a result of decisions made before or after the architects themselves were involved in the project. Poor siting of hospitals in the first instance, inadequate masterplans for growth and change, ad hoc decision making about changes in systems and servicing, and poor maintenance and grounds-keeping amid strained budgets all contributed to the degradation in quality of the hospital site and environment. Decisions about where resources should be allocated are inevitably very difficult. Thoughtfully landscaped hospital grounds cost significant sums of money and so expenditure on such qualities must be weighed against investment in other evidence-based treatments. High-end robotics and other medical machinery that is used with increasing frequency in hospitals today are some of things that compete for scarce resources. One of the most significant factors that works against investment or reinvestment in external environments at hospital sites is the fact that hospital managers are still very focused on moving people out of acute care institutions as quickly as is possible. By the time most inpatients are able to stroll outside and benefit fully from healing gardens, for example, they are being sent home.

Site planning in the era of the modern hospital was both agent and response, strategic thinking and tactical reaction. Rationalised systems of circulation were vital to what hospital planners and administrators conceived as the productive industrial enterprise of hospital-based healthcare. But sites were also required to undertake a huge range of unanticipated work due to changing technologies and habits. Car use and the growing demand for parking was one of the most notable. Just as important were shifting techniques for servicing the hospital. Power generation, the handling of deliveries and waste removal all changed significantly across the period 1920–1965. Finally, it was perhaps the shift away from a salubrious environment towards the collection of information and application of knowledge that exercised the greatest impact on hospital site planning in the twentieth century. While architects continued to understand and appreciate the value of enriching surrounds and natural prospects, the radical success of hospitals as institutions of knowledge tended to drive growth and overwhelm arguments that focused on the external environment. Against the continued demands of growth and medical innovation, the site as a healing environment has had to struggle for recognition and protection.

References

Betsky, Aaron. *James Gamble Rogers and the Architecture of Pragmatism*. Cambridge, MA: MIT Press, 1994.
Bluestone, E.M. "Unfinished Business: 'Chronic' Patients." *Modern Hospital* 51, no. 3 (September 1938): 82–4.
Bourke, Anne. "Domestic Residence to Multi-Storey Building: The Lived Experience of Hospital Grounds in Melbourne before World War II." *Health & Place* 18 (2012): 1015–24.
Cederström, Hjalmar. "A Report on the Municipal Conditions of Stockholm with a Proposal for a New General Hospital Accommodating 1,500 Patients." *Nosokomeion* 3 (1932): 320–5.
Cederström, Hjalmar. *Södersjukhuset*. Stockholm: Rydahls Boktryckeri A-B, c. 1946.
de la Riviere, R. Dujarric. "Evolution des Idées pour la Construction des Hôpitaux en France." *Nosokomeion* 2, no. 4 (1931): 1109–31.
"The Designing Procedure of Coolidge, Shepley, Bulfinch & Abbott, Architects of the New York Hospital: Cornell Medical College Buildings." *Architectural Forum* 58, no. 2 (February 1933): 87–117.
D'Hooghe, Alexander. *The Liberal Monument: Urban Design and the Late Modern Project*. New York: Princeton Architectural Press, 2011.
Doyle, Barry M. "Healthcare before Welfare States: Hospitals in Early Twentieth Century England and France." *Canadian Bulletin of Medical History* 333, no. 1 (Spring 2016): 174–204.
Doyle, Barry M. "Pie in the Sky? Paul Nelson's Design for the *Cité Hospitalière De Lille*." Accessed 1 December 2017. https://bmdoyleblog.wordpress.com/2014/02/06/pie-in-the-sky-paul-nelsons-design-for-the-cite-hospitaliere-de-lille-1932/.
"A Fortress of Health." *Modern Hospital* 29, no. 5 (November 1927): 122.
French Ministry of Culture. "Hôpital Pasteur." Accessed 3 June 2014. www2.culture.gouv.fr/culture/inventai/patrimoine/.
Gerlach-Spriggs, Nancy, Richard Enoch Kaufman and Sam Bass Warner. *Restorative Gardens: The Healing Landscape*. New Haven, CT: Yale University Press, 1998.
Gmur, Silvia and Livio Vacchini. *Bauen fur die Gesundheit: Kantonspital Basel – Klinikum 1*. Basel: Christoph Merian Verlag, 2004.
Grover, Dorothy and "Imhotep". "A Great University Medical Centre for Melbourne: Full Details of a Far-Sighted Plan to Safeguard Posterity's Health." *Argus* (14 October 1944 (1944a)).
Grover, Dorothy and "Imhotep". "Staff and Patients of a Melbourne Medical Centre: Coordinated Training Facilities Would Provide Knowledge at Minimum Cost." *Argus* (21 October 1944 (1944b)).

Heskell, Julia. *Shepley Bulfinch Richardson and Abbott: Past to Present.* Boston: Shepley Bulfinch Richardson and Abbott Inc., 1999.

"The Hospitals of Western Reserve University." *Modern Hospital* 37, no. 3 (September 1931): 11–30.

"Hospital at Haifa, Palestine." *Architect and Building News* 161 (2 February 1940): 139–41.

Hughes, Jonathan. "Hospital-City." *Architectural History* 40 (1997): 266–88.

"Jerusalem's New and Modern Medical Centre." *Hospital Magazine* (September 1939): 16.

Longstreth, Richard. *City Center to Regional Mall: Architecture, the Automobile and Retailing in Los Angles, 1920–1950.* Cambridge, MA: MIT Press, 1997.

Longstreth, Richard. *The Drive-In, the Supermarket, and the Transformation of Commercial Space in Los Angeles, 1914–1941.* Cambridge, MA: MIT Press, 1999.

Marcus, Clare Cooper and Naomi A. Sachs. *Therapeutic Landscapes: An Evidence-Based Approach to Designing Healing Gardens and Restorative Outdoor Spaces.* Hoboken, NJ: Wiley, 2014.

Millburn Jr., William. "Modern German Hospital Construction." *RIBA Journal* 19 (1911–12): 33–56, 93–108, 121–42.

Moretti, B. Franco. *Ospedali.* Milan: Editore Ulrico Hoepli, 1951.

Nelson, Paul. *Cité Hospitalière de Lille.* Paris: Editions Cahiers d'art, 1933.

Ortega y Gasset, José. *The Revolt of the Masses.* New York: Norton, 1932.

Overy, Paul. *Light, Air and Openness: Modern Architecture between the Wars.* London: Thames & Hudson, 2007.

Peterkin, Janet. "Manhattan's Colossus of Medical Centers." *Modern Hospital* 31, no. 1 (July 1928): 55–66.

Peterkin, Janet. "Latest Equipment, Efficient Layout Feature Chicago Hospital." *Modern Hospital* 40, no. 6 (June 1933): 63–70.

Robinson, G. Canby. "The Principles of Planning: The New York Hospital: Cornell Medical College Buildings." *Architectural Forum* 58, no. 2 (February 1933): 85–6.

Royal Melbourne Hospital. *Annual Report, 1937–38.* Melbourne: The Royal Melbourne Hospital, 1938.

Schlink, Herbert H. *The National Medical Centre for New South Wales.* Camperdown, NSW: Royal Prince Alfred Hospital, 1946.

Sloan, Raymond P. "Vast New Medical Centre Guards New York's Health." *Modern Hospital* 40, no. 3 (March 1933): 49–56.

Stevens, Edward F. *The American Hospital of the Twentieth Century.* New York: Architectural Record Publishing Company, 1918.

"The Structure and Equipment of the New York Hospital." *Architectural Forum* 58, no. 2 (February 1933): 118–24.

Teale, Ruth. "Schlink, Sir Herbert Henry (1883–1962)." In *Australian Dictionary of Biography*, National Centre of Biography, Australian National University. Accessed 3 January 2018. http://adb.anu.edu.au/biography/schlink-sir-herbert-henry-8359/text14551 (first published in hardcopy 1988).

Turner, Paul Venable. *Campus: An American Planning Tradition.* Cambridge, MA: MIT Press, 1984.

Ventura, Paolo. "L'ospedale nuovo di Brescia di Angelo Bordoni." Accessed 31 January 2017. www.bresciacity.it/storia-spedali-civili-di-brescia/.

Verderber, Stephen and David J. Fine. *Healthcare Architecture in an Age of Radical Transformation*. New Haven, CT: Yale University Press, 2000.

Wagenaar, Cor (ed.). *The Architecture of Hospitals*. Rotterdam: NAi Publishers, 2006.

Wallenstein, Sven-Olov. *Bio-Politics and the Emergence of Modern Architecture*. New York: Princeton Architectural Press, 2008.

Willis, Julie. "The Healthy City: Stephenson & Turner's Postwar Plans." In *Green Fields, Brown Fields, New Fields: Proceedings of the 10th Australasian Urban History, Planning History Conference*, 610–21. Melbourne: The University of Melbourne, 2010.

9 The modern hospital
The rise, fall and rise again of architecture

The twentieth century saw profound changes to the design of hospitals. Once places for caring for the sick and injured (*Nosokomeion*), by the mid-twentieth century they had become the centrepieces of health systems (*Hygeia*), in which medical and technological advances meant patients could not only expect treatment, but potentially also a cure for what ailed them. Architecture and design, explored here in seven sites from the scale of the bed to the campus, was at the heart of this transformation, playing, at the very least, an important role in the facilitation of such changes and, at times, an active role in the therapeutical regimes prescribed for patients. Hospitals became behemoths, great, rationalised healthcare campuses, shaping whole districts of cities – and in the process, they also became central to the social meaning and physical infrastructure of the modern welfare state.

Yet in the twenty-first century, the reputation of the modern hospital is equivocal. The ethos of rationalised planning led critics to dismiss the great institutions created in the twentieth century as inhumane monstrosities. But however flawed many individual hospital buildings were and are, it should not be forgotten that the project of the modern hospital was one directed at dramatically transforming the health of whole populations, an ambition that was realised to a remarkable degree. Moreover, as this book has demonstrated, the modern hospital was not a singular entity that found a fixed form. Architectural experiment in hospital and healthcare settings continued throughout the period from the 1920s until the 1960s. As some elements faded into medical obscurity, such as the balcony and solaria, other elements such as flexibility in servicing and planning became more important. And architects have continued to be cognisant of the needs and amenities of patients. The modern hospital, in other words, was the product of a distinct period with a clear unifying aspiration. But it was not a fixed entity architecturally. Indeed, the modern hospital was characterised by its organisational dynamism, a characteristic which explains some of its formal failings and its lack of architectural appeal in the conventional sense.

The design of the hospital: the patient, the doctor and the architect

Annmarie Adams structured her book on the development of modern hospitals in Canada, *Medicine by Design* (2008), around four figures: the patient, the nurse, the doctor and the architect. These figures represent distinct interests in the process of conceptualising the hospital, and in a certain sense they vie for control of what the hospital should be as object and environment. Over time, and particularly so in the period examined in this book, the comparative role or influence of each main player in shaping the design of hospitals has also waxed and waned. Hospitals, therefore, reflect the relative power of each of these groups in any given period.

In the twentieth century, the patient remained mostly mute – a body to which medical things were done, space was given and amenity provided, but contained and bound to the bed, disempowered, controlled, passive and largely without a voice. Yet the patient was the measure by which a hospital could be considered a success: their recovery and successful treatment was paramount, and it was a unit by which the value of medical practice could be quantified and the environment of the hospital could be determined. The continuing rise of the expert medical practitioner in the hospital is seen in the increasing specialisation and expertise of doctors and nurses in this period. While Florence Nightingale's proposals that became the model for the so-called Nightingale ward in the pavilion hospital placed the nurse at the heart of patient care, it was the doctor in the twentieth century who became the locus of power in the hospital, whose medical decisions were the primary driver of patient care. And, finally, the architects were the ones who realised the various demands, which became exponentially more complex as the century progressed, as a finished building. The waxing and waning of influence, or the swing of the pendulum between the demands of the doctors versus that of the patient, unsurprisingly see design and architectural responses change over time.

This book's consideration of the rise of the modern hospital from the end of World War I starts at the point when the near ubiquitous hold of the pavilion hospital, stacked or otherwise, was being challenged by new ways of thinking about the relationships and configurations of wards, departments and services. The pavilion plan had placed the patient, in bed, in a standard configuration, with a specified amount of space, light, ventilation and nursing attention, with architectural inventions perhaps limited to the exterior style of the building. But as hospitals required more spaces for treatment, therapy and equipment, the demands on the designs of their buildings prompted new architectural possibilities. The rise of the hospital as the locus for specialist medical expertise saw greater demands for hospital-based treatment from all sections of society. As a result, architects looked to models of efficiency and service for inspiration for a new generation of hospitals, finding such models in contemporary factories and hotels in particular. But neither example provided simple lessons for new hospitals. Architects had to grapple with the increasing complexity involved in planning, equipping and servicing the twentieth-century hospital. New hospital briefs in the 1920s and 1930s encapsulated not only bed-bound patients, but also specialist medical spaces containing equipment for diagnosis and treatment, such as X-rays and Sitz baths, and services, such as boilers, generators, air conditioning, kitchens and laundries. That complexity – and the growing size of hospitals, particularly in built-up urban areas – saw the emergence of the skyscraper hospitals in the late 1920s and foregrounded the concept of the "health city" (Figure 9.1).

In the early decades of the twentieth century, a newly influential figure emerged in response to this growing complexity – the hospital consultant, epitomised by American figures such as S.S. Goldwater (1873–1942), physician and medical administrator, and Malcolm T. MacEachern (1881–1956), surgeon and hospital management expert. It was the consultant's role to coordinate and balance the needs and preferences of the other key

Figure 9.1 Rear view, Hôpital Beaujon (Beaujon Hospital), Clichy, France. Architects: Walter, Plousey & Cassan, 1932–1935. Photograph: Henri Manuel, c. 1935.

Source: Moretti, B. Franco. *Ospedali*. Milan: Editore Ulrico Hoepli, 1951: 276.

players in the hospital and to do so in a way that accorded with the highest standards of efficiency. But it was also true that a number of architects made it their business in the 1920s, 1930s and 1940s to become experts in their own right – to hold their own with these consultants, who were mostly medical men, in establishing the most efficient programme for the modern hospital. So hospital expertise became a kind of interdisciplinary art requiring knowledge of – and the ability to coordinate – physical spaces, organisational structures and medical systems. The role of the hospital consultant and hospital specialist architect in realising a properly modern hospital, therefore, was to make medical knowledge the centrepiece of hospitals and the healthcare system.

The power of architecture was thus twofold in the modern hospital. First, it was in the making of the plan, as American hospital architect Edward F. Stevens had insisted as early as 1918 (Stevens 1918). Architects were charged with bringing spatial clarity and rationality to a proliferating set of hospital functions. Second, architects also took on the task of making the expressive dimensions of hospital buildings an element of treatment itself. The use of sunlight (heliotherapy) as a specific treatment for tuberculosis patients meant that increasingly the architectural responses for hospitals included bespoke spaces for therapy, where the building element, such as the balcony, was not just the site of the treatment, but was integral to it. Led by progressive European thought from the mid-1920s, architects designed hospitals that not only played a significant role in the treatment and comfort of patients, but also embodied in their aesthetics the ideas and look of hygiene, efficiency and functionalism. The use of materials – new types of "healthful" glass, noiseless flooring that discouraged the buildup of static electricity and seamless metal that could be completely disinfected – also played an important role in the design of hospitals.

From the 1930s, the possibilities of architecture playing an active role in the treatment and curing of patients also saw architects bring a new fervour of experimentation to the most complex hospital spaces, such as the operating theatre. Solving problems was not just seen in the overtly medical spaces, such as the positioning and protection of places for radiation and X-ray departments, but also in the spaces of service: how did oxygen, conditioned air, steam and hot water optimally reach the service point? How did food, scientifically determined from diet kitchens on a huge scale, arrive hot or cold to the bedside? And how did linen – an essential commodity in the healthcare environment – circulate efficiently from laundry to bed and back again? The confluence of design and need, particularly in the 1930s, saw creative and inventive solutions and an imagining of the hospital as a complete system of inputs and outputs that, above all, needed efficient management. Change in one area – such as the use of strong electric light in the operating theatre – prompted further change, such as the switch from white to green linens to reduce eye fatigue and glare, design decisions which have become so universal that the reasons for them have become lost.

Architecture in the hospital, from the 1920s to the 1940s, was in the active service of promoting the best medical care in the most efficient manner possible. Care at the time was significantly spatialised, scientific and mechanical, with much of the medical treatment physical – where something was done *to* the body – rather than the subcutaneous treatments of drug therapies and vaccinations that would rise from the 1950s, where the site of treatment was often *within* the body. Architecture followed the same path: it moved from a robust physical external expression in the 1920s and 1930s, but from the 1950s, along with changes in medical treatment, it too took a subcutaneous turn. Closing up the hospital, hermetically sealing the building as though it were one giant clean room, was a gradual process: air conditioning, while starting in the spaces where the body was most exposed, such as operating theatres and morgues, spread to other treatment spaces and finally on to patient wards. With that sealing of the building, the capacity for architectural experimentation at the skin of the building – something that architects had revelled in throughout the 1930s and early 1940s – was frequently, though not always, diminished to the point of extinction.

Design-wise, by the 1960s, the hospital needed efficient, fit-for-purpose spaces that were appropriately serviced. But the need for new creative architectural solutions for sunlight, fresh air and infection control were a thing of the past. Some problems, once a standard solution was arrived at, simply didn't need further reinvention. Efficiency and flexibility were the order of the day, and the heyday of the architect as a driver of innovation in hospital design, as opposed to an effective facilitator, had passed. The hospital had dramatically grown in size from the late 1910s and, rather like the functionalist city of the 1960s, the 1960s hospital was not in crisis, but architecturally, it was in stasis.

It is unsurprising that during this period, 1918–1960, there emerged the specialist hospital architect (and consultant) whose expertise and solutions were considered essential in conceiving and commissioning new hospital buildings. Medical processes, techniques and practices changed comparatively quickly during this period, and it was not uncommon to see hospitals that had been completed in the mid-1910s being considered completely obsolete by the mid-1930s. Corresponding with the rise of the hospital architect, an international community of practice grew up with loci in North America, Europe and Australia that shared ideas and knowledge through tours, meetings, conventions and journals. High points of influence and ideas in hospital architecture swung between different locations: innovations in North America would be overtaken by new ideas emerging from Europe, and developed in Australia and Scandinavia, before a new wave of influence emerging from the United States, and then from the United Kingdom.

The relevance of the architect in the hospital

By the mid-1960s, the role of the architect in designing the modern hospital was enmeshed in facilitating a myriad of complex systems that, by necessity,

The modern hospital 219

drove what had become an extremely sophisticated organism. To a significant degree, the specialist hospital architects of that period, working hand in hand with medical experts and administrators, had successfully achieved the functional and technical resolution of all parts of the modern hospital. But now a growing list of new challenges became evident. Given the giant scale of the contemporary hospital, its complex servicing and often decade-long building programmes, and the constant need for an ongoing evolution of the hospital campus, questions of wayfinding, humanisation, flexibility, environmental amenity and symbolic identity became ever more pressing – not that these questions had ever been absent from the minds of hospital designers. Architects from the 1920s to the 1950s were acutely aware of these issues and addressed them in often creative and innovative ways. But hospital architects now had to face that many of these questions appeared to lie outside their control.

Some architects, craving relevance, came up with mad or even fanciful schemes, such as E. Todd Wheeler's inverted multistorey pyramid that was to magically respect historic inner-city fabric below it or his scheme for an underwater hospital (both published in 1971) that would produce the perfect environmentally stable internal environment (Figure 9.2). Others, like Bertrand Goldberg, focused on the patient-bed experience as the driver for radical formal change. The intention was to subvert formal expectations of the modern hospital and invite debate and speculation on what had become, to many, a design hegemony based on functional

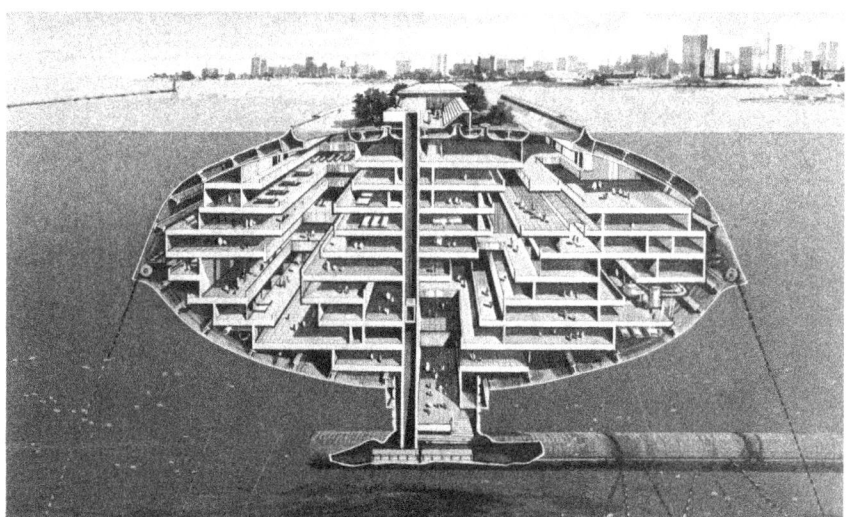

Figure 9.2 A speculative design for an underwater hospital. Architects: E. Todd Wheeler/Perkins & Will, 1971. Delineator: E. Todd Wheeler, 1971.

Source: Wheeler, E. Todd. *Hospital Modernization and Expansion*. New York: McGraw-Hill, 1971: 215.

Courtesy: McGraw-Hill Education.

arrangement and an all too ready acceptance of what constituted an image of modernity for health. Part of the challenge was that some architects had begun to lose confidence in modern architecture's ability to speak to a broader community and comfortably merge with the existing city. At the same time, others saw new aesthetic possibilities in the expression of servicing and structure, which in the 1960s had reached a point of apotheosis, and which, with emerging Cold War issues of potential atomic destruction, environmental pollution and a looming energy crisis, suggested architectural strategies of self-containment and self-subsistence organisms, discrete and detached from the city. Bold megastructural strategies like McMaster University Health Sciences Centre, Ontario, Canada (Architects: Craig, Zeidler & Strong, 1967–1972) and Universitätsklinikum (University Hospital), Aachen, Germany (Architects: Weber & Brand, 1972–1982) were thus logical endpoints, seemingly invincible machines that paralleled the completion of Piano & Rogers' Centre Pompidou (1971–1977) in Paris, France: giant technocratic behemoths that provided idealised value-free and completely flexible floor space within. In the history of twentieth-century architecture, the hospital at Aachen has been largely overlooked and its status as an exemplar of a campus-city that actively engages with its immediate designed and distant landscapes and is flexible internally, technically adaptive and able to expand deserves greater recognition (Figure 9.3). But

Figure 9.3 Aerial view, Universitätsklinikum (University Hospital), Aachen, Germany. Architects: Weber & Brand, 1972–1982. Photograph: Hans Blossey, 2015.
Courtesy: ImageBROKER via Getty Images.

not everyone wanted to accept an image of healthcare as an enormous, self-referential machine. Just as in the broader realm, beyond the design of hospital buildings, the aesthetics and ethics of architecture was, arguably, on the verge of crisis.

Influences on the design of the hospital: evidence-based research

If it can be argued on the basis of examples that were constructed or even projected as hypothetical possibility that hospital design reached a point of stasis by the mid-1960s, there were also other mechanisms at work in the 1950s that would quietly come to have influence on hospital design as it emerged in the 1970s and 1980s. Some were not always for the good. In the United States, for example, the introduction of the Hospital Survey and Construction Act (known as the Hill-Burton Act) in 1946, as Jeanne Kisacky notes, "ensured that postwar hospital construction would be based on prewar designs", with federal funding made available to communities across the country predicated on following pre-war medical practices and minimal standards (Kisacky 2017: 338, 340). More than four thousand projects in the United States over twenty years adhered to this push for standardisation, which led to "an oversupply of functionally obsolete hospitals". If innovation and keeping up with the latest in medical knowledge was the aim, then more often than not, hospital administrators and architects had to be willing to give up any form of government funding (Kisacky 2017: 340). It was only the widespread take-up of antibiotics, which made the link between infection and surroundings meaningless, and the concomitant rise and increased cost-effectiveness of air conditioning, that hospital design was gradually freed from such regulatory strictures.

By contrast, one powerful mechanism for positive change was the instigation of new empirical research into the practices, use and design of hospital spaces. While the manual-like hospital discourse of the late 1940s and early 1950s efficiently and expertly captured technical data, there was little critical reflection and scientific evaluation of that data. In United Kingdom, despite the establishment of the National Health Service (NHS), the construction of sophisticated hospital buildings after World War II was either absent or delayed, which meant that British developments and innovations in the hospital field came late. But – as had occurred in British postwar school design (Franklin 2012) – a practice of critical international comparison and empirical research, especially on contemporary North American and European examples – engendered a new research-based mentality in design from the early 1950s. This was encouraged by the Nuffield Provincial Hospitals Trust, which was established in 1939 but only began to produce research documents on health centres and hospitals in earnest after 1949 – initially under the guidance of John Madge but, more significantly, under the leadership of architect Richard Llewelyn-Davies (1912–1981) and collaborator John Weeks (1921–2005), who worked within a multidisciplinary team of architects, statisticians, a physician and a nurse (McLachlan 1992; Hughes 1996). The 1955 report *Investigations into the Functions and Design of Hospitals*, produced in collaboration with the University of Bristol, made use of international cooperation through contact with Sweden's Central Board of Hospital Planning and Equipment and the US Department of Public Health. It employed, as Jonathan Hughes has written:

> questionnaires, time & motion studies and environmental research in order to consider hospital design from first principles. Their enquiries ranged over nursing routine and medical technique, architectural design and their financial implications.
>
> (Hughes 1996: 52–3)

The report was internationally significant as were later reports on laboratories (1961) and children's hospitals (1963) (Nuffield Foundation 1961, 1963). This evidence-based research was important because it continued the tradition of the international network of shared discourse around the question of hospital design that had existed since the 1920s, but which was now translated as a more focused scientific study of environmental needs. John Weeks's subsequent articles on indeterminacy and obsolescence, and the need to plan for unforeseen change and flexibility in healthcare design, further reinforced emerging British expertise in the field. At the same time, the emphasis on indeterminacy, while theoretically robust and topical at the time, further downplayed the roles of humanisation and symbolic identity in the modern hospital. While Weeks introduced useful concepts, such as "geography", "village" and "streets" in approaching the generation of hospital design, these did not always translate well in aesthetic terms. Northwick Park Hospital, Harrow, England (Architects: Llewelyn-Davies & Weeks, 1962, 1966–1970), for example, demonstrated his ideas:

> Northwick Park has been designed from the outset to be "indeterminate", that is not only internally flexible but never to reach a "final" size or form. There is no concept of finality built into the design of an indeterminate hospital; at the beginning only the directions and method of growth are decided and not the precise form, which appears as a result of the erosion of time on the original programme. An indeterminate design allows for continuous change and growth of the whole complex without its ceasing function, within limits set by the capacity and shape of the communications' and service network, and the total size of the hospital site itself.
>
> (Weeks 1966: 338)

The physical result was a multistorey glazed circulation spine to which volumes could be added at will, determined only by a 7-metre span of column-free space (relating to the width of a four-bed room) and an external skin of exposed concrete floor slabs and structural mullions – essentially a neutral frame (Figure 9.4). It was a suitable demonstration of Weeks's theory and indubitably influential in polemical terms (Hughes 1999). In

Figure 9.4 The elevated main hospital "street", Northwick Park Hospital, Harrow, England. Architects: Llewelyn-Davies & Weeks, 1962, 1966–1970. Photograph: Henk Snoek, 1973.
Courtesy: Henk Snoek/RIBA Collections.

1976, Peter Stone (a member of the original firm) proudly declared: "Today – some 14 years after its inception – the creeping extension of the building continues, and the interior is subject to endless small alterations" (Stone 1976: 1135). Certainly its architectural significance has been recognised (Harwood 2015), but as a facility that maximised human experience and environmental amenity, it was less than ideal, described by hospital staff as comparable to a "Russian nuclear reactor" (Abramson 2016: 140).

At the same time in the United Kingdom, there were occasions whereby specific, formally innovative architectural results were combined with new hospital functions. The Nuffield Transplantation Surgery Unit (Architect: Peter Womersley, 1963–1968) at Edinburgh's Western General Hospital, Scotland, was the first purpose-designed facility of its kind in the world to be built for human organ transplants (Figure 9.5). The building was connected by an overhead bridge to the main hospital and as such, it was a discrete unit. It had a main floor with perimeter circulation so that the building's central core of functions could be kept completely sterile. Fully air conditioned and with a deep ceiling space above and service floor below, any maintenance could be kept entirely separate from the protected sterile zone, essential for organ transplants. This very distinct programme

Figure 9.5 Exterior, Nuffield Transplantation Surgery Unit, Western General Hospital, Edinburgh, Scotland. Architect: Peter Womersley, 1963–1968. Photograph: Sam Lambert, 1968.

Courtesy: Architectural Press Archive/RIBA Collections.

was expressed architecturally by cantilevering inverted U-shaped concrete beams to support the perimeter circulation and above at ceiling level to form an expressed eave with exposed U-shaped brackets. The U-shaped beams could also house service ducts. ("Nuffield Transplantation Surgery Unit, Edinburgh" 1968; Fair 2017). The building's very tall lift and air-intake tower with its curved projections combined with the sand-coloured concrete brackets, beams and panels to echo the stone of the building next door, and as such its overall sculptural virtuosity also echoed Edinburgh's castellated and picturesque building traditions. However, this was a rare case in the 1960s whereby aesthetics and the most up-to-date medical care met with such productive results.

The aesthetic problem of the hospital

Recognition of the aesthetic problem of the modern hospital came late to the discourse of architecture. While important though partial histories of the modern hospital emerged, such as John Thompson and Grace Goldin's *The Hospital: A Social and Architectural History* (1975), and individual local accounts such as Peter Stone's exposition on the self-proclaimed "heroic years" (the 1950s and 1960s) of British hospital architecture (1976) have filled in some historical gaps (Stone 1976: 1121), these texts did not promote design directions for the modern hospital. It wasn't until after 2000 that visual and linguistic analogies such as the shopping mall, and references to the historic city and even the hospital's modernist history that came to be associated with the modern hospital in the 1980s and 1990s, were documented. David Sloane and Beverlie Sloane's *Medicine Moves to the Mall* (2003), for example, is important as it emphasised the decisive shift in approach to hospital design from the early 1980s evidenced by hospitals like the Dartmouth Hitchcock Medical Center, Lebanon, New Hampshire, USA (Architects: Shepley, Bulfinch, Richardson & Abbott, 1992). A slew of books in the 2000s on healthcare and hospital design signalled a new shift towards patient-centred care and the environment, in effect zeroing in on the intimate and macro scales of the seven sites of inquiry that form the structure of this book, and also returning in no small part to the ideals and aspirations that drove the development of the modern hospital in the 1920s and 1930s, which itself was driven by a reappreciation of the importance of the human body and the patient as a doubly reflective agent. Wayfinding, humanisation, flexibility, environmental amenity and symbolic identity have all returned to the fore as key design requirements of the modern hospital.

The rise of patient experience

Catering to the needs of patients under the dominance of the medical expert in the design of hospitals inevitably meant some limitations to the patient experience. While architects had made efforts in the 1910s and 1920s to make hospitals attractive places for patients, the rules of efficiency and hygiene soon overrode these efforts, and hospitals became the epitome of "clinical" spaces: ruthlessly institutional; functional to the point of being bare; clean but lifeless. The relative loss of architectural influence on the design of the hospital corresponded to a declining interest in the psychological wellbeing of the patient. The measurable medical benefits that could be made by providing amenable spaces, such as balconies and gardens, was hugely outweighed by the provision of the most up-to-date treatments and by hard-nosed hospital administrators with an eye on their balance sheets. But something was lost in that process. While health outcomes improved, patients' blind faith in the power of the hospital to cure their ailments began to diminish from the late 1960s.

In recent years, the pendulum has swung back to the potential for expressive architectural design to play an active and meaningful role in the hospital. As popular taste began to move away from functional modernism and anti-institutional feeling grew, particularly from the late 1960s, the designers of hospitals sought to distance the hospital from its overly institutional look and feel. A revised approach to hospital design was evident from the 1980s (Sloane and Sloane 2003), which saw the public spaces of hospitals consciously "de-institutionalised" and often modelled on shopping malls – busy places of apparent normality. Yet, while the intention of this strategy was to repersonalise the scale of the very large general hospital, this was not specifically a focus on patient wellbeing across the broad spectrum of the hospital spatial experience, from admission to bedside.

Serious interest in the built environment's effect on human behaviour and perception gained traction in the 1960s, and from the 1970s there was increasing interest in the interconnections between humans, health and environments. The work of Aubrey R. Kagan and Lennart Levi (1974) and Aaron Antonovsky (1979) laid the foundation for understanding the psycho-social connections between people, health and places, and was followed by studies that began to validate the links between patient outcomes and the design of the buildings which housed them, such as Roger Ulrich's seminal 1984 study of the positive benefits to patients who had visual access to nature (Ulrich 1984). The work of Marcus and Barnes (1999) and Franklin Becker (2008) also demonstrated links between designed environments and patient health and wellbeing.

The work of Heidi Salonen et al. (2013) on improved health and wellbeing points to over two hundred studies examining links between various design and environmental factors and patient wellbeing in healthcare environments. The authors identify nine key design elements that are important in healthcare facilities – ranging from primary responsibilities, such as safety and ergonomy of furniture and equipment, to a re-emergent interest in elements like ventilation, thermal environment, acoustic environments, construction material and spatial layout – and include more recent interests in wayfinding and the visual environment that forms part of the patient journey. Within this, they note particular aspects, including daylighting, colour, artworks and floor coverings. What is evident from their review is that there is now a weight of evidence supporting the idea that a well-designed hospital environment can have a positive effect on reducing anxiety and stress and promoting patient wellbeing.

In the twenty-first century, a series of new hospitals is now placing architectural thought and innovation at the forefront of requirements for their new facilities and extraordinary emphasis on what is called a patient-centred model of care (Figure 9.6). The value of an amenable, well-designed environment on patient wellbeing and faith in the medical system is increasingly understood (that is, that in dealing with human beings, one cannot just rely on the rational power of science, but must also deal with feelings and perceptions), and that a patient who finds their surroundings comfortable and suitable for their needs, and whose stress levels are not inadvertently inflated by them, is likely to be more receptive to treatments and more likely to undertake or complete such treatments.

Revisiting the seven sites of design

This book has examined the changing design of hospitals through seven sites of design, from the bed to the campus. Some of these sites remain just as valid as places of innovation, whilst others have lessened in importance and influence in the spatial design of the hospital. As a final gesture, each is briefly revisited:

The bed

The bed is still an essential unit of care, and a key place of ministration to the patient. But, increasingly, patients are treated in a range of settings and it is no longer standard that a patient is automatically assigned to a bed for treatment within a hospital. For one, the crippling costs of providing each patient with residential care within the hospital has encouraged the rise of outpatient and ambulatory care programmes, decreasing significantly the time in which patients spend in the hospital environment. Those patients in beds for long periods of time are often very unwell, yet their overall amenity has increased with more attention paid to their comfort. Beds are now advanced technological instruments, capable of multitudes of adjustments – which the patient can manage themselves – but they have not dramatically changed in their function or design. The arrangement of beds, however, has seen significant changes, with ward design moving towards single rooms, replete with private connected ablution and toilet facilities. The bed is no longer the exclusive site of treatment of the patient in the hospital.

Figure 9.6 The hospital in the twenty-first century: the atrium of the Royal Children's Hospital, Melbourne, Victoria, Australia. Architects: Bates Smart and Billard Leece Partnership, 2006–2011. Photograph: Shannon McGrath, 2012.

© Shannon McGrath, used with permission.

The nurse

The position of the nurse within the hospital has seen significant change. While the immediate patient-nurse interaction at the bedside has not largely changed in a spatial or design sense, the spaces the nurse occupies in the hospital have. Nurses have moved from being generalist carers – handmaidens to the hospital – to being highly professionalised specialists and experts who bring dedicated skills to each department of the hospital. The origins of the nursing profession in nunneries and convents, and social expectations about how and where women were permitted to work in the late nineteenth and early twentieth centuries, had meant that nurses were generally staff who lived on the hospital site, accommodated in large nurses' homes. Just as they have thrown off their stylised uniforms of starched caps and all-white dress, the restrictive, self-contained life of nursing staff is a thing of the past, and they no longer have their entire lives circumscribed by the design of the hospital. Yet, the nurses' station, as the marshalling and command point for wards, remains an essential element of the hospital.

The operating theatre

The operating theatre moved to become a highly specialised instrument in the period examined by this book, where hygiene, lighting, humidity, air purification and observation were all carefully controlled to ensure maximum outcomes for the patient at their most vulnerable. Once the site of the most inventive designs to manage these aspects, the operating theatre still demands highly specialised technology, but it no longer needs specific architectural treatment to accommodate this. Aside from its HEPA-filtered, positive-pressure air conditioning and specialist lighting, operating theatres no longer need to occupy particular locations in the hospital to access daylight and outside air, and are more akin to specialist engineering workshops than moments of architectural expression.

Spaces of diagnosis and therapy

The spaces of diagnosis and therapy are still vitally important in the hospital, but the nature and size of the equipment has changed over time. Few hospitals still have extensive hydrotherapy or heliotherapy spaces, but ultraviolet (UV) or light therapy is still used for patients with skin conditions such as psoriasis. The machines of physiotherapy, once torturous-looking contraptions, are no longer the specialist tools of the hospital but ubiquitous equipment seen in gymnasiums everywhere. Oxygen therapy, however, is still relatively common and can be seen in forms such as hyperbaric chambers for the treatment of decompression sickness as well as wounds. Radiation treatments still require a distinct architectural response, located underground in bunkers. Spaces for X-ray departments have shrunk, as the machines have become smaller, but other forms of "looking inside", such as computed tomography (CT), magnetic resonance imaging (MRI) and positron emission tomography (PET), are huge and heavy machines that need particular spatial responses. So do very recent therapies, such as proton beam therapy, which requires its own particle accelerator for operation, demanding complex engineering and architectural responses as a result. But increasingly, architects have sought to make those forbidding spaces pleasant through visible connections to the outside where possible and by introducing artwork and distractions into them for the wellbeing, indeed calming, of patients.

Services

The servicing of the hospital is still crucially important, but the days of cavernous spaces set aside for housing the plant, kitchen or laundry are mostly past. Air conditioning, with high-performance filters, zoning and isolation, has moved from the province of specialist spaces to being an essential service for the whole hospital building. Nevertheless, interest in patient amenity has meant a return to the availability of courtyards and balconies, and even, perhaps, the openable window. Air conditioning largely manages both temperature and humidity, eliminating the need for separate heating systems. Giant in-house laundries have largely been overtaken by outsourced linen services. And while there are still hospital kitchens, in some hospitals patients have the capacity to reheat prepared food for themselves, and hospital cafes have moved from large institutional cafeterias to sophisticated purveyors of food and coffee that even attract passers-by as part of their clientele. Where once the provision of motorised trucks for moving supplies around was an exciting revelation, there are now autonomous robotic vehicles servicing the hospital. Finally, in relation to the bed, where once a jack for a bedside radio was regarded as the epitome of progress, now even television is redundant with wi-fi available and patients able to bring their own devices.

The look of the hospital

Once, the exterior aesthetics of the hospital sought to convey the intention of the care contained therein. Architecturally, the exterior design of the hospital echoed general architectural trends, but hospitals were seen as particularly suitable for the clean lines of modernism. But the failure of modernism, and the turn away from the exterior in later hospitals, led to an era of utilitarian skins that did little to express the idea of the hospital except to reinforce their institutional aura. The re-enlivening of hospitals, by introducing concepts of the shopping mall and more, began changes that saw hospitals open up externally and engage more with their local community. Hospitals needed to shift gear, to become more welcoming. Recently, many new hospitals have set new aesthetic and experiential benchmarks, with the engagement of non-hospital specialist firms to introduce new ways of thinking about the architectural possibilities of the hospital's look and feel.

The hospital campus

The hospital campus is still big and complex; many hospitals have accreted extra services over time, threatening the institutional clarity of the original plan and making traversing the site more difficult. But the rise of models of patient-centred care have seen much greater emphasis on gardens, courtyards and even balconies, as well as the means by which hospitals are entered. The hospital is almost inevitably no longer a series of isolated buildings in a park-like setting – few cities have big enough greenfield or brownfield sites close enough to the populations to be served to achieve this. So, hospital sites are now more about careful siting of buildings and achieving appropriate access: for patients and visitors (both on foot and by car), for staff, for ambulance arrivals, for supplies and for waste removal.

Envoie

The modern hospital, that which developed in the mid-1920s to the mid-1960s, was a site of radical transformation and experiment, in which design and architecture played a pivotal part. Far from being places in which the architecture spoke of institutional control, the design of hospitals saw innovations in their design utilising the ideas of modernism for the greater good. The architecture and spaces of the modern hospital had to keep pace with rapid advances in medicine and medical research in the twentieth century, and, in large part, this matching of physical accommodation and the delivery of a maximised health service was achieved. The modern hospital was, in short, a success story. Hospitals grew and grew to become vast citadels or campuses to which people flocked, encouraged by the guarantee of a beneficent, reliable and expert care, and in many cases, the most up-to-date medical technologies and instrumentation.

The corollary between advances in medicine and the architecture to house them, however, has not ceased to be relevant. As such, many of the hospitals examined in this book have reached a point of obsolescence or have been reconfigured to meet contemporary needs – or they have been altered and added to beyond recognition. It would be easy to dismiss such hospitals from what in hindsight can now be described as the heroic period of hospital building as irrelevant and unequal to today's expectations of healthcare. In many cases, this is a logical and correct conclusion. However, across the world, a substantial number of these hospitals like the Universitätsspital (University Hospital) Basel, Switzerland (formerly Kantonsspital (Cantonal Hospital), 1939–1945) (Figure 9.7) and the Södersjukhuset (Southern Hospital) in Stockholm, Sweden (1937–1944) function and adapt to change with relative ease and continue to perform key roles as vital foci for their

Figure 9.7 Interior, Universitätsspital Basel (formerly Kantonsspital [Cantonal Hospital]), Basel, Switzerland. Architects: H. Baur, E. & P. Vischer and Bräuning Leu Dürig, 1939–1945. Photograph: Cameron Logan, 2010.

© Cameron Logan, used with permission.

communities and their cities (Figure 9.6). A number, like Paul Nelson's Centre Hospitalier Mémorial France États-Unis (France United States Memorial Hospital) at Saint-Lô, France (1946–1956), have also been recognised as important heritage sites from social, technical and aesthetic perspectives

Figure 9.8 Centre Hospitalier Mémorial France États-Unis (France United States Memorial Hospital), Saint-Lô, France. Architect: Paul Nelson, 1946–1956. Photograph: studio Henri Baranger, 1959.
Courtesy: Conseil dép. de la Manche, arch. dép., 4 Fi 20/12–1–4.

(Logan, Goad and Willis 2010) (Figure 9.8). However, it must be recognised that the disappearance of many modern hospitals and the disfavour they earned is a necessary part of the essential progressiveness and flux that underlie approaches to and the understanding of medicine, healthcare and its research. The positive hopes that inspired the global network of hospital administrators and hospital architects in the first half of the twentieth century to collaborate and actively embrace change was an intrinsic part of their mission. This book has thus documented a defining episode in what must always be a long and constantly unfolding story of hospital architecture.

References

Adams, Annmarie. *Medicine by Design: The Architect and the Modern Hospital, 1893–1943*. Minneapolis, MN: University of Minnesota Press, 2008.
Abramson, Daniel M. *Obsolescence: An Architectural History*. Chicago, IL: University of Chicago Press, 2016.
Antonovsky, Aaron. *Health, Stress and Coping*. San Francisco, CA: Jossey-Bass Publishers, 1979.

Becker, Franklin. *The Ecology of the Patient Visit: Physical Attractiveness, Waiting Times and Perceived Quality of Care*. Ithaca, NY: Department of Design & Environmental Analysis, College of Human Ecology, Cornell University, 2008.

Fair, Alistair. "Peter Womersley: Nuffield Transplantation Surgery Unit, Western General Hospital, Edinburgh, Great Britain." In *SOS Brutalism: A Global Survey*, edited by O. Elser, P. Kurz and P.C. Schmal, 430–1. Zurich: Park Books, 2017.

Franklin, Geraint. "'Built-in Variety': David and Mary Medd and the Child-Centred Primary School." *Architectural History* 55 (2012): 321–67.

Harwood, Elain. *Space, Hope and Brutalism: English Architecture 1945–1975*. New Haven, CT and London: Paul Mellon Centre for Studies in British Art, Yale University Press in association with Historic England, 2015.

Hughes, Jonathan. "The Brutal Hospital: Efficiency, Identity & Form in the National Health Service." PhD diss., Courtauld Institute of Art, University of London, London, 1996.

Hughes, Jonathan. "The Indeterminate Building." In *Non-Plan: Essays on Freedom, Participation and Change in Modern Architecture and Urbanism*, edited by Jonathan Hughes and Simon Sadler, 90–103. Oxford: Architectural Press, 1999.

Kagan, Aubrey R. and Lennart Levi. "Health and Environment: Psychosocial Stimuli: A Review." *Social Science & Medicine* 8, no. 5 (May 1974): 225–41.

Kisacky, Jeanne. *Rise of the Modern Hospital: An Architectural of Health and Healing, 1870–1940*. Pittsburgh: University of Pittsburgh Press, 2017.

Logan, Cameron, Philip Goad and Julie Willis. "Modern Hospitals as Historic Places." *Journal of Architecture* 15, no. 5 (2010): 610–19.

Marcus, Clare Cooper and Marni Barnes (ed.). *Healing Gardens: Therapeutic Benefits and Design Recommendations*. New York: John Wiley, 1999.

McLachlan, Gordon. *A History of the Nuffield Provincial Hospitals Trust, 1940–1990*. London: Nuffield Provincial Hospitals Trust, 1992.

Nuffield Foundation: Division for Architectural Studies. *The Design of Research Laboratories*. London: Oxford University Press, 1961.

Nuffield Foundation: Division for Architectural Studies. *Children in Hospitals: Studies in Planning*. London: Oxford University Press, 1963.

"Nuffield Transplantation Surgery Unit, Edinburgh." *Architectural Design* 38, no. 4 (April 1968): 156–63.

Salonen, Heidi, Marjaana Lahtinen, Sanna Lappalainen, Nina Nevala, Luke D. Knibbs, Lidia Morawska and Kari Reijula. "Design Approaches for Promoting Beneficial Indoor Environments in Healthcare Facilities: A Review." *Intelligent Buildings International* 5, no. 1 (2013): 26–50.

Sloane, David and Beverlie Sloane. *Medicine Moves to the Mall*. Baltimore and London: Johns Hopkins University Press, 2003.

Stevens, Edward F. *The American Hospital of the Twentieth Century*. New York: Architectural Record Publishing Company, 1918.

Stone, Peter. "Hospitals: The Heroic Years." *Architects' Journal* (15 December 1976): 1121–48.

Thompson, John D. and Grace Goldin. *The Hospital: A Social and Architectural History*. New Haven, CT: Yale University Press, 1975.

Ulrich, Roger S. "View Through a Window May Influence Recovery from Surgery." *Science* 224, no. 4647 (1984): 420–1.

Weeks, John. "Indeterminate Hospital Design on Urban Sites." *Hospital Management, Planning and Equipment* (June 1966): 338–41.

Index

Aalto, Aino Marsio 47
Aalto, Alvar 7, 8, 21, 44, 47–50, 53, 54, 161, 168
Acoustics 18, 29, 47, 48, 137, 145, 226
Action for Cities: A Guide for Community Planning 94
Adams, Annmarie xvi, 13, 16, 27, 44, 56, 62, 63, 79, 215
Ahlbom, Sven 183
air conditioning 47, 52, 85, 89–91, 98, 123, 132–6, 139, 173, 177, 178, 209, 216, 218, 221, 229, 230
Albert Kahn & Associates 157; *see also* Kahn, Albert
Allied Architects' Association 64, 158, 199, 202
Alter, Wilhelm C.F. 3–4, 5–6, 9, 11, 203
American Hospital Association 4, 153, 159, 161, 168
The American Hospital of the Twentieth Century 9, 120
Andrews, C.D. 176
Antonovsky, Anton 226
Archer, Bruce 33
The Architecture of Hospitals 16
Architectural Forum 64, 129, 130, 167
Arter & Risch 169
Australia xiv, 1, 9, 11, 12, 20, 25, 27, 29, 52, 53, 65, 67, 72, 85, 87, 89, 91, 111, 112, 117, 118, 152, 153, 155, 160, 164, 166, 167, 168, 181, 203, 205, 207, 208, 218, 228
automobiles 20, 192, 199, 210; *see also* car parking; cars

Babcock, Florence 68
Bacon, Asa A. 52, 153
Bardin, J. 46
Barnes, Marni 226
Bartning, Otto 162
Bates Smart 228
Baum, Dwight James 157
Baur, H. 105, 146, 169, 203, 232
Becker, Franklin 226
bed *see* hospital bed
Beem, Marvel Darlington 33
Befreites Wohnen: Licht, Luft, Oeffnung 35, 163
Berlin & Swern 153
Bernhard, Oskar 110, 111
Betsky, Aaron 6, 198, 199
Bijvoet, Bernard 161, 165
Billard Leece Partnership 228
Biopolitics and the Emergence of Modern Architecture 16
Birch-Lindgren, Gustaf 168
Blalock, Alfred 96
Boeck-Hansen, K. 178
boiler houses 19, 129, 131, 136–7, 164, 167
Bordoni, Angelo 193, 194
Boston 16
Both, Donald 52
Both, Edward T. 52
Bourke, Anne 207
Boyd, Stanley 79
Breines, Simon 48
Brescia 193, 194, 195, 196, 198
Bruegmann, Robert 14, 129
Brunfaut, Gaston 7, 168
Brunfaut, Maxime 168
Buchbinder, Leon 39
Bunshaft, Gordon 7, 175, 177, 200
Burle-Marx, Roberto 175
Butler, Charles 7, 9, 46, 73, 89, 92, 94, 98, 121, 131, 137, 143, 144
Butler & Kohn 196

Campbell, Margaret 6, 112, 163
Campbell, Stuart 125
campus *see* hospital campus
Canada xiv, 16, 27, 148, 149, 152, 153, 182, 183, 215, 220
Canadian Medical Association Journal 9
Carbon Arc Solarium Units 113, 115
car parking 178, 192, 208
cars 207; *see also* automobiles; car parking
Case Western Reserve University 192, 197
CAT scan *see* CT scans
Cederström, Hjalmar 11, 13, 14, 48, 51, 71, 112, 146, 173, 174, 203, 204, 208, 210
Centre Pompidou 220
"A Century of Progress" exhibition 83, 84
Chicago 7, 9, 10, 37, 51, 65, 68, 69, 72, 80, 96, 97, 108, 120, 137, 140, 153, 154, 156, 157, 161, 181, 182, 191, 192
Chromofar lamps 81
CIAM *see Congrès Internationaux d'Architecture Moderne*
city planning *see* urban planning
civic design 152, 157, 160, 175, 179, 188, 193, 194, 196, 197, 201, 209
Colmar 193, 194, 195, 196, 198
Colomina, Beatriz 6, 163
colour 44, 47, 82, 83, 108, 160, 164, 227
Columbia University 39, 200
Columbia University Medical School 198
computed tomography 123–4, 230; *see also* CT scans
Congrès Internationaux d'Architecture Moderne 6–8
Coolidge, Shepley, Bulfinch & Abbott 57, 58, 137, 138, 139, 141, 157, 158, 172, 197
Coolidge & Shattuck 197
Cooper, Gail 132, 133
Copenhagen 45, 89, 113, 178
Corbett, Harvey Wiley 198
Cormack, Allan 124
Cornell Medical College 133, 150
Costa, Lucio 175
Craig, Zeidler & Strong 14, 148, 149, 182, 183, 220

CT scans 123, 124, 125, 230
Curtis & Davis 179

Daiber, Hans 80, 90
Das Deutsche Krankenhaus 1925 9
Das Krankenhaus 9
Davis, Arthur Q. 179
Davis, Audrey B. 101, 103
Denmark 45, 89, 160, 178
Design and Construction of General Hospitals 95
diagnosis 3, 19, 101–4, 114–26, 177, 216, 229
Distel, Hermann 11, 161, 168
Döcker, Richard 7, 35–6, 111, 162, 163
Donati, Mario 44
Dorney, J.H. Esmond 65, 181
Dudok, Willem 160, 170
Duiker, Jan 7, 161, 165
Dunham, George C. 147
Dürig, Bräuning Leu 105, 146, 169, 203, 232

Eastman Kodak Co. 117
Elcock, C.E. 9
Elzner & Anderson 157
Erdman, Addison 9, 46, 89, 92, 94, 98, 121, 131, 137, 143, 144
Erikson, Carl 83–5, 86, 87, 89, 96, 109, 161
Erikson, Carl Jr. 96
eugenics 4, 5
Eveready National Carbon Company 113, 115

Failla, G. 121
Favier, Marcel 46
Ferriss, Hugh 199
Fietz, H. 169
Fine, David J. 16, 182
Finland 7, 8, 21, 48, 49, 160, 161, 164, 174
Finsbury Borough Health Centre 7
Finsen, Niels Ryberg 110, 113
Finsen lamp 113, 114
Finsen Medical Light Institute of Copenhagen 113
Flagg, Paluel J. 82, 83
fluoroscopy 120, 134
food 13, 29, 56, 70, 131, 144–6, 147, 196, 217, 230
Forty, Adrian 61, 62, 63
Foucault, Michel 4

France 4, 11, 85, 86, 87, 88, 89, 98, 107, 133, 144, 145, 146, 147, 148, 152, 160, 162, 163, 172, 178, 188, 189, 193, 194, 195, 199, 216, 220, 232, 233
Frey, Hans 48, 50
Friedman, D.S. 163
Friedmann, Carl A. 29, 31
Fritschel, Herman L. 52

Gaberel, Rudolf 27, 28
Galton, Douglas 25, 26
Ganster, William A. 171
Gardella & Martini 168
Garfield, Sidney 181
Gargiani, Roberto 40
Gatch, Willis Dew 31
Germany xiv, 5, 11, 21, 36, 47, 61, 62, 80, 90, 101, 107, 109, 111, 123, 160, 161, 162, 163, 168, 178, 179, 182, 183, 190, 220
germ theory 25
Giedion, Sigfried 6, 7, 21, 35, 163
Gläserner Mensch see Transparent Man
glass blocks 81
glass bricks *see* glass blocks
Goldberg, Bertrand 65, 181, 219
Goldhagen, Sarah Williams 47
Goldin, Grace 16, 25, 27, 45, 61, 63, 70, 131, 225
Goldwater, S.S. (Sigismund Schultz) 4, 73, 92, 112, 153, 170, 197, 216
Golub, Jacob J. 70
Goodfriend, Jacob 29
Great Depression 166
Gropius, Walter 7, 21, 168
Grubbe, Emil 120

Haefeli, Max Ernst 7, 169
Haefeli, Moser & Steiger 169
Haldane, John Scott 126
Haldane equipment 109, 126
Hall, E. Stanley 35, 63
Hamlin, Talbot 7
Harland, J.B. 170
Harrison & Abramowitz 175
Hart, Deryl 91
Harvard Medical School 197
Harwood, Elain 180, 224
Healthcare Architecture in an Age of Radical Transformation 16
heating 39, 48, 88, 109, 123, 129, 130, 131, 132, 133, 134, 136, 137, 139, 230

heliotherapy 17, 34, 35, 103, 104, 109–11, 113, 217, 229
Henderson, A. & K. 117, 118
Henle, Fritz 57, 59, 60
Hill-Burton Act 221
Hilversum xiv, 161, 165
Hirsch, G.M. 65, 181
Hockett, A.J. 91
Hoffman, Josef 7
homeliness, concepts of 25, 26–7, 37, 43, 44, 52, 72, 156, 162, 170
Hood, Raymond 198
The Hospital: A Social and Architectural History 16, 225
hospital bed 17, 19, 24–52; in-built bedpan 31, 32; call systems 17, 41, 42, 66; castors 29, 30; Circ-O'lectric Bed 33, 34; Gatch Bed 31, 33; Humidicrib 52, 53; lighting 43; King's Fund Bed 33; Push Button Bed 31, 33
hospital campus xv, 1, 14, 17, 18, 20, 24, 73, 149, 156, 176, 181, 182, 188–211, 214, 219, 220, 227, 231
hospital design: block hospital 14, 15, 17, 64, 75, 152, 154, 157, 159, 201; *Breitfuß* (*see* hospital design, podium and slab); comparison with hotel 3, 13, 24, 27, 51, 73, 123, 144, 146, 152, 154, 156, 174, 177, 216; "matchbox on a muffin" (*see* hospital design, podium and slab); Pavilion plan 20, 24, 25, 47, 56–63, 64, 75, 131, 132, 154, 157, 190, 193, 195, 205; podium and slab 174, 176, 177, 178, 179, 180, 181; styling (classical 157, 162, 170, 175; Collegiate Gothic 191, 192; Gothic 157, 158, 160, 162; Gothic Revival 157; Neo-Gothic 157; Neoclassical 193, 197; traditional 1, 13, 45, 152, 157, 162, 168, 193, 195); modern (moderne 157; modernist 6, 20, 45, 112, 143, 152, 160, 162, 163, 166, 167, 168, 170, 208, 209)
Hospital Design and Function 182
Hospital Modernization and Expansion 182, 219
Hospital Planning 9, 46
hospitals: Australia (Alfred Hospital, Prahran, VIC 117, 118; Echuca Base Hospital, Echuca, VIC 53; Frankston Children's Hospital, Frankston, VIC 112; Freemason's Hospital, East

Melbourne, VIC 166; King George V Hospital for Mothers and Babies, Camperdown, NSW 85, 87, 167; Mercy Hospital, East Melbourne, VIC 111, 164, 167; Prince Henry's Hospital, Melbourne, VIC 11, 12, 72; Queen Victoria Hospital, Melbourne, VIC 160; Royal Children's Hospital, Melbourne, VIC 228; Royal Melbourne Hospital, Melbourne, VIC 1, 2, 22, 141–3, 151, 167, 168, 184, 203, 205–6, 212; Royal Prince Alfred Hospital, Sydney, NSW 167, 207; Sandringham and District Hospital, Sandringham, VIC 65, 181; St George's Hospital, Kew, VIC 67; United Dental Hospital, Sydney, NSW 167; Yaralla Military Hospital, Concord, NSW 167); Austria (Allgemeines Krankenhausder Stadt Wien (AKH) (Vienna General Hospital), Vienna 180; Sanatorium Purkersdorf, Purkersdorf 7; Stadt Krankenhaus (State Hospital), Vienna 162, 164, 166; Universitäts-Kinderklinik (University Children's Hospital), Vienna 116); Belgium (Institut Jules Bordet, Brussels 168; Sanitarium Joseph Lemaire, Tombeek 168); Brazil (German Hospital, Rio de Janeiro 170; Hospital da Lagoa (Hospital Sul America), Rio de Janeiro 176); Canada (Health Sciences Centre, McMaster University, Hamilton, ON 148–50, 182, 183, 220; Royal Victoria Hospital, Montreal, QC 16); Czechoslovakia (Foyers Masaryk, Prague 144); Denmark (Copenhagen County Hospital, Glostrup 89; Rigshospital, Copenhagen 45; University Hospital, Odense 178); Egypt (Al Moasset Hospital, Alexandria 183; Tuberculosis Clinic, Alexandria 168); England (Aintree University Hospital, Liverpool 180; Atkinson Morley Hospital, Wimbledon 124; Birmingham Hospital, Birmingham 168; Charing Cross Hospital, London 79; Fazakerley Hospital (*see* hospitals, England, Aintree University Hospital); Guy's Hospital, London 83; Hull Royal Infirmary, Hull 180; Infectious Diseases Hospital, Isleworth 170; Infectious Diseases Hospital, Tolworth 170; Leeds Hospital, Leeds 63; London Hospital, London 113, 114; Northwick Park Hospital, Harrow 222–3; Poole Sanatorium, Nunthorpe 170; Queen Elizabeth II Hospital, Welwyn 176; Rochford Hospital, Rochford 170; Royal Herbert Hospital, Woolwich 25, 26; Royal Masonic Hospital, London 160; St Thomas' Hospital, London 15, 28, 61; Wexham Park Hospital, Slough 180); Finland (Helsinki Sanatorium, Helsinki 164; Paimio Tuberculosis Sanatorium, Paimio 7, 8, 21, 48–50, 161, 162, 164; Turku University Central Hospital, Turku 173); France (Centre Hospitalier Mémorial France États-Unis (France United States Memorial Hospital), Saint-Lô 87, 88, 194, 232, 233); Cité Hospitalière (Hospital Complex) (unbuilt project), Lille 123, 133, 149, 177–8, 188–91, 195, 207, 209; Cité Hospitalière de Lille (Lille Hospital Complex), Lille 85, 86, 87, 162, 191, 194; Hôpital Beaujon (Beaujon Hospital), Paris 144, 145, 146, 147, 148, 162, 172, 194, 199, 216; Hôpital Louis Pasteur (Louis Pasteur Hospital), Colmar 194, 195–6; Hotel de Dieu, Paris 190; La Maison Medicale de Châtillon-sous-Bagneux, Châtillon 46); Germany (Charité Berlin-Campus Klinikum Benjamin Franklin (Benjamin Franklin Campus Clinic), Berlin 178, 179; Chirurgische Universitätsklinik (University Surgical Clinic), Tübingen 80, 81, 90; Cologne University Hospital, Cologne 178; Deutsches Rotes Kreuz Kliniken (Red Cross Surgical Hospital), Berlin 162; Krankenhaus Waiblingen, Waiblingen 35, 36, 111, 123, 162, 163, 171; Martin Luther Hospital, Berlin 183; Protestant Hospital, Gütersloh 183; Rudolf Virchow Krankenhaus (Rudolf Virchow Hospital), Berlin 61–3, 190, 193, 209; Universitätsklinikum (University Hospital), Aachen 182, 220; West

End Hospital, Berlin 190); Iran (University Hospital, Tehran 183); Iraq (Hospital, Khademain 183; Southern Base Teaching Hospital, Basrah 183); Israel (Government Hospital, Haifa 170, 201; Hadassah University Medical Centre, East Jerusalem 201); Italy (Columbus Clinic 44; Nuovo Ospedale Maggiore di Brescia, Brescia 193, 194; Venice Hospital (unbuilt), Venice 7, 40, 52); Japan (Tokyo Teisin Hospital, Tokyo 170); Latvia (Sanatorium, Tervete 168); Netherlands (Diaconessenhuis (Deaconess House), Eindhoven 178; Haga Ziekenhuis locatie Leyweg (*see* hospitals, Netherlands, Leyenburg Ziekenhuis); Leyenburg Ziekenhuis (Leyenburg Hospital), The Hague 178; Zonnestraal Sanatorium, Hilversum xiv, 161, 162, 164, *165*, 167); New Zealand (Wellington Hospital, Wellington 168); Northern Ireland (Altnagelvin Hospital, Londonderry 176); Peru (Maternity hospital, Lima 168); Poland (Neusalz Oder Distric Hospital, Nowa Sol 183); Scotland (Ninewells Teaching Hospital, Dundee 89; Nuffield Transplantation Surgery Unit, Edinburgh 224, 225; Western General Hospital, Edinburgh 224); Sweden (Karolinska Hospital, Stockholm 183; Södersjukhuset (Southern Hospital), Stockholm 11, 48, 51, 71, 112, 146, 173, *174*, 202, 203, 204, 205, 231; Uppsala Sanatorium, Uppsala 168); Switzerland (Kantonsspital (Cantonal Hospital), Basel 104, 105, 146, 168, 169, 203, 204, 205, 231, 232; Kantonsspital (Cantonal Hospital), Lucerne 168; Kantonsspital (Cantonal Hospital), Zurich 169; Loryspital, Bern 104, 111, 162, 168; Maternity Hospital, Bern 168; Universitätsspital Basel (*see* Kantonsspital (Cantonal Hospital), Basel); Zürcher Höhenklink (Zurich Heights Clinic), Clavadel 27, 28); United Kingdom 14, 26–27, 33, 35, 107, 160, 176, 218, 221, 224; United States (Albany Hospital, Albany, NY 153; Bataan Hospital, Albuquerque, NM 91; Bellevue Hospital, Manhattan, NY 135; Beth Israel Hospital, Manhattan, NY 110; Butterworth Hospital, Grand Rapids, MI 153; Central Kansas Medical Center, Great Bend, KS 65; Children's Hospital, Cincinnati, OH 157; Children's Memorial Hospital, Chicago, IL 140; Cincinnati General Hospital, Cincinnati, OH 107, 113; Columbia-Presbyterian Medical Center, Manhattan, NY 6, 119, 154, 157, 159, 198, 202; Dartmouth Hitchcock Medical Center, Lebanon, NH 225; Doctors Hospital, Manhattan, NY 157; Eagleville Sanatorium, West Norriton, PA 157; Fifth Avenue Hospital, Manhattan, NY 154, 155; Fort Hamilton Veterans' Administration Hospital, Brooklyn, NY 134, 175, 199, 200; German Hospital, Chicago, IL 80; Harborview Hospital, Seattle, WA 158; Harkness Intermediate Hospital, Manhattan, NY 198; Highland Hospital, Alameda, CA 154, 157; Hospital for Chronic Diseases, Welfare Island, NY 170, 171, 197; Hospital of the Good Samaritan, Los Angeles, CA 157; James M. Jackson Memorial Hospital, Miami, FL 80; Johns Hopkins Hospital, Baltimore, MD 68, 96, 131; Kaiser Foundation, Panorama City, CA 181; Lake County Tuberculosis Sanatorium, Waukegan, IL 171; Lorain Community Hospital, Lorain, OH 65; Los Angeles County General Hospital, Los Angeles, CA 29, 63, 64, 158, 199, 201, 202, 203; Lovelace Clinic, Albuquerque, NM 91; Lying-In Hospital, Chicago, IL 69, 153, 157, 191, 192; Lying-In Hospital, Manhattan, NY 80; Lying-In Hospital, Providence, RI 154; Maimonides Health Center, San Francisco, CA 202; Meadowbrook Hospital, Long Island, NY 112, 170; Memorial Hospital, Manhattan, NY 121; Michael Reese Hospital, Chicago, IL 7; Milwaukee Hospital, Milwaukee, WI 52; Montefiore

Hospital for Infectious Diseases, Manhattan, NY 29; Mount Sinai Hospital, Manhattan, NY 73, 74, 133; New York University–Bellevue Medical Center, Manhattan, NY 176; New York Hospital–Cornell Medical Center, Manhattan, NY 44, 57, 58, 113, 137, 138, 139, 141, 157, 158, 197, 206; Northwest Community Hospital, Arlington, VA 134; Northwestern University hospitals, Chicago, IL 65, 156; Passavant Memorial Hospital, Chicago, IL 108, 156; Prentice Women's Hospital, Chicago, IL 65, 181; Presbyterian Hospital, Chicago, IL 51; Providence Hospital, Mobile, AL 182; Providence Lying-In Hospital, Providence, RI 154; Springfield Hospital, Springfield, MA 137; St Joseph's Hospital, Tacoma, WA 181–2; St Luke's Hospital, Chicago, IL 96, 97; St Luke's Hospital, San Francisco, CA 83; Swedish Hospital, Seattle, WA 81; Syracuse Memorial Hospital, Syracuse, NE 157; University of Chicago Clinics, Chicago, IL 68, 69; University Hospitals of Cleveland, OH 146, 191, 197; University of Michigan Hospital, Ann Arbor, MI 68, 82, 153, 146, 157; Washington Hospital, Washington, PA 156; Water Reed Hospital, Washington, DC 122; White Memorial Hospital, Temple, TX 65; White Plains Hospital, White Plains, NY 171; Women's Hospital, Detroit, MI 157)

Hospitals: Integrated Design 9, 46, 129

Hospital Survey and Construction Act *see* Hill-Burton Act

hot water 131, 136, 137, 139, 217

Hounsfield, Godfrey 124

Howell, Joel D. 2, 68, 103

Hughes, Jonathan 14, 176, 190, 191, 222, 223

humidicrib *see* hospital bed

humidity 52, 79, 89, 90, 91, 109, 130, 132, 133, 134, 209, 229, 230

Hunter, S.D. 156

hydrotherapy 104, 106–8, 126, 229; Hubbard bath 107, 108; Sitz bath 107, 216

hygiene 6, 7, 19, 25–7, 78, 79, 101, 136, 139, 152, 162, 163, 190, 217, 226, 229

IHA *see* International Hospital Association

IHF *see* International Hospital Federation

Imhäuser, Hermann 11, 48, 51, 71, 112, 146, 173, 174, 203, 204

incinerators 19, 147

International Hospital Association 3, 4, 5, 6, 8, 149, 161, 168, 202, 203; conferences 4–5

International Hospital Federation 8

International Hygiene Exhibition 101

Ireland, Charles 83

Irwin, Leighton 11, 12, 13, 67, 72

Jacobsen, Arne 178

Japan 91, 170

Jasinski, Stanislas 168

Jenkins, Austin 72

Johnson, Reginald D. 157

Judtmann, Fritz 162, 166

Kagan, Aubrey R. 226

Kahn, Albert 82, 153, 157; *see also* Albert Kahn & Associates

Kaiser Permanente 181

Katz, Waisman, Blumenkranz, Stein & Weber 135

Keck, George Fred 37, 39

Kellein, Thomas 47

Kellog, Alfred 129, 130, 149

Kidder Smith, G.E. 169, 170, 173, 174

King, Anthony 61

Kisacky, Jeanne 15, 16, 61, 66, 96, 133, 221

kitchens 17, 19, 56, 73, 75, 131, 143–6, 150, 153, 196, 216, 217, 230

Klinklāvs, Aleksandrs 168

Koch, Robert 61

Kodak *see* Eastman Kodak Co.

Kogel, Marcus 153

Kopp, Ernst 170, 183

Kozak, Bohumiz 144

Kozlowskiego, Mieczyslawa 168

Kreis, Wilhelm 101

Lahiji, Nadir 163

Lamplough, Francis Everard 35, 37

Lanchester & Lodge 168

Index 241

Landolt, R. 169
laundries 17, 19, 56, 75, 129, 131, 137, 139–43, 144, 145, 150, 153, 167, 196, 207, 216, 217, 230
Lavender, Jerry 107
Le Corbusier 6, 7, 21, 40, 52, 163, 168, 175, 190
Léger, Fernard 178
Leighton Irwin & Company 12, 72; *see also* Irwin, Leighton
Lenoble, J. Guy 87
Levi, Lennart 226
light 15, 18, 25, 35, 39, 40, 47, 57, 67, 79, 83, 85–6, 90, 96, 98, 131, 139, 143, 152, 160, 175, 189, 209, 215, 227, 229; artificial 18, 19, 33, 43, 48, 80, 81–2, 84, 88, 98, 109, 135, 217; daylight 39, 81, 94, 121, 123, 135, 144, 162, 229; Glare 43, 45, 46, 48, 81, 82, 98, 217; Holophane Multiple Controlens Lighting System 81; ultraviolet 113, 229; *see also* sunlight
Lille 85, 86, 87, 123, 133, 149, 162, 177, 188, 189, 190, 191, 194, 195, 196, 207, 209
Lister, Joseph 61
Liverpool Regional Hospital Board 180
Llewelyn-Davies, Richard 221, 222, 223
Llewelyn-Davies, Weeks & Partners 180, 222, 223
Llewelyn-Davies & Weeks 222, 223
London 7, 15, 28, 33, 35, 61, 79, 83, 113, 114, 160, 170
Longstreth, Richard 199
Lorne, Francis 136, 146, 160
Ludlow, William F. 83
Luenenberger & Flückiger 169
Lugthart, W. F. 178
lupus 110, 114

MacEachern, Malcolm T. 4, 97, 153, 216
Madge, John 221
magnetic resonance imaging 125, 230
Malmio, Veikko 89
Marcus, Clare Cooper 207, 208, 226
Mayhew, Clarence 181
McCulloch, William F. 112, 170
McIntyre, William 52
Melbourne 2, 11, 12, 65, 72, 111, 142, 153, 160, 164, 166, 167, 168, 206, 228

medical records 18, 67–9, 108, 117, 119, 120, 122
Medicine by Design 215
Medicine Moves to the Mall 225
Mendelsohn, Erich 7, 170, 201–2, 203
Meyers, Henry H. 154, 157
Mies van der Rohe, Ludwig 47, 54, 137, 160, 163
Milburn, W. & T.R. 170
Model Operating Room 83, 96
Moderne Bauformen 81, 90
Modern Hospital xiv, 4, 9, 10, 29, 31, 44, 70, 73, 87, 91, 96, 108, 137, 156, 159, 160, 161, 168, 172, 191, 198, 202
modernism xiv, 1, 6, 7, 11, 13, 14, 26, 123, 150, 152, 160–6, 168, 170, 172, 173, 195, 196, 209, 226, 230, 231
Montreal 16
Moretti, B. Franco 9, 25, 27, 51, 85, 86, 89, 104, 105, 144, 171, 193, 194, 195, 216
morgue 26, 131, 133, 146, 147, 148, 196, 218
morgue caravan 147, 148
Moser, Werner M. 7, 169
MRI *see* magnetic resonance imaging

National Health Service 221
Nelson, Paul 7, 87, 88, 123, 133, 149, 177–8, 183, 188–91, 194, 195–6, 207, 209, 232, 233
Neutra, Richard 172
Niemeyer, Oscar 175, 176
Nightingale, Florence 25, 56, 57, 59, 61, 71, 75, 132, 215
Nightingale ward 25, 26, 45, 46, 61, 154, 215
Nissen lamps 81
North West Metropolitan Regional Hospital Board 176
Nosokomeion 3–4, 5, 9, 11, 21, 146, 161, 202, 203
Notes on Hospitals 25, 59
Nuffield Foundation 222
Nuffield Provincial Hospitals Trust 136, 221
nurses' homes 17, 56, 57, 59, 72–4, 167, 229
nurses' stations 18, 25, 41, 43, 56, 57, 63–4, 65, 66, 71, 181, 182, 229

occupational therapy 104, 107, 126
operating theatres 17, 18, 19, 26, 60, 75, 78–98, 120, 131, 133, 134, 140, 143, 161, 167, 177, 178, 217, 218, 229
Ortega y Gasset, José 190
Osler, William 125
Overy, Paul 163, 209
oxygen 70, 83, 89, 91, 126; reticulated 17, 19, 41, 131, 217; tent 109, 110; therapy 104, 108–9, 229

Paatela, Jussi 173
Padua 78
Parker, Paul 57, 58
Pasteur, Louis 61, 194, 195
pathology 103, 120; departments 120; laboratories 2, 17, 19, 94
penicillin 39, 111
Pereira, William L. 7, 171
Perkins & Will 14, 182, 219
Perret, Auguste 196
PET *see* positron emission tomography
Pevsner, Nikolaus 7, 61
photography 57, 103, 114, 116, 117
phototherapy 111, 112; *see also* heliotherapy
physiotherapy 19, 34, 75, 104–6, 107, 108, 126, 229
Piano & Rogers 220
Pomerance & Breines 135
Ponti, Gio 44, 168
Pope, John Russell 112, 170
positron emission tomography 230
Powell, Philip 180
Powell & Moya 180
Poyet, Bernard 61
Prague 144
Priestley, Joseph 108, 109

radiation departments 17, 217
radiation therapy 19, 34, 120–5, 229
radio 17, 41, 230
radiography 114, 117
radiotherapy 120, 122; *see also* radiation therapy
Ray, Man 189
records *see* medical records
Reich, Lilly 47
Reiser, Stanley 103, 104, 125, 126
Richard E. Schmidt, Garden & Martin 153, 154
Richards, J.M. 7
Richardson, Henry Hobson 197

Rigs ward *see* wards
Rio de Janeiro 170, 175, 176
Rise of the Modern Hospital 15
Riss, Egon 162, 166
Robert Matthew, Johnson-Marshall & Partners 89
Robertson, Robert H. 80
Robinson & Campan 153
Rockefeller Center 157, 197
roentgenology 68
Roentgen rays *see* X-ray
Rogers, James Gamble 6, 119, 154, 157, 159, 198, 202
Rollier, Auguste 9, 110–11
Roosevelt Island *see* Welfare Island, New York
Rorem, C. Rufus 3
Rosellini, Ana 40
Rosenfield, Butler & Kohn 171
Rosenfield, Isadore 7, 9, 39, 40, 45, 46, 47, 63, 121, 122, 129, 134, 135, 143, 171, 179, 180
Rüdin, Ernst 5

Sachs, Naomi A. 207, 208
Sadar, John 37
Saint-Lô 85, 87, 88, 178, 194, 232, 233
Saint Ouen 88
Salonen, Heidi 226
Salvisberg, Otto 104, 111, 162, 168
sanatoria *see* tuberculosis sanatoria
Sand, René 149
Sarkis, Hashim 40
Schlink, Herbert 207
Schmidt, Garden & Eriksen 80, 96, 157, 161, 191, 192
Schmidt, Garden & Martin 153, 154
Schmidt, Richard E. 80, 96, 153, 154, 157, 161, 191, 192
Schulze & Weaver 171
Schütz, J. 169
Sekula, Allan 103
Shanken, Andrew 13, 94
Shepley, Bulfinch, Richardson & Abbott 225
Shepley, Rutan & Coolidge 197
Sherman, Harry 83
Sijmons, K.L. 178
Simon & Simon 157
Sir John Burnet, Tait & Lorne 160
Skidmore Owings & Merrill 7, 134, 175, 177, 199, 200, 209
Skislewicz, Anton 80

Index 243

Skylights 40, 79, 80, 84, 88, 94
Sloan, Raymond P. 44, 157, 158, 198
Sloane, Beverlie 44, 225, 226
Sloane, David 44, 225, 226
smell 1, 45, 131, 132
Smith, Carrol & Johansen 81
Smith, F.W. 170
Solaria 17, 34, 48, 111, 162, 164, 167, 168, 170, 173, 214
South America 9, 170
Stanford University 197
Stanley Hall, Easton & Robertson 35, 63
steam 19, 88, 90, 129, 131, 136–9, 150, 217
Steiger, Rudolf 7, 169
Stephenson, Arthur xiv, 11, 71, 76, 86–7, 100, 153, 155, 160–2, 164–8, 184, 186, 209, 210
Stephenson & Meldrum 111, 112, 166, 167
Stephenson & Turner 85, 86, 87, 153, 166, 168, 183, 203, 205, 206
Stevens, Edward F. 9, 11, 13, 16, 62, 63, 66, 70, 89, 98, 120, 129, 130, 133, 134, 137, 154, 168, 192, 193, 217
Stevens, Curtin & Mason 168
Stevens & Lee 16, 137, 154
Stockholm 13, 48, 51, 71, 112, 146, 173, 174, 183, 202, 204, 205, 231
Stone, J.E. 9, 11
Stone, Peter 224
storage 67–8, 94, 104, 117, 131, 140, 144, 145–6, 208
Stryker, Homer Hartman 33, 34
Studebaker, Glenn R. 140
Stuttgart xiv, 3, 9, 36, 111, 123, 161, 162, 163
sunlight 6, 18, 28, 35, 37, 39, 48, 109–11, 113, 163, 164, 170, 171, 172, 206, 217, 218
Sweden 11, 13, 48, 51, 71, 112, 146, 152, 160, 168, 173, 174, 183, 202, 204, 205, 222, 231
Switzerland 6, 21, 27, 28, 48, 104, 105, 110, 111, 146, 152, 160, 162, 168, 169, 203, 231, 232

Tatton-Brown, William 14
Taylor, Frederick Winslow 2, 19, 70, 131
Tecton 7
Teleoptic Corporation of Racine 41, 42, 66

television 18, 41, 84, 86, 96, 97, 230
Tenon, J.R. 61
Terrazzo 86, 144
Theodore, David 71
Thiers, Albert 46
Thomas, Grainger & Thomas 158
Thompson, John D. 16, 25, 27, 45, 61, 63, 70, 131, 225
Thompson, W. Gilman 68
Toronto 149, 168
Transparent Man 101, 102, 123, 126
Trendelenburg position 33, 53
Truesdale, Philemon E. 91, 92, 93
tuberculosis 9, 26, 35, 39, 103, 110, 113, 120, 133, 163, 172, 196, 217
tuberculosis pavilion 162, 164
tuberculosis sanatoria xiv, 6–8, 21, 26, 48–50, 103, 111–12, 157, 161, 162, 164, 165, 168, 170, 171
Turner, Paul Venable 191, 197

Uklein, Vladimir 4
Ullberg, Uno 173
Ulrich, Roger 226
United Kingdom 9, 14, 20, 26, 27, 33, 35, 40, 107, 160, 170, 176, 218, 221, 224
United States xiv, 2, 9, 16, 37, 39, 50, 52, 72, 73, 87, 91, 98, 125, 134, 152, 153, 160, 161, 170, 179, 189, 191, 218, 221
University of Bristol 136, 222
urban planning 63, 94, 190
US Department of Health, Education and Welfare 41, 94, 95, 147
US Department of Public Health 222
US Office of War Information 57
USPHS *see* US Public Health Service
US Public Health Service 9, 41, 94, 95, 140

Vanderbilt University Medical School 197
Venice Hospital (unbuilt) *see* hospitals, Italy
ventilation 25, 47, 85, 89, 121, 131, 134, 144, 215, 226; mechanical 18, 19, 90, 98, 123, 129, 132, 133, 136, 139, 143; natural 37, 48, 132, 133, 136, 143
Ventura, Paolo 193, 194
Verderber, Stephen 14, 16, 65, 178, 182, 208

244 *Index*

Vetter, William (Willy) 194, 195, 196
Vischer, P. 105, 146, 169, 203, 232
Vita glass 35, 37–8

Wagenaar, Cor 14, 16, 178, 180, 207
Wallenstein, Sven-Olov 4, 6, 16, 190, 191
Walter, Cassan & Madeline 85, 86
Walter, Jean 9, 11, 71, 85–7, 89, 98, 144, 145, 146, 147, 148, 162, 167, 172, 191, 194, 199, 208, 216
Walter, Plousey & Cassan 144, 145, 146, 147, 148, 162, 172, 199, 216
wards: Nightingale (*see* Nightingale ward); Rigs 46–8, 51, 63; Spanish 46
waste 131, 132, 144, 145–6, 147, 196, 210, 231
Waterworth, Eric 52
Waterworth Infant Respirator 52
Watson, B.P. 9
Weatherwax, J.L. 114
Weber & Brand 182, 220
Weeks, John 180, 221, 222, 223
Weideli, H. 169
Weissenhof Siedlung xiv, 161, 163, 164
Welfare Island, New York 143, 171, 197
Westman, Carl 183
Wheeler, E. Todd 182, 219
Wigley, Mark 163
Wilinsky, Charles F. 70, 71

Wilk, Christopher 101, 163
Williams, Louis R. 67
Willis Carrier 133
Winslow, Charles Edward 1, 23
Wolff, Alfred R. 133, 150
Womersley, Peter 224
World War I, effect of 3, 17, 56, 61, 109, 215
World War II, effect of 8, 11, 13, 20, 52, 57, 64, 111, 120, 122, 134, 144, 153, 166, 172, 173, 175, 193, 205, 221
Wright, Frank Lloyd 168

X-ray 19, 94, 104, 114, 116, 117, 120–2, 124–6; departments 75, 116, 117–19, 121–2, 134, 143, 177, 216, 217, 229; *see also* radiography

Yamada, Mamoru 170
Yerbury, Francis 160
Yorke, Rosenberg & Mardall 15, 176, 180
York & Sawyer 154, 155, 171
Ypyä, Martta 89
Ypyä, Ragnar 89

Zander, Gustav 106
Zander Machines 106
Zeidler, Eberhard 14, 148, 149, 182, 183, 220
Zervos, Christian 177

For Product Safety Concerns and Information please contact our EU
representative GPSR@taylorandfrancis.com
Taylor & Francis Verlag GmbH, Kaufingerstraße 24, 80331 München, Germany

www.ingramcontent.com/pod-product-compliance
Lightning Source LLC
Chambersburg PA
CBHW071821300426
44116CB00009B/1391